Illumination and Interpretation

Illumination and Interpretation

The Holy Spirit's Role in Hermeneutics

M. X. Seaman

WIPF & STOCK · Eugene, Oregon

ILLUMINATION AND INTERPRETATION
The Holy Spirit's Role in Hermeneutics

Copyright © 2013 M. X. Seaman. All rights reserved. Except for brief quotations in critical publications or reviews, no part of this book may be reproduced in any manner without prior written permission from the publisher. Write: Permissions. Wipf and Stock Publishers, 199 W. 8th Ave., Suite 3, Eugene, OR 97401.

Scripture quotations are from The Holy Bible, English Standard Version® (ESV®), copyright © 2001 by Crossway, a publishing ministry of Good News Publishers. Used by permission. All rights reserved.

Wipf&Stock
An Imprint of Wipf and Stock Publishers
199 W. 8th Ave., Suite 3
Eugene, OR 97401

www.wipfandstock.com

ISBN 13: 978-1-62032-842-2

Manufactured in the U.S.A.

This book is dedicated to the Church
for the purpose of direction, exhortation, and transformation
by the power of the Holy Spirit,
to the exaltation of Christ Jesus,
for the glory of God the Father.
2 Cor 4:15

I acknowledge, O Lord, with thanksgiving, that thou hast created this thy image in me, so that, remembering thee, I may think of thee, may love thee. But this image is so effaced and worn away by my faults, it is so obscured by the smoke of my sins, that it cannot do what it was made to do, unless thou renew and reform it. I am not trying, O Lord, to penetrate thy loftiness, for I cannot begin to match my understanding with it, but I desire in some measure to understand thy truth, which my heart believes and loves. For I do not seek to understand in order to believe, but I believe in order to understand. For this too I believe, that "unless I believe, I shall not understand."

—Anselm, *Proslogion* (from Chapter 1: The Awakening of the Mind to the Contemplation of God)

Contents

Acknowledgments | ix
Abbreviations | xi

1. The Necessity of the Holy Spirit and His Work | 1
2. Illumination and Hermeneutics | 15
3. Initial Illumination | 54
4. Progressive Illumination | 83
5. Transformative Illumination | 127
6. Conclusion | 165

Bibliography | 171
Scripture Index | 185
Subject Index | 191

Acknowledgments

To Missy—in every way you are my perfect counterpart. The Lord has been tremendously gracious to me, because everything that I lack you fill up with your compassion, support, patience, even temperament, intelligence, and many more intangibles. I still remember the day of your salvation—there is not a more joyous day in our lives together than that day! You have had an incredibly intensive discipleship experience and because of that you are an encouragement to me in both faith and practice as you are truly a model of the virtuous woman in Prov 31. Thank you for being the epitome of a godly wife. May I love you always as Christ loved the Church.

To Emerson and Reagan—your mommy and I are so incredibly blessed by both of you. Thank you for truly being gifts from above! I pray that we would model the life of Christ before you so that you would imitate us as we imitate our Lord. We have prayed for your souls from the day that each of you were born. May the illumination of the Holy Spirit be realized in your hearts!

To Mom & Dad—you have always loved and supported me, rebuked and chastised me as it was necessary, encouraged and exhorted me in times of trouble, and you have taught me to rely on the Lord at all costs. You have done what parents should do, but I recognize that not all parents are this way. You have truly been a tremendous blessing and gift from above and this is recognized by all who meet you. Dad, I would not be the man of God that I am today were it not for your stern instruction and your caring demeanor. And Mom, your timely exhortation and your selfless attitude have shown me how to be a more godly man. I love you with all my heart and take comfort in the fact that what is pleasing in your sight is likewise pleasing in the Lord's.

To my God—truly without you this would not have been possible. I am utterly amazed that you would choose to use me in such a manner as this, for I am nothing without you. Thank you for the salvation that I have in Christ Jesus and the deposit of the Holy Spirit that guarantees my salvation. May the fruit of my studies be used for your glory.

Abbreviations

Reference Works
(Full information included in the Bibliography)

BDAG   *A Greek-English Lexicon of the New Testament and Other Early Christian Literature*, third edition. Revised and edited by Frederick William Danker.

BDB   *Hebrew-Aramaic and English Lexicon of the Old Testament*. Complete and unabridged. By Francis Brown, S. R. Driver, and Charles Briggs.

BECNT   *Baker Exegetical Commentary on the New Testament*. Edited by Robert W. Yarbrough and Robert H. Stein.

EBC   *The Expositor's Bible Commentary*. Edited by Frank E. Gæbelein.

EDT   *Evangelical Dictionary of Theology*. Edited by Walter A. Elwell.

ICC   *The International Critical Commentary*. Edited by Samuel Rolles Driver, Alfred Plummer, and Charles Augustus Briggs.

NAC   *The New American Commentary*. Edited by E. Ray Clendenen.

NIBC   *New International Biblical Commentary*. Edited by W. Ward Gasque.

NICNT   *The New International Commentary on the New Testament*. Edited by Ned B. Stonehouse, F. F. Bruce, and Gordon D. Fee.

NIGTC   *The New International Greek Testament Commentary*. Edited by I. Howard Marshall and W. Ward Gasque.

NTC   *New Testament Commentary*. By William Hendricksen and Simon J. Kistemaker.

TNTC   *The Tyndale New Testament Commentaries*. Edited by Leon Morris.

WBC   *Word Biblical Commentary*. Edited by David A. Hubbard and Glenn W. Barker.

Abbreviations

Primary Sources

All references to Calvin's *Institutes* will be footnoted by book number, chapter number, section number, and page number(s) and cited from John Calvin, *Institutes of the Christian Religion* (trans. Henry Beveridge; Peabody, Mass.: Hendrickson, 2008).

All references to the works of Owen, unless otherwise noted, will be footnoted by book title, volume number, chapter number, and page number from John Owen, *The Works of John Owen* (vols. 3-4, ed. William H. Goold; Johnstone & Hunter, 1856; Repr., Carlisle, PA: The Banner of Truth Trust, 1967).

1

The Necessity of the Holy Spirit and His Work

ACCORDING TO THE SCRIPTURES, the Holy Spirit is essential for the faith and practice of the believer.[1] In a different sense, another vital aspect of the believer's faith and practice is a proper framework for interpreting the Scriptures. All too often though, the Holy Spirit is divorced from the life of the believer and thus, from the practice of hermeneutics. This separation results in a severe neglect of the Spirit's indispensable role in the interpretive process and an avoidable misunderstanding of the doctrine of illumination as a whole.

Generally, the role of the Holy Spirit in biblical interpretation is nebulous at best and outright rejected at its very worst. Contributing to this anemic state is the physical invisibility of the Holy Spirit and his relative anonymity as he seeks to exalt the Son to the glory of the Father.[2] Despite this, the Spirit's work in the life of the believer as it pertains to his work of illumination is clearly visible when equipped with a proper understanding of this activity. As a result, it is necessary to establish briefly my preliminary assumptions concerning the deity and personhood of the Spirit, as they bear upon our understanding of the doctrine of illumination.[3]

---

1. For example, see Rom 8:1–30 and Gal 5:16–25.

2. Letham, *The Holy Trinity*, 56, alludes to this in his section on the Holy Spirit, and the Evangelist John speaks to this in John 16:13–15.

3. Torrance, *The Christian Doctrine of God*, 147–8, presents a well-formed understanding of the deity and personhood of the Holy Spirit in reference to the Triune Godhead. He writes, "A distinction must be drawn between thinking of the Spirit absolutely and thinking of him relatively. Absolutely considered the Spirit is God of God, and like the Son whole God of whole God, so that the Being of the Spirit is the Being ... of the Godhead. . . . In this absolute sense 'Spirit' refers to the Deity, without

Illumination and Interpretation

The Deity and Personhood of the Holy Spirit

In order for the indispensability of the Holy Spirit's role in the hermeneutic process to be substantiated, it is necessary that he is recognized as God. The deity of the Holy Spirit has been affirmed in orthodox Christianity since the early days of the church.[4] Moreover, contemporary theologians like Millard Erickson have maintained a belief in the deity of the Spirit with such statements as, "The Holy Spirit is God in the same fashion and to the same degree as are the Father and the Son."[5] The underpinning of this statement is derived from Scripture's attestation to the divine attributes,[6] activity,[7] and identification[8] of the Holy Spirit. Consequently,

---

distinction of Persons, and is equally applicable to the Father, the Son and the Holy Spirit. Considered relatively, however, the Spirit is Person ... who in distinction from and together with the Persons of the Father and the Son belongs with them to the one Being of God. The Holy Spirit is, then, like the Father and the Son, both *ousia* and *hypostasis*, and with the Persons of the Father and the Son is eternally in God and inseparable from him who is *one Being, three Persons*."

4. See Basil of Caesarea, "*De Spiritu Sancto*," 1–50, for an extended treatise defending the deity of the Holy Spirit. Also see Walvoord, *The Holy Spirit*, 8, for an attestation to this statement, and Yarnell, "The Person and Work of the Holy Spirit," 626–58, for a brief, but comprehensive historical theology of the doctrine of the Holy Spirit.

5. Erickson, *Christian Theology*, 873.

6. The Scriptures attest to the Holy Spirit's possession of the four distinctly divine attributes of eternality (Heb 9:14), omnipresence (Ps 139:7–10), omniscience (1 Cor 2:10–11; John 16:13), and omnipotence (Luke 1:35; Rom 15:19; and John 3:5–8). Concerning the passages in reference to the Spirit's omnipotence, Erickson, *Christian Theology*, 874, astutely notes, "While these texts do not specifically affirm that the Spirit is omnipotent, they certainly indicate that he has power that presumably only God has."

7. The Scriptures also affirm the Spirit's divinity by attributing to him the three uniquely divine activities of God—the act of creation (Gen 1:1–3; Job 33:4), the impartation of life (John 6:63; Rom 8:11), and the authorship of divine prophecy (2 Pet 1:21).

8. The deity of the Holy Spirit is also validated by his identification with God. Based on the work of John L. Dagg, Yarnell, "The Person and Work," 660, argues that the deity of the Holy Spirit is confirmed through the association of the Spirit with the Father and the Son in the baptismal formula (Matt 28:19–29), by the benedictory prayer offered to Him along with the Father and the Son (2 Cor 13:14), by the assertion that the temple of God is the temple of the Holy Spirit (1 Cor 3:16), by the statement that sin against the Holy Spirit is sin against God (Acts 5:3–4), and by the affirmation that OT texts pertaining to God are applied to the Holy Spirit by the authors of the NT (cf. Exod 17:7 with Heb 3:9; Isa 6:8–10 with Acts 28:25; Jer 31:31–34 with Heb 10:15–17). In addition, although grace is an attribute that is normally conjoined with the Lord Jesus Christ, the Spirit is also distinguished as the source of grace (Heb 10:29). Similarly, the love of God is specified as not only coming from the Father, but also the Spirit (Rom 15:30), and the characteristic of

the Holy Spirit is one person in the trinitarian Godhead which is one God in three persons. More specifically, his divine being is the same as and equal to that of God the Father and God the Son.

Not only is the deity of the Holy Spirit an essential part of the foundation for a proper formulation of the doctrine of illumination, but the personhood of the Holy Spirit is as well. This is vital because many Christians do not have a problem affirming the deity of the Holy Spirit, but the line of distinction between the person of the Holy Spirit and the persons of the Father and the Son is blurred.[9] Just as the Scriptures affirm the deity of the Holy Spirit, likewise, the Scriptures attest to the unique personhood of the Holy Spirit as a member of the triune Godhead.[10] To be sure, if the Spirit is fully God, then it follows that he is not merely one-third God, but he is one person of the triune Godhead who possesses fully the identical nature of God. As Bruce Ware avers, "Because of this, what distinguishes the Spirit from the Father and the Son is not the divine nature of the Holy Spirit . . . what distinguishes the Spirit is his particular *role* as the Holy Spirit in relation to the Father and to the Son and the *relationships* that he has with each of them."[11] In light of this, the truth of the personhood of the Holy Spirit is of fundamental importance for his role in the hermeneutic process.

Accordingly, the Holy Spirit's divinity and personhood suggest the crucial nature of his role in biblical interpretation. However, there is an apprehensive ambiguity surrounding the purpose of the Spirit's ministry of illumination. To clarify the Holy Spirit's role in view of a trinitarian framework, Torrance articulates:

> It is only through Christ and in the Spirit that we are given access to the Father, and thereby may know God in his one yet three-fold revelation as Father, Son and Holy Spirit. While this

---

fellowship that is generally associated with the Holy Spirit, is sometimes identified with the Father (1 John 1:3, 6) and the Son (1 Cor 1:9).

9. Toon, *Our Triune God*, 175–6.

10. In the Scriptures, the distinctive characteristics of personhood consisting of knowledge (John 14:26; 1 Cor 2:10–11; Eph 1:17), emotion or sensibility (Rom 8:27; 15:30; Eph 4:30), and will (1 Cor 12:11; cf. Acts 16:6–11), are credited to the Holy Spirit. Also the use of the masculine pronoun (John 15:26; 16:13–14; cf. Eph 1:14) as opposed to the neuter pronoun to represent the neuter noun *pneuma* evidences the personhood of the Holy Spirit along with the mention of the Spirit in the baptismal formula (Matt 28:19) and the benedictory prayer in 2 Cor 13:14.

11. Ware, *Father, Son, & Holy Spirit*, 103. Köstenberger and Swain, *Father, Son, and Spirit*, 135, 144, also affirm this point and base it upon the deity of the Holy Spirit.

> knowledge of God is actualised in us through the Communion [*sic*] of the Holy Spirit, who is the Spirit of the Father and of the Son, its content is determined and informed by what has once for all taken place in Jesus Christ, the Lord and Saviour of mankind, for in him and through him, the one Word of God, all our thinking and speaking of God are brought into faithful conformity to him as the incarnate self-articulation and self-communication of God to mankind. Thus as the Word of God made flesh Jesus Christ embodies in himself not only the exclusive language of God to mankind but the faithful response in knowledge and obedience of humanity to God.[12]

Indeed, the Spirit works in the believer through the Word of God so that by means of the knowledge of God conformity to Christ will result.

Therefore the Holy Spirit's work of illumination is necessary for biblical interpretation so that it results in transformation in the life of the believer.[13] The doctrine of illumination is often misunderstood due to its apparently enigmatic nature. However, if a suitable proposal for understanding illumination is set forth through a properly constructed biblical framework, then the Holy Spirit's role in biblical interpretation will no longer be considered a pariah to disregard, but it will be considered in its proper right, i.e., as indispensable for the believer's hermeneutic.

First, this argument needs to be founded upon a clear distinction between two types of illumination: the initial illumination of the Holy Spirit and the progressive illumination of the Holy Spirit.[14] A lack of definition between these two very distinct types of illumination contributes

---

12. Torrance, *The Christian Doctrine*, 17.

13. It is imperative to note that when speaking of the doctrine of illumination and the concept of transformation, I am referring to the transformative effect that the text has on the reader. I am not referring to the transformation of the text by the reader. As Thiselton, *New Horizons in Hermeneutics*, 31, writes, "Texts can also suffer transformation at the hands of readers and reading communities. Readers may misunderstand and thereby misuse them; they may blunt their edge and domesticate them; or they may consciously or unconsciously transform them into devices for maintaining and confirming prejudices or beliefs which are imposed on others in the name of the text." As will be discussed in much greater detail later, the purpose of the illumination of the Holy Spirit is not the transformation of the text, but the transformation of the reader by the text.

14. The terms initial and progressive illumination are used by Gray Poehnell, "The Relationship of Illumination to the Interpretation of Scripture" in order to distinguish between the two types of the Spirit's work. Although the language of initial illumination is seldom utilized in other works, the language and/or understanding of progressive illumination is recognized by others. For example, this understanding is displayed by Jeff Ingle, "A Historical and Scriptural Survey of the Doctrine of Illumination."

The Necessity of the Holy Spirit and His Work

to a convoluted understanding of the doctrine as a whole. Both initial and progressive illumination are necessary components of the Holy Spirit's work that is needed for proper biblical interpretation.

In view of these definitions, this study will develop a proposal for understanding the doctrine of illumination that will be termed transformative illumination. It is important to recognize that this will not be an attempt to introduce an entirely new type of illumination, for this would only serve to confuse matters further. Transformative illumination is a framework for understanding the doctrine of illumination as a whole. Hence, it is a synthesis of the doctrine which encompasses both initial and progressive illumination.

Furthermore, transformative illumination, as the name suggests, highlights the transformative aspect of the Holy Spirit's work in illumination. As much as the doctrine of illumination is neglected in hermeneutic scholarship, the goal of illumination, i.e., transformation, is disregarded as the necessary outcome of the Holy Spirit's work. It is recognized that the Spirit's illumination may aid the interpreter in understanding the biblical material, but seldom is this understanding conveyed as a transformative work in the heart and life of the reader. L. Gregory Jones addresses this concern when he writes, "Readers who attempt to remain detached and neutral in their interpretation of the Bible will typically understand it less deeply than those who discipline their lives by studying Scripture as the vehicle of God's Word. Scripture bears witness to the God of Jesus Christ so that we may be transformed by the power of the Holy Spirit into the likeness of Christ."[15] To be clear, the goal of the Spirit's work of illumination in conjunction with the Scriptures is transformation in the faith and practice of the believer.

These remarks signal another oft-neglected issue in the practice of hermeneutics that must be treated with greater depth, viz., the difference between the biblical interpretation of the regenerate and the unregenerate. There are very few works that address this issue adequately.[16] Nevertheless, this matter is a crucial piece in the discussion surrounding the doctrine of illumination and will greatly contribute to a proper understanding of the Holy Spirit's role in biblical interpretation.

Connected to this issue is the position of the doctrine of illumination in relation to hermeneutics. It is vital to understand the relationship

---

15. Jones, "Formed and Transformed by Scripture," 31.

16. An example of a work with a brief section on this topic is Maier, *Biblical Hermeneutics*, 53–5.

of illumination with hermeneutics by addressing the association between illumination and revelation, illumination and inspiration, illumination and perspicuity, illumination and sufficiency, and illumination and authority. In order to establish the doctrine of illumination as an important component, if not the most important component, in the discipline of hermeneutics, it is essential to recognize and gain a proper understanding of its relationship to these doctrines pertaining to Scripture.

Foundationally, this doctrine is built on the extensive biblical record that witnesses to the illumination of the Spirit. Therefore, it is necessary to evaluate the witness of the OT and the NT for the purpose of constructing a biblical theology of the doctrine of illumination that results in an understanding of transformative illumination.[17] The specific biblical texts that are treated have been chosen based upon their reference to the Holy Spirit's work as it pertains to illumination, and also because of their historical-theological usage for the development of the doctrine. Each passage will be treated briefly, but adequately on the contextual, exegetical, and interpretive levels in order to serve as the foundation for the framing of a proper biblical-theological understanding of the Holy Spirit's work in biblical interpretation. Although the entire biblical witness is taken into account, because of the role of the Holy Spirit in the process of illumination and the post-ascension dispensation of the Spirit of God, the NT and its representative texts will be evaluated to a greater extent.[18]

The Neglect of the Holy Spirit

As noted above, the Holy Spirit is consubstantial with the Father and the Son in the divine essence and is also a distinct person of the triune

---

17. For initial illumination, the passage 2 Cor 3:12–4:6 was chosen based upon the emphasis of the Spirit's work in relation to unbelievers, and the texts Eph 1:18; Heb 6:4; 10:32 were chosen based upon the employment of the term *phōtizō* as it pertains to salvation. For progressive illumination, the texts Ps 119:18, 33–34; Ezek 11:19–20; 36:26–27; Luke 24:45; John 14:26; 15:26; 16:13; 1 Cor 2:6–16; Eph 1:17; 1 John 2:20, 27; 5:20, were chosen based upon the Spirit's work of granting the believer understanding of the Scriptures. For understanding the concept of transformative illumination, the texts 2 Cor 3:18; Rom 8:1–11; 12:1–2; Gal 5:16–25; and Eph 4:17–24, were chosen based upon the Spirit's work of transformation in the life of the believer.

18. For a treatment of the Holy Spirit's role in the OT see Cole, *He Who Gives Life*, 95–145, and Hamilton, *God's Indwelling Presence*, 9–55. For a brief, but comprehensive assessment of Holy Spirit's role in the OT see Veenhof, "Holy Spirit and Holy Scripture," 70–2.

Godhead. However, even though many Christians would affirm the previous statement, according to an incisive observation made by Letham, "Today most Western Christians are practical modalists."[19] That is, they lack the proper understanding of the three persons of the Trinity, which results in a distorted view of God. Contributing to and resulting from this circuitous misunderstanding is the neglect of the Holy Spirit as the third person of the Trinity in the Christian life, and more specifically in the realm of hermeneutics.

The Neglect of the Holy Spirit in the Christian Life

In general, an assessment of the Christian life reveals a stark imbalance in reference to the value attributed to the presence of the Holy Spirit and his ministry in the life of the believer. Wayne House and Gordon Carle remark, "In the realm of Christian theology, the twentieth century can best be described as the century of the Holy Spirit. Never before in the history of the church had so much attention been given to the third Person of the Trinity."[20] Although this may prove true, the Holy Spirit remains surrounded by a cloud of obscurity, which hampers an adequate comprehension of his person and work. House and Carle go on to say, "Christian thought regarding the nature and work of the Holy Spirit has been intermittent and irregular."[21] Indeed, a vicious cycle of ignorance and neglect regarding the Holy Spirit has contributed to the deprivation of the Spirit in the Christian life.

Furthermore, the Holy Spirit's role may have inadvertently contributed to his neglect in the faith and practice of the regenerate. Referencing volume one of the *B.C.C. Report*, John Thompson writes, "The dominance of Christology over pneumatology in our interpretation of God's working in the world emerges . . . in what is often held to be a weakness of the theology of the Spirit in the West, where the Spirit sometimes appears to be little more than an appendage of Christ."[22] The Spirit's role of empowerment and exaltation of the name of Christ Jesus to the glory of the Father certainly draws attention to the other two persons of the

---

19. Letham, *The Holy Trinity*, 5.
20. House and Carle, *Doctrine Twisting*, 102.
21. Ibid.
22. Thompson, *Modern Trinitarian Perspectives*, 6.

Trinity; however, it does not excuse an underdeveloped pneumatology and an understated place for the Holy Sprit in the Christian life.

To be sure, there exist Christians on both ends of the spectrum concerning the Holy Spirit, in which he is completely disregarded in matters of faith and practice on one end and in which he is overly emphasized to the depreciation of the Father and the Son on the other end. A balance needs to be struck that recognizes the Holy Spirit as the third person of the one true God while also acknowledging the function of the Holy Spirit in relation to the Godhead as it pertains to the Christian life.

The Neglect of the Holy Spirit in Hermeneutics

Hermeneutics has in the past and remains to be a topic of much debate. Certainly, a proper hermeneutic is essential in order to arrive at a proper interpretation of the Scriptures; however, the major component that ought to constitute a proper hermeneutic is often overlooked by both those in academia and in the pew, viz., the role of the Holy Spirit. In the past few hundred years with the rise of the historical-critical method and its various offshoots, and the historical-grammatical method and its various manifestations there has been a tremendous surge of scholarship devoted to hermeneutical studies. The desire to access the biblical world and to discover the author's original intention for his original audience has propelled this scholarship to a large degree. Furthermore, with the advent of biblical archaeology and the insights of biblical geography, the aspiration to discover the historical situation of the text in order to place oneself within the context of the original audience has influenced the majority of hermeneutical study.[23]

However, despite the vastness of this scholarship, the corpus as a whole is anemic concerning the role of the Holy Spirit in the process of biblical interpretation.[24] Many hermeneutics texts devote an insignificant

---

23. See Frei, *The Eclipse of Biblical Narrative*, 1–65, for the development of this hermeneutical shift. Also, Klein, Blomberg, and Hubbard, *Biblical Interpretation*, 23–62, present a history of interpretation that represents this trend.

24. For example, Klein, Blomberg, and Hubbard, *Biblical Interpretation*, 139–41, is one of the few texts that include a section on illumination, but in their 563 page, twelve chapter book this section only spans three pages. Also see, Osborne, *The Hermeneutical Spiral*, 435–7, in which there are two pages devoted to the place of the Holy Spirit in hermeneutics, but only half of which is devoted to the doctrine of illumination in his eighteen chapter, 624 page book.

amount of attention to the Holy Spirit's role in biblical interpretation, while some exclude the discussion altogether.[25] The necessity of the activity of the Holy Spirit for a proper interpretation of the Scriptures is relegated to a place of subservience to a large extent.[26]

Consequently, Bruce Waltke asserts, "The doctrine of illumination demands that Scripture be read in a spirit that is harmonious with God's Spirit; it cannot be read and understood in the same way one relates to other purely human books . . . but the contemporary literature on hermeneutics does not deal seriously with this personal dimension, emphasizing instead reading the Bible as literature."[27] More specifically, the role of the Holy Spirit as it pertains to the doctrine of illumination is often dismissed as merely a spiritual endeavor that has no claim to the historical nature of interpretation.[28] Thus, the person of the Holy Spirit is at best a mere afterthought in the mind of the interpreter and the role of the Holy Spirit in biblical interpretation is reduced to being that of a meager bystander. Certainly, the principles that are utilized in a proper hermeneutic are designed to yield the immeasurable riches of the Word of God; but not without diligent study, long hours, proper exegesis, *and* the illumination of the Holy Spirit.

In modern biblical scholarship, the scientific study of the Scriptures has overtaken the force of the biblical world established in the Scriptures by the Holy Spirit.[29] As a result, biblical scholars have not only neglected

---

25. Some examples of hermeneutic texts that exclude any significant discussion pertaining to the Holy Spirit's role of illumination include Terry, *Biblical Hermeneutics*; Poythress, *God Centered Biblical Interpretation*; and Tate, *Biblical Interpretation*.

26. Concerning this, De Young, "The Holy Spirit," 1, comments, "For many Christians nothing seems to be more esoteric than the work of the Holy Spirit in the understanding and communication of divine truth . . . a common attitude is to take for granted his work in communicating truth."

27. Waltke, *An Old Testament Theology*, 81.

28. De Young, "The Holy Spirit," 1, writes, "When it comes to scholarly methods of interpreting the Bible, the Holy Spirit may as well be dead. . . . For while we believe that the Holy Spirit is alive and active and we invite his participation, our method of interpretation has no concrete role for him."

29. See Auerbach, *Mimesis*, 3–23, for a discussion concerning the biblical world. According to Auerbach, the biblical world portrayed in the text of Scripture is wholly different from any other literary world. He illustrates this by juxtaposing two different styles of literature that serve to represent reality. The first of these is the Homeric epic which presents a fully externalized description placed in the foreground for the reader. In this style, nothing is left to interpretation as the author explicitly presents both meaning and perspective to the reader. The other of these styles is the biblical narrative

Illumination and Interpretation

the progressive illumination of the Spirit, but have altogether discharged the initial illumination of the Holy Spirit as a necessary prerequisite for interpreting and understanding the Word of God.[30] Increasingly, biblical commentaries are being authored by biblical scholars who are devoid of the Holy Spirit, and through scientific method and hermeneutical tools have produced works which contend with commentaries written by believers in exegesis and interpretation.[31] However, Auerbach is clear that

---

that is "fraught with background" (p. 12). In this style, only that which is "necessary for the purpose of the narrative" is externalized for the reader, while "all else [is] left in obscurity" (p. 11). As a result, the biblical narrative, unlike the Homeric epic where nothing is left concealed, requires interpretation on the part of the reader. The basis for this is the Scripture's claim that the world portrayed in the text is not just the biblical world, but is indeed the real world itself. Auerbach asserts, "The Bible's claim to truth is not only far more urgent than Homer's, it is tyrannical—it excludes all other claims. The world of the Scripture stories is not satisfied with claiming to be a historically true reality—it insists that it is the only real world" (pp. 14–15). Therefore, the Bible is not merely a representation of history, it is history—God's history, in which all other reality must conform. Indeed, it is through the Scriptures that there is access to the one real world and the meaning of historical reality. Also see Sailhamer, *Introduction to Old Testament Theology*, 216, who agrees and posits that certainly, the events that are presented in the text of Scripture are real, meaningful, historical events, but "the clear intent of the biblical narratives is to establish the fact that this is the only true account of the world." Likewise, see Frei, *Eclipse*, 2–3, who corresponds with Auerbach and presents three elements for this realistic reading of the text of Scripture: the biblical narratives are to be read literally as they refer to actual historical occurrences, the biblical world is "a single world of one temporal sequence," and the biblical world is the one and only real world.

30. De Young, "The Holy Spirit," 1, cites a couple reasons for the disavowal of the Holy Spirit's role in hermeneutics. He argues, "First the grammatical-historical hermeneutic defined as discovering the intention of the human author treats the Bible just like any other book. Its divine authorship makes no difference in how we are to interpret it. . . . Second, the work of the Holy Spirit is usually confined to convincing us of the truth of what Scripture says and applying it to our lives. He does not help us to understand the meaning of the text (which even an unbeliever can do through the grammatical-historical hermeneutic)."

31. Examples of such commentary series include *Hermeneia—A Critical and Historical Commentary on the Bible*, the *International Critical Commentary*, and *The Anchor Bible*, which states in its foreword that it is "a project of international and interfaith scope: Protestant, Catholic, and Jewish scholars from many countries contribute individual volumes." More specifically, Michael V. Fox in his commentary *Character and Ideology in the Book of Esther*, writes in the introduction, "The Esther story is a metaphoric world . . ." (p. 4), "Esther (I mean the Esther of the book, not a woman who might have actually lived in Achemenid Persia) exists solely in the words spoken about and by her" (p. 6), "How do we judge the adequacy of evidence in proving . . . hypotheses about something that (in our world) never existed? . . . The author of Esther has projected a world from his imagination . . ." (p. 9), and ". . . I doubt the historicity of the Esther story . . ." (p. 11).

the biblical narratives can only produce the effects on the reader that they seek if they are believed to be true.[32] Concerning this dilemma, John Watson insightfully remarks, "[They] do not lack knowledge but [they] do lack divine wisdom—knowledge tempered with spiritual character."[33]

This presents an interesting dilemma for the study of hermeneutics and specifically for the doctrine of illumination. Is the Holy Spirit needed for a proper interpretation of the text? Is a proper understanding of the Scriptures contingent upon regeneration? What constitutes a proper understanding of the Scriptures? What exactly is the role of the Holy Spirit in biblical interpretation?

The Indispensability of the Holy Spirit

The Indispensability of the Holy Spirit for the Christian Life

The neglect of the Holy Spirit oftentimes constitutes a sad commentary on the Christian life, but the indispensability of the Spirit for the faith and practice of the regenerate is a wondrous truth that the Christian should behold. The Scriptures attest to this indispensability first of all, as the Spirit is proclaimed to convict the world concerning sin, righteousness, and judgment (John 16:8–11). Without this work of the Holy Spirit, conversion and Christian life cannot take place.[34] Also, the Spirit is promised to indwell the believer and empower him for matters of faith and practice (John 14:16–17; Rom 8:1–11). Erickson speaks to this when he writes, "The Spirit . . . is able to affect one more intensely because, dwelling within, he can get to the very center of one's thinking and emotions, and lead one into all truth."[35] Hence, a major work of this indwelling is the continued transformation of the life of the believer, in which he is conformed to the image of Christ.

Specifically, the aforementioned activities of the Spirit display his inherent indispensability for the Christian life, but there are two general reasons that bolster the Spirit's importance as well. First, in the words of Erickson, "The Holy Spirit is active within the lives of believers; he is resident within us. He is the particular person of the Trinity through whom the

---

32. Auerbach, *Mimesis*, 14.
33. Watson, "The Holy Spirit and the Bible," 280.
34. Erickson, *Christian Theology*, 888.
35. Ibid., 889.

entire Triune Godhead currently works in us."[36] This is a powerful statement because many believers speak as if Jesus Christ is within their hearts. Whether this is an issue of semantics or not, it reflects an errant understanding of the person of Christ and the work of the Holy Spirit, resulting in an unintended dismissal of one of the Spirit's most important activities. Jesus Christ is clear when he states that the Holy Spirit operates in his stead and is coming into the world because he is leaving it (John 16:5–7).

Subsequently, the second reason that supports the notion that the Holy Spirit is indispensable for the Christian life is that this is the age of the New Covenant, when the Spirit's presence and activity is more conspicuous than that of the Father or the Son.[37] With the fulfillment of the prophecies concerning the New Covenant (Joel 2:28–32) taking place in Acts 2, the inauguration of the eschatological presence of the Holy Spirit occurred and has continued to this day. Therefore, to neglect the Holy Spirit is to neglect God's true intentions for the Christian life. Thus, Daniel Migliore highlights the indispensability of the Holy Spirit in this way:

> Neglect and suspicion of the work of the Holy Spirit has damaging effects on both Christian life and Christian theology. It can lead to distortions in the understanding of God, the doctrine of Scripture, the significance of the natural order, the value of human culture, the interpretation of Christ and his work, the nature of the church, the freedom of the Christian, and the

---

36. Ibid., 862–3.

37. Ibid., 863. To be sure, it is necessary to guard against aberrantly exalting the person and place of the Holy Spirit above the Father and the Son by setting him in a proper trinitarian context. Yarnell, "The Person and Work," 682–3, states, "Those who worship God the Father must worship him in and with the second and third persons of the Trinity. Without the Spirit, man may not approach the Son, through whom the Father is approached. To worship God is to worship the trinitarian God in his one essence and three persons. The Holy Spirit is both the subject of worship and the object of worship. The subjectivity of the Spirit draws attention to his divine work in worship; the objectivity of the Spirit draws attention to his divine person in worship. . . . To say that the Holy Spirit is the object of worship is to recognize the full deity of the Spirit and to worship him. If the Spirit is God, and he is, then he must be worshipped together with the Father and the Son." Moreover, to guard against subordinating the Spirit's divinity in relation to the Father and the Son, Erickson, *Christian Theology*, 863–4, argues, in this New Covenant era, ". . . [T]he Spirit performs a ministry of serving the Father and the Son, carrying out their will (which is also his). In this respect, we are reminded of the Son's earthly ministry, during which he was subordinate in function to the Father. Now this temporary subordination of function—the Son's during his earthly ministry and the Spirit's during the present era—must not lead us to draw the conclusion that there is an inferiority in essence as well."

hope for the final fulfillment of life. When the work of the Holy Spirit is forgotten or suppressed, the power of God is apt to be understood as distant, hierarchical, and coercive; Christocentric faith deteriorates into Christomonism; the authority of Scripture becomes heteronomous; the church is seen as a rigid power structure in which some members rule over others; and the sacraments degenerate into almost magical rites under the control of a clerical elite.[38]

Indeed, the Holy Spirit is indispensable for all matters pertaining to faith and practice; a recovery of this mindset is much needed and appears to be on the theological horizon.[39]

The Indispensability of the Holy Spirit for Hermeneutics

Despite the scant attention that illumination receives in many hermeneutics texts, it is often asserted that the biblical interpreter would be remiss without the Holy Spirit's aid.[40] Arguably the impetus behind the interpretation of the Scriptures, the Spirit's work is of vital importance for a proper understanding of the Word of God. The biblical record attests to the essential nature of the doctrine of illumination[41] and there are several works that verify the extensive biblical witness of this doctrine.[42]

---

38. Migliore, *Faith Seeking Understanding*, 166.

39. Ibid, 166–8. Here, Migliore cites six factors regarding a renewed interest in the Holy Spirit and Christian spirituality. Notable among these factors is the hunger for a deeper faith, i.e., a faith that experiences God through the working out of theology in the life setting. Also, Migliore cites a recent resurgence in the interest surrounding the person and work of the Holy Spirit in both the OT and the NT as a contributing factor.

40. Calvin, *Institutes*, (3.2.33), 377, states, "Without the illumination of the Spirit, the word has no effect." Likewise, Owen, *Works*, "Causes" (4.1.124), writes, "The principal efficient cause" that allows believers to grasp a knowledge and understanding of the Word of God is "the Holy Spirit of God himself alone." Also, Klein, Blomberg, and Hubbard, *Biblical Interpretation*, 4, declare, ". . . the role of the Spirit in understanding God's Word is indispensable." Osborne, *Hermeneutical Spiral*, 436, similarly notes, "The person of God must strive for the Holy Spirit in exegeting . . . the Word of God." In addition, Zuck, "The Role of the Holy Spirit in Hermeneutics," 129, avers, "The Holy Spirit needs to be much involved in the process of a believer's efforts to comprehend and interpret the Bible."

41. Ps 119:18; Luke 24:45; John 14:26; 15:26; 16:13; 1 Cor 2:6–16; 2 Cor 3:12–4:6; Eph 1:17–18; 1 John 2:20, 27; 5:20.

42. See Jeff Ingle, "A Historical and Scriptural Survey of the Doctrine of Illumination;" Meador, "A Study in the Role of the Holy Spirit;" and Zuber, "What Is Illumination."

Illumination and Interpretation

The Holy Spirit's indispensability rests upon the distinction that the Bible is a certain kind of text, that is, one that cannot merely be picked up and understood without divine aid. In fact, Stanley Hauerwas asserts, "Rightly reading the Scriptures, is not a given, but requires the hard discipline of existing as a people constituted by the practices of the risen Lord."[43] To be clear, the Scriptures seek transformation in the life of the reader. Hauerwas continues, "So Scripture will not be self-interpreting or plain in its meaning unless we have been *transformed* in order to be capable of reading it."[44] As a result, this approach to reading the Scriptures needs to be consciously pneumatological, for as stated above, transformation in the life of the believer does not happen apart from the Holy Spirit. Those who desire to understand the Scriptures properly will set their minds on the Spirit for this leads to life and peace. And according to Hauerwas, "Only such a people will be capable of rightly reading the Scripture. Only such a people are capable of in fact performing the Scripture."[45]

As can be seen, there are many issues surrounding the doctrine of illumination and the lack of attention that this theological concept receives makes it notoriously difficult to define; and hence, notoriously difficult to understand. The doctrine of illumination is one that is often misunderstood and as a result, convoluted and disregarded in biblical interpretation. Therefore, the importance of this work is bolstered as it seeks to define adequately the doctrine of illumination and the Spirit's role in the hermeneutic process such that it is properly understood as essential for biblical interpretation and the Christian life. With the goal of transformation in mind, and through the establishment of distinctions in the doctrine in order to provide clarification, a proper understanding of the Holy Spirit's work of illumination will significantly inform one's hermeneutic.

---

43. Hauerwas, *The Hauerwas Reader*, 255. Hauerwas is arguing that discipleship in the context of a community of believers is directly proportionate to one's ability to interpret the Scriptures. This matter will be discussed in further detail in the concluding chapter of this book.

44. Ibid., 257; emphasis added.

45. Ibid., 265.

2

Illumination and Hermeneutics

THE DOCTRINE OF ILLUMINATION is a necessary component in the discipline of hermeneutics. If the Holy Spirit and his work of illumination are indispensable for biblical interpretation, then the Holy Spirit and hermeneutics ought to make a likely marriage. However, Claude Peifer, writing to assert that the studies of the biblical scholar and the illumination of the Holy Spirit are not mutually exclusive, but components of a "mutually complete" approach to interpreting the Scriptures, makes this analysis of the present state of biblical scholarship:

> But it was primarily philosophical developments which changed people's attitude toward the Bible and allowed it to be approached purely as a historical document. The Enlightenment made reason the sole arbiter of truth, whereupon rational criticism claimed the entire sphere of human thought and life, including religion, as its rightful domain. In the nineteenth century there was added a new awareness of the importance of evolutionary development in all human affairs, and consequently of the time-conditioned character of the biblical literature. Therefore, the way to understand the meaning of the biblical writers was to apply to their work the same scientific methods which illuminated any document from antiquity.... In any case, there grew a more or less widespread consensus as to what is necessary for the understanding of Scripture: it requires an increase of knowledge, to be obtained by the human effort of study, and made available, ultimately, by the application of scientific methodology to the Bible. While this may range all the way from the research scholar working on the original text to the schoolchild

Illumination and Interpretation

becoming acquainted with the most elementary features of biblical history, the difference is only one of degree. In every case it is supposed that our understanding of Scripture is dependent upon the use, to some degree, of biblical criticism, that is, upon the use of our reason to arrive at the author's meaning.[1]

Consequently, in light of Peifer's comments concerning the neglect of the Holy Spirit's role in biblical hermeneutics, it is necessary to uncover the obscured relationship between the doctrine of illumination and related biblical doctrines often found in the hermeneutical realm. In order to establish the foundation for the indispensability of the Holy Spirit in biblical interpretation, the connections between illumination and the revelation, inspiration, perspicuity, sufficiency, and authority of Scripture will be made clear.

Additionally, another issue regarding the relationship between the Holy Spirit and hermeneutics is of vital import. Based upon my definitions of meaning and understanding pertaining to the Scriptures, a discussion regarding the interpretation of the Scriptures by the unregenerate and the regenerate will be undertaken so that the necessity of the Spirit's illuminatory role is further bolstered.[2] The doctrine of illumination and the discipline of hermeneutics have experienced an unfortunate divorce in recent years, but there must be reconciliation if there is to be proper biblical interpretation.

Related Biblical Doctrines

Illumination and Revelation

A proper view of the doctrine of illumination is based upon its interconnectedness with the doctrine of revelation.[3] Maier states, "If we have

---

1. Claude Peifer, "The Experience of Sin, Salvation, and the Spirit," 4–6.

2. It is important to recognize here that I am not in any way alluding to the patristic distinction between the literal and "higher" senses of Scripture nor what was later developed into the fourfold sense of Scripture in the Middle Ages. I am merely referring to a meaning and understanding that speaks to the lexical-grammatical level of the text that constitutes a basic cognitive knowledge—an understanding that the unregenerate can only have of the Scriptures; and a meaning and understanding which is enacted by faith and requires the Holy Spirit's work of illumination that inevitably leads to transformation in the life of the believer—an understanding that only the regenerate can attain of the Scriptures.

3. For a brief overview of the doctrine of revelation, see B. Demarest, "Revelation,

rightly defined our task, namely, to understand the Bible in accordance with its own basic claim . . . then our guiding principle must be to proceed consistently from the revelation that encounters us in the form of the Bible. The starting point must strictly and consistently be revelation itself."[4] Specifically, the arena of special revelation is of significance as it encompasses the Scriptures. It is important to note though, that the Scriptures and special revelation are not synonymous. Indeed, the Scriptures are a form of special revelation, but they do not compose the doctrine in its entirety.[5] Subsequently, it is an undemanding task to discuss the bond between illumination and revelation since both doctrines are directly related to the Scriptures.

Without the illumination of the Holy Spirit, the objective revelation of God, viz., the Scriptures, cannot be properly interpreted.[6] In accordance with this, F. W. Camfield asserts, "The doctrine of the Holy Spirit is the coping-stone of the doctrines of revelation and faith. Apart from it, the whole structure lacks unity and coherence."[7] Likewise, without the doctrine of revelation, the illumination of the Holy Spirit cannot be properly employed. Camfield continues:

> The doctrine of the Holy Spirit is superfluous and in the last resort meaningless, unless it be considered in relation to the New Testament conception of revelation as a whole, and be made the category for the explicating of revelation. Considered apart and in itself as a doctrine that can be treated independently, it yields nothing and leads nowhere. And it is because it has been to a large extent isolated and considered in itself, that thought about it has been so extraordinarily sterile. Men take it as an idea, and pursue the developments of the idea in scripture and in historical theology, and when they have done that, they leave the matter, for they can get no farther. Or they attempt to evaluate it psychologically and speak of it as the 'expression of an experience;' and they thus inevitably come to the conclusion

---

General," 1019–21 and C. F. H. Henry, "Revelation, Special," 1021–23. For a more comprehensive introduction see Erickson, *Christian Theology*, 177–223, or Akin, Nelson, and Schemm, *A Theology for the Church*, 71–174.

4. Gerhard Maier, *Biblical Hermeneutics*, 34.

5. For a discussion concerning this distinction see Dockery and Nelson, "Special Revelation," 121–3. Also see Warfield, *Revelation and Inspiration*, 47–8.

6. See Kwok, "Benjamin B. Warfield's Doctrine of Illumination," and his section entitled "Revelation and the Work of the Holy Spirit" for someone who supports this assertion.

7. Camfield, *Revelation and the Holy Spirit*, 98.

> that it possesses only relative truth. . . . But the doctrine of the Holy Spirit is not simply *a* doctrine of the Christian religion, it is *the* doctrine in which all doctrine culminates. It is the doctrine which makes the other doctrines really doctrines of *revelation*.[8]

To be sure, the doctrine of revelation and the doctrine of the Holy Spirit's work of illumination are *vitally* connected to one another, such that to isolate one from the other, be deficient in one or the other, or be altogether devoid of one or the other seriously degenerates the hermeneutical task.

This unique relationship between the doctrines of illumination and revelation is further heightened when considering the purpose of revelation. As stated by Dockery and Nelson, "The primary purpose of revelation is not necessarily to enlarge the scope of one's knowledge about God. Yet the purpose of knowledge about God is coming to know God . . . [thus] the Spirit applies God's revelation to the minds and hearts of his people by helping them interpret and understand God's written Word (this is sometimes called illumination)."[9] Therefore, revelation is both propositional, i.e., it communicates knowledge about God, and personal, i.e., it seeks to establish a faith relationship with the recipient. Steve Lemke concurs, "Revelation in its fullest sense is both propositional and personal . . . [and] is impoverished when either of these aspects of truth is neglected. . . . In Scripture, God both reveals essential information about himself and provides the opportunity for persons to come into a personal relationship with him."[10] The Bible is a distinctive form of special revelation concerning God that seeks to transform the reader through an intimate relationship with God; and since the Spirit is God, it would behoove the interpreter to enlist his divine aid.[11]

Furthermore, Veenhof alludes to this inimitable relationship between the knowledge of God, revelation, and illumination. He highlights the fact that God's revelation is not discerned in purely cognitive, intellectual concepts. Rather, since God's revelation is not only a communication

---

8. Camfield, *Revelation*, 99–100; emphasis in original.

9. Dockery and Nelson, "Special Revelation," 120–1.

10. Lemke, "The Inspiration and Authority of Scripture," 176–7.

11. Packer, *Keep In Step With The Spirit*, 239–40, alludes to this, "The lordship of the Spirit was exercised in the whole process of producing the Bible and setting it before us, and that same lordship is exercised as the Spirit moves us to receive, revere, and study the Scriptures and to discern their divine message to us. . . . Negligence and one-sidedness either way could be ruinous, and since a proper balance in this as in other matters comes naturally to none of us, we do well to be on our guard."

about God, but is actually God's communication of *himself*, then God is not merely pursuing the intellect, but the whole of man. He argues, "Just so is the knowledge of God, which is given to man by illumination, not only a taking notice of God and his work, but rather the annexation of his thinking and willing and working. Illumination, revelation, knowledge are therefore 'relational' just because they are existential."[12]

Certainly, the relationship between illumination and revelation is a significant one, but it needs to be stated that the Spirit's illumination does not provide new revelation in addition to nor apart from the Scriptures. Fred Klooster affirms this from the outset in his article on illumination[13] and R. C. Sproul qualifies his statement by denying that any *normative* revelation has been given to the church by the Spirit since the close of the NT canon.[14] For Sproul, this qualification is of the utmost importance because he is quick to clarify that this does not mean that the work of the Holy Spirit has ceased in the leading and guiding of his people; rather, he means that private leadings and guiding by the Holy Spirit should not and do not carry the force of Holy Writ.[15] Regarding the relationship between revelation and illumination, Hunt explicates, "Illumination is the form in which God continues to speak by his Spirit once the Bible is written. God continues to speak, but so far as special revelation is concerned he speaks now primarily through scripture. . . . He enables the believer who responds in faith to hear what God through the scripture would say in the new situation of the believer."[16] Thus, the Spirit works through God's special revelation, i.e., the Scriptures, in order to communicate to the believer that which is in the text, so that the life and faith of the believer might be transformed for the sake of the gospel.

Attempting to define the relationship between revelation and the role of the Holy Spirit, Donald Bloesch arrives at a much different conclusion than stated above. He argues that evangelicalism allows for a different view, one in which the Bible is viewed as the ". . . divinely prepared medium or channel of divine revelation rather than revelation itself."[17] Bloesch's view

---

12. Veenhof, "The Holy Spirit and Hermeneutics," 121.
13. Klooster, "The Role of the Holy Spirit in the Hermeneutic Process," 451.
14. Sproul, *Scripture Alone*, 133.
15. Ibid.
16. Hunt, "The Holy Spirit and Revelation Today," 39.
17. Bloesch, *Holy Scripture: Revelation, Inspiration, & Interpretation*, 18.

Illumination and Interpretation

is founded upon his assertion that revelation is larger than the Scriptures.[18] Hence, he contends that the Scriptures are "at least one step removed from the revelation itself. Their witness points to revelation, but it also mediates revelation, since the Spirit acts through the persons and words that he inspires."[19] So instead of identifying the Scripture with revelation, which he concedes would make the task of interpretation much simpler,[20] Bloesch speaks of the text as a conduit in which revelation is received.

Bloesch's conception of revelation is greatly influenced by his theology of Word and Spirit. Indeed, he stresses the role of the Spirit and the experience of faith, such that in his understanding revelation is not merely cognitive, but "it is an act of communication by which God confronts the whole person with his redeeming mercy and glorious presence."[21] In Bloesch's understanding, his view of revelation is necessary in order to allow for this. Furthermore, he argues for the objectivity of that revelation by stating, "In this era when propositional or conceptual truth is being sacrificed for existential or emotive truth, it is incumbent on theology to reaffirm the conceptual side of divine revelation."[22] Bloesch is making a sincere attempt to not only include the Spirit in his hermeneutic, but define the work of the Spirit as an indispensable component of the hermeneutical endeavor. Some of Bloesch's convictions are not much unlike the conclusions that I affirm above,[23] but while Bloesch's intentions may be valid, his conclusions are aberrant.

Not only does Bloesch's conception of revelation unnecessarily suffer from his well-meaning intentions, but his views of scriptural inerrancy and infallibility are infected as well. In his efforts to conflate the "paradoxical unity" which he refers to as Word and Spirit, Bloesch redefines the concepts of inerrancy and infallibility in order to account for the work of the Spirit. He writes, "In my opinion it is wiser to speak

---

18. Ibid., 21–3. Bloesch bases this on a conviction that he asserts is evident throughout church history in the Fathers and the Reformers.

19. Ibid., 56.

20. Ibid., 173.

21. Ibid., 48.

22. Bloesch, *A Theology of Word & Spirit*, 19.

23. In addition to these, Bloesch, *Holy Scripture*, 42, also affirms what he calls a sacramental model of revelation in which he understands revelation as "God in action, God revealing the depth of his love and the mystery of his will to the eyes of faith. Revelation has a personal, a propositional and an experiential pole. What is revealed is a personal presence in conjunction with a spoken or written witness and received by a believing heart."

of the truthfulness or veracity of Scripture rather than of its inerrancy . . . [because] the perfect accuracy of the letter or text of Scripture is not an integral part of the Christian faith."[24] Concerning infallibility he comments, "The Bible contains a fallible element in the sense that it reflects the cultural and historical limitations of the writers. But it is not mistaken in what it purports to teach: God's will and purpose for the world. . . . [Therefore] I affirm the message of Scripture is infallible and that the Spirit interprets this message to people of faith."[25] For Bloesch, infallibility does not reside entirely in the text, but in the Spirit as he works in and through the Scriptures.[26] The source of this view can be traced back to his view of revelation, in which he purports that Scripture ". . . is not in and of itself divine revelation, but when illumined by the Spirit it becomes revelation to the believer."[27]

However, it is not necessary to affirm Bloesch's view of revelation in order to establish the Spirit's primary role in biblical interpretation. The view of the relationship between revelation and illumination purported by Bloesch is convoluted and unnecessary when considering that, as Watson asserts, "Since the Bible is the Word of God because it is the product of the influence of the Holy Spirit on men we may say that the Holy Spirit is the Author of the Bible and is also its interpreter in the minds of men, while, at the same time, since it was written by men for men, it is an ideal revelation for man who is spiritual because made in the image of God."[28] In this study's view, since the Holy Spirit is both the author and the interpreter of the divine revelation, inerrancy and infallibility can remain indwelt in the text and revelation can still be identified with the Scriptures.

Illumination and Inspiration

As a result of the close ties between the doctrines of revelation and inspiration, the relationship between illumination and inspiration can be discussed with relative ease. However, it is necessary to be aware of the distinction between illumination and inspiration because to equivocate

---

24. Bloesch, *Holy Scripture*, 116.
25. Ibid., 115–6.
26. Ibid., 117.
27. Bloesch, "The Primacy of Scripture," 119.
28. Watson, "The Holy Spirit and the Bible," 275.

Illumination and Interpretation

them presents a grave danger that could result in an aberrant and distorted theology.[29]

According to Erickson, simply defined, inspiration is "that supernatural influence of the Holy Spirit on the Scripture writers which rendered their writings an accurate record of the revelation or which resulted in what they wrote actually being the Word of God."[30] In this definition, it is important to note the Spirit's vital role in the process of inspiration. On the other hand, Lemke asserts, illumination refers to "the experience in which spiritual discernment of Scripture is provided by the Holy Spirit. God's Spirit opens human minds to perceive and understand the truth already made known through revelation and recorded in Scripture through inspiration. Illumination provides discernment of God's inspired canon, but never supersedes or supplements it."[31] Likewise, the Spirit's role is highlighted in this definition, thus connecting the two doctrines.[32]

As the Spirit is the author of Scripture (2 Tim 3:16–17; 2 Pet 1:19–21), he is also the interpreter and illuminator of Scripture. John Lewis notes that dependence upon the Spirit for one's interpretation of Scripture recognizes the Spirit's authorship of Scripture through inspiration; and similarly, affirmation of the Spirit's inspiration of the Scriptures, should compel the interpreter to depend on the Holy Spirit's aid.[33] It is essential that a careful distinction between inspiration as the past work of the Holy Spirit and illumination as his present work is recognized here.[34] Thus, the Spirit's work of illumination is contingent upon the Spirit's inspiration of the Scriptures. J. Theodore Mueller argues this point to the extent that,

---

29. For a brief overview of the doctrine of inspiration and its various views, see Erickson, *Christian Theology*, 224–45, and Dockery and Nelson, "Special Revelation," 141–62. This author holds to the verbal plenary view of inspiration as outlined in Dockery and Nelson, "Special Revelation," 153–4.

30. Erickson, *Christian Theology*, 225.

31. Lemke, "Inspiration and Authority," 177.

32. Another simple distinction between the definitions of inspiration and illumination is given by Finlayson, "Contemporary Ideas of Inspiration," 222, where he states, "By inspiration is meant that influence of the Holy Spirit on the minds of selected men which rendered them organs of God for the infallible communication of that revelation. By illumination is understood the divine quickening of the human mind in virtue of which it is able to understand the truth so revealed and communicated."

33. Lewis, *Revelation, Inspiration, Scripture*, 121–2.

34. Young, "The Holy Spirit and the Word of God," 41, emphasizes this point and explains, "The present work is always of a subordinate nature, and is not strictly a speaking through the Scripture to the reader or hearer; but rather a speaking to the mind of the reader or hearer, so that he can understand the truth of the written Word."

Illumination and Hermeneutics

"All who deny the plenary inspiration of the Scriptures and assume only a partial inspiration imperil the testimony of the Holy Spirit."[35]

Paul Achtemeier's doctrine of inspiration is differently nuanced than that affirmed in this work, but he is also aware of the essential connectivity between inspiration and illumination.[36] He writes, " . . . there is no place for appeal to the inner testimony of the Spirit to defend wholly subjective interpretations of Scripture, a practice which happens when the witness of the Spirit is detached from the content of Scripture and raised to independent importance. If the Spirit that bears witness to the reader of Scripture is the same Spirit who was at work in the production of the Scripture, then the witness of the two will correspond and reinforce one another."[37] Although Achtemeier readily acknowledges this relationship, it should be recognized that this is based upon a view of illumination that he describes as a continuing process of inspiration through the reading of Scripture.[38] Indeed, this reflects an undeveloped understanding of the doctrine of illumination that results in an unfounded doctrinal syncretism.[39] Certainly,

---

35. Mueller, "The Holy Spirit and the Scriptures," 272.

36. Achtemeier's view of inspiration is explicated in his work entitled *Inspiration and Authority*. In this work, in an effort to combine the divine and human elements in the process of inspiration, he holds to a form of the dynamic view in which the Spirit directs the writers of Scripture, while also allowing for the convergence of the components of tradition, situation, and respondent to be involved in the process. In doing so however, the locus of inspiration is slightly removed from the words of Scripture which the verbal plenary view seeks to emphasize.

37. Achtemeier, *Inspiration and Authority*, 125.

38. Ibid., 124.

39. Bloesch, *Holy Scripture*, 121, who holds to a similar view of inspiration to that of Achtemeier, likewise reflects an anemic understanding of the doctrine of illumination when he states, "Divine inspiration entails guidance or superintendence, illumination and even preservation." Perhaps Bloesch's understanding of inspiration can be better comprehended as he explicates the relationship it has with revelation: "Inspiration concerns the reliability of the scriptural witness; revelation refers to the self-disclosure of Jesus Christ in the biblical witness. Inspiration signifies the election of the biblical witness; revelation, the uniting of the biblical witness with God's self-witness. Inspiration is the overseeing and directing of the biblical writing; revelation is the rendering of the biblical testimony transparent to its divine content. Inspiration means that the Bible is penetrated and filled with the Holy Spirit; revelation occurs when the Bible transmits the Word of God by the action of the Spirit. Inspiration has to do mainly with the form of the Bible; revelation, the thing signified. Revelation is the shining of the light of God through the prism of Scripture; inspiration is ensuring that Scripture can be a prism for God's light. Inspiration reaches its goal in revelation; revelation finds its springboard in inspiration" (p. 126).

Illumination and Interpretation

these two doctrines are fundamentally connected, but as previously noted they are also significantly distinctive.[40]

In addition, the concepts of the infallibility and inerrancy of Scripture are often projected out of the doctrine of inspiration. It is important to note that though these two concepts are corollaries of the doctrine of inspiration and refer to the inherent dependability of the Scriptures, they do not relate to the doctrine of illumination in the same manner. Zuck makes this clear when he stresses:

> In inspiration the Holy Spirit superintended the authors in order to override any human error. In interpretation the Holy Spirit guides but He does not guard against infallibility. To elevate one's interpretations to the level of infallibility would blur the distinctions between inspiration (a past, now completed work of the Spirit in the recording of Scripture) and interpretation (a present, ongoing work of the Spirit in helping interpreters in the comprehending of Scripture).[41]

Consequently, though the same Spirit is at work in illumination as was at work in the process of inspiration the concepts of infallibility and inerrancy are not communicable attributes to the process of interpretation.[42] However, without the Holy Spirit's illumination, it is impossible to arrive at a proper interpretation of the infallible and inerrant Word of God.

Illumination and Perspicuity

The biblical doctrine of perspicuity may be the one that is most closely aligned to the doctrine of illumination because it treats the clarity of

---

40. Vanhoozer, *The Drama of Doctrine*, 226, affirms, "The Scriptures are the Spirit's work form first to last. The Spirit is involved in the very messy historical process of producing Scripture—prompting, appropriating, and coordinating human discourse to present God's Word—as well as in the process of bringing about understanding of Scripture among present-day readers. The traditional names for these modes of participation are *inspiration* and *illumination*, respectively;" emphasis in original.

41. Zuck, "The Role of the Holy Spirit in Hermeneutics," 122.

42. Even though Bloesch, *Holy Scripture*, 121–2, and Achtemeier, *Inspiration and Authority*, 45–63, deny the connectivity between inspiration and the inerrancy/infallibility of Scriptures, Dockery and Nelson, "Special Revelation, 142–9, combat this with a good summary of the role that human authorship plays in regard to divine inspiration and also highlight and explain some improper deductions that are often reached concerning the human authorship of Scripture. These improper conclusions are the phenomena of Scripture, the accommodation of Scripture, the salvation emphasis, textual criticism, and sinful humanity.

Scripture as it relates to the purpose of understanding.[43] A common misconception concerning illumination is that the Holy Spirit serves to illumine the text of Scripture. However, the light of Scripture requires no further illumination according to its own testimony.[44] Instead, it is the reader of Scripture that is the object of the Spirit's activity. John Webster states, "The setting of the clarity of Scripture is the effective illuminating presence of God the revealer who is in himself light and whose mighty work of reconciliation overthrows the darkness and ignorance of sin, restoring us to fellowship and establishing the knowledge of himself."[45] The neglect of the doctrine of illumination and a misunderstanding of Scripture's perspicuity has fueled the misconception that the text requires illumination. Thus, it is of vital import to discuss both the interrelatedness and distinctiveness of these two doctrines.

A concise definition of the principle of perspicuity is given by Walter Kaiser, who writes that it simply means, "... the Bible is sufficiently clear in and of itself for believers to understand it."[46] He further explains that Scripture is sufficiently perspicuous to inform the reader of the essential message of the Christian faith and despite some difficulties it is likewise sufficient to disciple the believer.[47] In a similar vein, building off the assumption that God is communicative, Mark Thompson asserts that it is God's desire to be

---

43. For a historical, theological, and biblical overview of the doctrine of perspicuity see Baldwin, "The Perspicuity of Scripture," and Roberts, "The Relationship Between the Perspicuity of Scripture and the Nature of Spiritual Illumination," 6–22.

44. Deuteronomy 29:29 states, "The secret things belong to the Lord our God, but the things that are revealed belong to us and to our children forever, that we may do all the words of this law." Psalm 19:7–8 states, "The law of the Lord is perfect, reviving the soul; the testimony of the Lord is sure, making wise the simple; the precepts of the Lord are right, rejoicing the heart; the commandment of the Lord is pure enlightening the eyes." Psalm 119:105 states, "Your word is a lamp to my feet and a light to my path." Second Timothy 3:15–17 states, "... and how from childhood you have been acquainted with the sacred writings, which are able to make you wise for salvation through faith in Christ Jesus. All Scripture is breathed out by God and profitable for teaching, for reproof, for correction, and for training in righteousness, that the man of God may be competent, equipped for every good work."

45. Webster, "Biblical Theology and the Clarity of Scripture," 358. Also, Ingle, "A Historical and Scriptural Survey of the Doctrine of Illumination," 100, contends, "It should be noted that it is the *person* who is illuminated by the Spirit to understand the Word. The problem lies within man, not in God's Word. There is some sense in which illumination takes place in conjunction with the revealed truth of God's Word. But it is man who has the sin problem that keeps his eyes veiled from the truth" (emphasis in original).

46. Kaiser, "Legitimate Hermeneutics," 128.

47. Ibid.

Illumination and Interpretation

known by his creatures and Scripture exists for that very purpose, thus it is perspicuous.[48] Certainly, latently foundational to this statement is Martin Luther's familiar refrain when considering the objective of revelation in which he argues that since God desires that we know him, he would not have a purpose in making his revelation obscure.[49]

Although these statements are accurate, especially according to the Bible's own testimony, this does not suggest that Scripture is free from being misunderstood nor does it indicate that everything in Scripture is equally comprehensible.[50] To be sure, the process of interpretation is still required in order to understand Scripture. According to Osborne, this misunderstanding of the perspicuity of Scripture often results when the doctrine is applied to the hermeneutical process instead of the gospel message itself.[51] Admittedly, the task of interpretation is complex and demanding, but the clarity of Scripture's content as it resides in the person of Jesus Christ is unaffected by the complexity that often accompanies the hermeneutical endeavor.

Accordingly, Luther's distinction between external and internal perspicuity is helpful and reveals the integral role that the Holy Spirit plays:

> The perspicuity of Scripture is twofold, just as there is a double lack of light. The first is external, and relates to the ministry of the Word; the second concerns knowledge of the heart. If you speak of *internal* perspicuity, the truth is that nobody who has not the Spirit of God sees a jot of what is in the Scriptures. All men have their hearts darkened, so that, even when they can discuss and quote all that is in Scripture, they do not understand or really know any of it. They do not believe in God, nor do they believe that they are God's creatures. . . . The Spirit is needed for the understanding of all Scripture and every part of Scripture. If, on the other hand, you speak of *external* perspicuity, the position is that nothing whatsoever is left obscure or ambiguous, but all that is in the Scripture is through the Word brought forth into clearest light and proclaimed to the whole world.[52]

---

48. Thompson, *A Clear and Present*, 51, 79.

49. Luther, *The Bondage of the Will*, 128.

50. See 2 Pet 3:14–18 for an apostolic attestation to this fact. Also, Zuck, "The Role of the Holy Spirit," 128; Grudem, *Systematic Theology*, 108–9; Baldwin, *Perspicuity*, 15; Osborne, *The Hermeneutical Spiral*, 27; and Dockery and Nelson, "Special Revelation," 163, affirm this statement.

51. Osborne, *Hermeneutical Spiral*, 27.

52. Luther, *Bondage*, 73–74; emphasis in original.

In Luther's delineation, he describes external perspicuity as being an inherent property of the text, i.e., it is external to the reader of the text. This being the case, he likewise grants that some *passages* of Scripture are difficult to understand, but this "does not prevent our knowing all the *contents* of Scripture."[53] Therefore, since external perspicuity refers to the linguistic and grammatical clarity of Scripture, it is due to our own ignorance if some portions of Scripture appear obscure.

Moreover, it is evident in Luther's explanation of Scripture's perspicuity that the Holy Spirit maintains an internal role in the heart of the reader. Indeed, this establishes the link between illumination and perspicuity. Luther recognizes that apart from the Holy Spirit's illumination on the darkened heart of the *reader*, the Scriptures *appear* clouded in obscurity; ". . . but that is due, not to any lack of clarity in Scripture, but to their own blindness and dullness, in that they make no effort to see truth which, in itself, could not be plainer."[54] Dockery and Nelson agree at this point and support the Spirit's indispensability for biblical interpretation by contending, "In this sense, Scripture is only clear to those who believe the gospel. The work of the Spirit is necessary to illuminate darkened minds and blinded eyes, enabling them to understand."[55]

Granting the above argument, Grudem's more qualified definition of the perspicuity of Scripture may be more appropriate for our understanding of the relationship between illumination and perspicuity. Note the emphasis he places on divine aid as he writes, "The clarity of Scripture means that the Bible is written in such a way that its teachings are able to be understood by all who will read it seeking God's help and being willing to follow it."[56] For Grudem, the clarity of Scripture and the illumination of the Holy Spirit are naturally connected. Only when the reader is properly illumined by the Holy Spirit and devoid of obscurity within himself, can the clarity of Scripture truly reflect upon the reader and his ability to understand it. To sum up, Webster states, "The act of interpretation repeats the basic motif of Christian existence, which is being drawn out of the darkness of sin and turned to the light of the gospel. *Holy Scripture is clear*; but because its matter is that to which we must be reconciled, readers can only discern its clarity if *their* darkness is *illuminated*. . . .

---

53. Ibid., 71; emphasis in original.
54. Ibid., 72.
55. Dockery and Nelson, "Special Revelation," 163.
56. Grudem, *Systematic Theology*, 108.

Illumination and Interpretation

Interpretation of the clear Word of God is therefore not first of all an act of clarification but the event of being clarified."[57] It is in light of this that the illumination of the Holy Spirit and the inherent perspicuity of the Scriptures share an intimate bond, such that the Spirit's ministry of illumination enables the perspicuous nature of Scripture by enlightening the mind and heart of the reader.

Illumination and Sufficiency

The illumination of the Holy Spirit and the sufficiency of Scripture[58] share a common bond, i.e., comparatively speaking, they are both neglected among hermeneutical doctrines. Nonetheless, both doctrines are vital to the hermeneutical endeavor and are more closely linked than appears at first take.

Grudem defines the sufficiency of Scripture as follows: "... [it] means that Scripture contained all the words of God he intended his people to have at each stage of redemptive history, and that it now contains all the words of God we need for salvation, for trusting him perfectly, and for obeying him perfectly."[59] In light of our present discussion, this definition serves as a suitable foundation because it speaks directly to the Scriptures and their purpose. However, it does lack one crucial element, viz., the role of the Holy Spirit.

Again, the end of the Spirit's illumination is transformation in the life of the believer, which in essence is the appropriation of the Scripture's message. Hence, illumination is inherently connected to the sufficiency of the Scriptures. Dockery and Nelson explain, "The doctrine of sufficiency entails the affirmation that Scripture is itself sufficient for doctrine and life (2 Tim 3:16-17) inasmuch as the Scriptures are learned with the illuminating assistance of the Holy Spirit (John 14:26; 16:13; 1 Cor 1:6ff.) and life is lived by the empowerment of the Holy Spirit (2 Pet 1:3)."[60]

Accordingly, Timothy Ward observes that the Reformers made much of the sufficiency of Scripture and that the central issue at stake was "the

---

57. Webster, *Confessing God*, 63–4; emphasis added.

58. For a discussion concerning the biblical basis of the sufficiency of Scripture see Smith, "The Doctrine of the Sufficiency of Scripture," 8–11. For a discussion concerning the historical-theological basis of this doctrine see Johnson, "Time, Scripture and Tradition."

59. Grudem, *Systematic Theology*, 127.

60. Dockery and Nelson, "Special Revelation," 163.

nature of the Holy Spirit's ongoing activity in relation to Scripture."[61] In reaction to the Church on the one hand and the Radical Reformation on the other hand, the Reformers advocated the sufficiency of the Scriptures by taking the middle road and arguing that "the Scripture the Holy Spirit authored in the past receives its authority in the present from the fact that God the Holy Spirit continues to speak in it and through it the same message he once uttered."[62] In view of this, the sufficiency of Scripture is not only founded upon the Holy Spirit's inspiration of the Scriptures, but is indeed established by the Holy Spirit's continual work of illumination.

Additionally, Ward offers a helpful rubric for understanding the sufficiency of the Scriptures in terms of the actions of the Holy Spirit. He writes:

> The text itself cannot produce faithful response; it is sufficient for *notitia* ('intelligent cognition' of 'intelligible information'), but insufficient for the two stages of faithful response, for both of which the Holy Spirit is required: *assensus* ('cognition passed into conviction . . . truth believed as applicable to ourselves, as supremely vital and important for us') and *fiducia* ('conviction passed into confidence . . . the engagement of person to person in the inner movement of the whole man to receive and rest upon Christ alone for salvation').[63]

This rubric foreshadows the upcoming discussion concerning cognitive meaning and understanding and transformative meaning and understanding in which the Holy Spirit is shown to be indispensable for a proper interpretation of the Scriptures. Suffice it to say for now that the Scriptures are sufficient for the faith and practice of the believer, in cooperation with the Holy Spirit.

Illumination and Authority

Normally, the doctrines of inspiration and authority go hand-in-hand. However, in this study the hermeneutical doctrine of authority has been transferred to the final position because it serves as an anchor to the doctrines of revelation, inspiration, perspicuity, and sufficiency and especially to the doctrine of illumination. Each of these doctrines relies upon and is influenced in some way by the authority of Holy Scripture,

---

61. Ward, *Words of Life*, 110–1.
62. Ibid., 110.
63. Ward, *Word and Supplement*, 202.

Illumination and Interpretation

and it is in the relationship between illumination and authority that the lucidity of this interdependence will be brought to fruition.

To begin, a point of clarification is in order. Here, when speaking of authority, we are referring specifically to the authority of the Scriptures. There are other sources of authority that have been recognized by believers throughout the annals of church history,[64] but as the Spirit works in direct cooperation with the Word, so the illumination of the Spirit operates in conjunction with the authority of the Scriptures.[65]

As affirmed by Dockery and Nelson, the proper place to begin a discussion on biblical authority is with God himself, for it is in God that all authority is ultimately located.[66] Therefore, it should be established that biblical authority is based sturdily upon the divine provenance of the Scriptures. As shown above, the Holy Spirit is indeed divine, as he is the third person of the triune Godhead,[67] and as the author and interpreter

64. The sources of authority that are traditionally recognized at different levels by the Christian faith are reason, tradition, and the church, along with the Scriptures. Maier, *Biblical Hermeneutics*, 167–9, briefly treats reason and the interpretation/teaching of the church as various sources of authority in light of their relationship with the Scriptures. Saucy, *Scripture*, 230–40, addresses the authorities of human spiritual experience and the teaching authority of the church in relation to the authority of the Scriptures.

65. The Scriptures attest to their own authority in a few passages: 2 Tim 3:16–17 which states, "All Scripture is breathed out by God and profitable for teaching, for reproof, for correction, and for training in righteousness, that the man of God may be competent, equipped for every good work;" 2 Pet 1:19–21 which states, "And we have something more sure, the prophetic word, to which you will do well to pay attention as to a lamp shining in a dark place, until the day dawns and the morning star rises in your hearts, knowing this first of all, that no prophecy of Scripture comes from someone's own interpretation. For no prophecy was ever produced by the will of man, but men spoke from God as they were carried along by the Holy Spirit;" John 5:39–40 which states, "You search the Scriptures because you think that in them you have eternal life; and it is they that bear witness about me, yet you refuse to come to me that you may have life;" John 10:35 which states, ". . . Scripture cannot be broken;" and Matt 5:17–19 which states, "Do not think that I have come to abolish the Law or the Prophets; I have not come to abolish them but to fulfill them. For truly, I say to you, until heaven and earth pass away, not an iota, not a dot, will pass from the Law until all is accomplished. Therefore whoever relaxes one of the least of these commandments and teaches others to do the same will be called least in the kingdom of heaven, but whoever does them and teaches them will be called great in the kingdom of heaven."

66. Dockery and Neslon, "Special Revelation," 162.

67. Although we are emphasizing the Holy Spirit and his work, it is vital to recognize that biblical authority is a trinitarian authority that rests upon the triune Godhead as averred by Hatchett, "The Authority of the Bible," 204, and also Ward, *Words of Life*, 129, when he writes that Scripture is the means "by which the Father presents himself to us as the faithful God of the covenant, and by which the Son, the Word of God,

of the Scriptures he transmits his authority to the written Word.[68] Ward concurs with this point:

> The phrase 'the authority of Scripture' must be understood to be shorthand for 'the authority of God as he speaks through Scripture.' To speak about the authority of Scripture is really to say more about God, and about the ways he chooses to act and speak in the world, than it is to say something directly about Scripture itself. The authority of Scripture is dependent entirely on the authority of God, and comes about only because of what God has chosen to do in the way he authored Scripture, and because of what he continues to do in presenting himself to us through Scripture as a God we can know and trust.[69]

Ward's comments provide an adequate segue into the relationship between illumination and authority since he references God's continued work through the Scriptures today. Likewise, Achtemeier stresses that biblical authority, since it is established upon the divine, is not to be relegated to the past, but continues in the present as God speaks through the Scriptures.[70] This present working of God through the Scriptures connects the doctrines of illumination and authority. Accordingly, in his theology, Erickson inherently links the doctrines of illumination and authority by addressing the doctrine of illumination in his chapter on

---

speak his words to us, and whose message and words the Holy Spirit himself spoke, oversaw and now illumines for us."

68. Studebaker, "'The Authority of the Holy Spirit' in Contemporary Theology," 303, supports this point when he writes, "Such authority [biblical authority], however, ultimately emerges from the Spirit's authority as a divine Person. The mind of God as revealed in the Bible is ultimately non-accessible without the Spirit, who has the authority to search and reveal this mind to us." Likewise, Achtemeier, *Inspiration and Authority*, 144, agrees, "To raise the question of authority within a context of the canonical collection of inspired Scripture is to be pointed by that entity not to itself and the documents of which it is comprised, but rather to be pointed to One who lies beyond the documents, and from whom the documents derive such authority as they have." Bloesch, *Holy Scripture*, 129, also contends this point: "Scripture is authoritative because it is penetrated and filled with the Holy Spirit. It is God-breathed, and the creative breath of God remains in and with Scripture." Migliore, *Faith Seeking Understanding*, 46, is also in agreement, asserting, "To speak of the authority of the Bible rightly is to speak of its power by God's Spirit to help create and nourish this new life in relationship with God and with others."

69. Ward, *Words of Life*, 128.

70. Achtemeier, *Inspiration and Authority*, 145–6.

Illumination and Interpretation

biblical authority.[71] To be sure, the same Holy Spirit who inspired the Scriptures thereby imputing authority to them is the same Holy Spirit who illuminates the Scriptures such that they are authoritative in the life of the believer. As J. I. Packer states, "So those who would live under the authority of the Spirit must bow before the Word as the Spirit's textbook, while those who would live under the authority of Scripture must seek the Spirit as its interpreter."[72] The Spirit's ministry of illumination is thus directly proportional to the perpetuity of Scripture's authority. Again, Ward's comments are *a propos*:

> The doctrine of the illumination of Scripture by the Holy Spirit is usually defended as the only means by which the authority of Scripture can be made to rest, as it must rest, on God himself alone. . . . God is in Scripture in the sense that the speech acts of Scripture are an aspect of his active presence; it is then quite natural that the ongoing illuminatory work of the Holy Spirit should occur in and through those words.[73]

However, the authority of the Scriptures as derived from the inspiration of the Spirit is not synonymous with the authority that the Scriptures maintain today by the illumination of the Spirit. Certainly, both forms of authority find their origin in the divine, but it is vital that they are properly distinguished lest our understanding of authority become unbalanced.

Lemke explicates this distinction with the terms intrinsic authority and extrinsic authority. Intrinsic authority refers to the biblical authority that has been imputed to the Scriptures by their divine provenance; whereas, extrinsic authority refers to a believer's acknowledgement of the Scripture's authoritativeness as a normative guide for faith and practice.[74] In concurrence with Lemke, Ned Stonehouse states, "We should keep in view, first of all, that the divine authority of the Bible as Scripture is an intrinsic authority rather than one superimposed upon it, and that, therefore, possession of the attribute of divine authority does not have to wait upon the recognition thereof to be valid."[75] This understanding is crucial because it is not Scripture's extrinsic authority that makes it

---

71. Erickson, *Christian Theology*, 266–85.
72. Packer, *Keep In Step With The Spirit*, 240.
73. Ward, *Words of Life*, 94.
74. Lemke, "Inspiration and Authority," 189.
75. Stonehouse, "Special Revelation as Scriptural," 84.

authoritative; on the other hand, as a result of Scripture's intrinsic authority, it also possesses an extrinsic authority in reference to the regenerate.

Bernard Ramm offers a helpful framework for understanding the biblical doctrine of authority in relation to the illumination of the Holy Spirit as he speaks about the bond between Word and Spirit. Concerning this bond he argues, "The *duality* of the Word and the Spirit must always be maintained, for it is in this *duality* that the Protestant and Christian principle of authority exists."[76] In order to explain this duality as it is innately interconnected with biblical authority, Ramm suggests a trinitarian pattern of authority that involves at its very essence the illuminatory work of the Holy Spirit.[77] In his view, "The objective Word of the Father [the Scriptures], and the subjective ministry of the Spirit [illumination] intersect in the heart of the believer to create a true knowledge of God and to call into being the Christian principle of authority."[78] To make cer-

---

76. Ramm, *The Pattern of Authority*, 30. To support his thesis, Ramm cites a number of theologians including Calvin and the chapter in his *Institutes* entitled, "The Testimony of the Spirit Necessary to Confirm the Scripture, in Order to the Complete Establishment of Its Authority. The Suspension of Its Authority on the Judgment of the Church, an Impious Fiction" (*Institutes*, 1.7); Luther, who avers, "I believe that I can not by my own reason or strength believe in Jesus Christ my Lord or come to him; but the Holy Ghost has called me through the Gospel, enlightened me by his gifts, and sanctified and preserved me in the true faith" (*Small Catechism*); Kuyper, who comments, "Not, of course, as though the Bible, by itself, were sufficient to give, to every one who reads it, the true knowledge of God. We positively reject such a mechanical explanation: and by their teaching of the witness of the Holy Spirit as absolutely indispensable for all *conviction* concerning the Scripture, by their requirement of illumination for the *right understanding* of the Scripture, and by their high esteem of the ministry of the Word for the *application* of the Scripture, our fathers have sufficiently shown that such a mechanical explanation cannot be ascribed to them" (*Principles of Sacred Theology*, 360; emphasis in original); and Arminius, who declares, ". . . the Holy Spirit, by whose inspiration holy men of God have spoken this word, and by those whose impulse and guidance they have, as his amanuenses, consigned it to writing; that this Holy Spirit is the author of that light by the aid of which we obtain a perception and an understanding of the divine meaning of the word, and is the Effector of that *Certainty* by which we believed those meanings to be truly divine; and that He is the *necessary Author, the all sufficient Effector*" (*The Writings of Arminius*, I. 140; emphasis in original).

77. Ramm, *Authority*, 36, outlines his pattern of authority as follows: "(1) *Christ*, who is the living, personal Word of God, the supreme revelation of God, the supreme depository of the knowledge of God (Col 2:3); (2) *The Holy Spirit*, who conveys revelation, who delegates its authority, and who witnesses to its divinity; (3) *The Sacred Scriptures*, which are inspired by the Holy Spirit and therefore the document of revelation, which witnesses supremely to Jesus Christ, and which are the Spirit's instrument in effecting illumination" (emphasis in original).

78. Ibid., 62.

Illumination and Interpretation

tain, the Scriptures possess an intrinsic authority derived from the Spirit of God, which translates into an extrinsic authority in the life of the believer through the Holy Spirit's work of illumination. Thus, illumination and authority share a special bond because of the authoritative Word and the authoritative Spirit.

Naturally, a discussion about the internal testimony of the Holy Spirit is fitting since the Spirit's work in this regard is directly related to the recognition of Scripture's authority. Certainly, according to Erickson, these two concepts are interrelated. He writes, "It is a combination of these two factors that constitutes authority. Both are needed. The written word, correctly interpreted, is the objective basis of authority. The inward illuminating and persuading work of the Holy Spirit is the subjective dimension."[79] For the present time, it is sufficient to merely recognize the inherent connection between the inner testimony of the Spirit and biblical authority. Following this chapter, a more prolonged discussion concerning the inner testimony of the Spirit and its relationship with illumination will ensue.

Finally, in light of the bond between illumination and authority, it is necessary to address the effect of transformation that this should have on the faith and practice of the regenerate. Martyn Lloyd-Jones states, "Only when the authority of the Holy Spirit comes to bear upon us do all these things [the authority of Christ and the authority of the Scriptures] become real and living and powerful to us. More than that, all that we believe about the Scriptures and about the Lord Himself can only be applied in our ministry, and so become relevant to the world and its situation, as we are under the authority and power of the Holy Spirit."[80]

Hence, when biblical authority is accepted and the authority of the Holy Spirit is communicated, transformation is the inevitable result. Dockery and Nelson call for a "renewed commitment to biblical authority" which is prompted by the Holy Spirit because it bears on every aspect of the believer's life such that the outcome is a transformed faith and practice that serves as motivation for engagement in the expansion of God's kingdom.[81] As previously mentioned, the end of illumination is transformation in the

---

79. Erickson, *Christian Theology*, 278.

80. Lloyd-Jones, *Authority*, 62.

81. Dockery and Nelson, "Special Revelation," 173. Similarly, Weeks, *The Sufficiency of Scripture*, 88, notes a correlation between the all-encompassing nature of redemption and the pervasiveness of Scripture's authority: "The moment you admit that all of it [human life] needs to be redeemed, then you can no longer limit the range of Scripture's authority."

life of the believer. And now considering the interconnectedness of the doctrines of revelation, inspiration, perspicuity, sufficiency, and ultimately authority with the doctrine of illumination, the transformative work of the Spirit can be properly addressed regarding biblical interpretation.

The Interpretation of the Scriptures

Unregenerate Interpretation

A vital issue associated with the bond between the Spirit's illumination and hermeneutics that is often left untouched is the interpretation of the Scriptures by the unregenerate as opposed to biblical interpretation by those who are regenerate. If the Holy Spirit is indispensable for biblical interpretation, then are the Scriptures accessible to those who are devoid of the indwelling presence of the Spirit? To be more specific, can the unregenerate attain a proper understanding of the Scriptures?

First, informing our understanding of this intriguing question is the reality of sin and its noetic effects. Human nature is sinful and thoroughly corrupted, which encompasses its volition, its mind, and its heart.[82] As the Scriptures attest, ". . . none is righteous, no, not one; no one understands; no one seeks for God. All have turned aside; together they have become worthless; no one does good, not even one" (Rom 3:10–12).[83] It is this sinful nature that is predominantly recognized as the primary reason for the Spirit's work of illumination although there are different viewpoints concerning the extent of sin's corruption upon the faculties of

---

82. Kwok, "Benjamin B. Warfield's Doctrine of Illumination," 62, agrees with this affirmation when he writes, ". . . because of the corruption of sin, the human soul, including the mind and heart, cannot understand the message of the revelation without the illumination of the Holy Spirit."

83. Other Scripture passages that bolster this assessment of mankind's sinful nature are Rom 5:12 which states, "Therefore, just as sin came into the world through one man, and death through sin, and so death spread to all men because all sinned;" Rom 3:23, "For all have sinned and fall short of the glory of God;" Eph 2:1–3 which states, "And you were dead in the trespasses and sins in which you once walked, following the course of this world, following the prince and power of the air, the spirit that is now at work in the sons of disobedience—among whom we all once lived in the passions of our flesh, carrying out the desires of the body and the mind, and were by nature children of wrath, like the rest of mankind;" and Eph 4:18 which reads, "They are darkened in their understanding, alienated from the life of God because of the ignorance that is in them, due to their hardness of heart."

Illumination and Interpretation

man.[84] Erickson states, "Illumination is necessary because of sin's effect on the noetic powers of human beings. Some of the countering of this blindness takes place at the point of new birth, but some of it is a direct spiritual work at the point of exposure to the content of Scripture."[85]

It is necessary then to state beforehand my affirmation that the effects of sin upon mankind are pervasive, i.e., affecting all of man's faculties and therefore causing the Holy Spirit to be indispensable for the

---

84. Calvin, *Institutes* (3.2.33), 377, highlights the culpability of sin that produces the requirement for the Spirit's work of illumination. He maintains that humans are darkened in their understanding to such an extent that ". . . such is the proneness of our mind to vanity, that it can never adhere to the truth of God, and such is its dullness, that it is always blind even in his light. Hence without the illumination of the Spirit the word has no effect; and hence also it is obvious that faith is something higher than human understanding." Likewise, according to Owen, *Works*, "Causes" (4.5.176), man's deficiency in these areas is primarily the result of the effects of sin. He posits, "The first and general cause of all ignorance, error, and misunderstanding of the mind and will of God, as revealed in the Scripture, among all sorts of men, whatever their particular circumstances are, is the *natural vanity and darkness with which the minds of all men are depraved*. The nature of this depravation of our minds [is] by the fall, and the effects of it" (emphasis in original). Also, Owen argues that among other corruptions, sin adversely taints the affections, garners pride or "carnal confidence" in man's heart, and engenders a spiritual slothfulness in the interpreter's work (pp. 174–84). Additionally, Hodge, "The Witness of the Holy Spirit to the Bible," 42, contends, ". . . that sin, obscuring and distorting our natural knowledge of God, and darkening man's heart or mind, has rendered him incapable of seeing God in His works, and no less capable of truly seeing Him in the special revelation of Scripture by which He has restored and completed His revelation of Himself. There is need, therefore, of a complete renewal and illumination of the sinner." In the same manner, Erickson, *The New Evangelical Theology*, 72–3, asserts that because of the sinful nature of mankind one cannot properly interpret the Scriptures apart from the aid of the Holy Spirit. He writes, "Indeed, he [the unbeliever] is unable to understand or grasp the true significance of Scripture because of the effect of sin upon his thinking." Also, Goldsworthy, *Gospel-Centered Hermeneutics*, 307, writes, "The Spirit enables us to overcome the effects of sin on the rational process. He makes it possible for the reader to use every faculty to discern the word of God and apply it." In a different manner, Fuller, "Do We Need the Holy Spirit To Understand the Bible?", 22–3, attempts to explicate the reason behind the illumination of the Holy Spirit. He maintains that the interpreter of the Scriptures needs the Spirit's work of illumination because of his sinfulness. However, in Fuller's limited view, man's sinfulness is not considered a corruption of his noetic capabilities, but merely a corruption of his volitional capabilities (p. 23; also see McKinley, "John Owen's View of Illumination, 94). What he means by this is that man's pride, which is the focal point of his depravity, hinders his acceptance of the truth of Scripture and ". . . without realizing it, the natural man seeks to revise the biblical message so it will not be so offensive to him" (p. 23). Thus, it is on this volitional aspect of man that the Holy Spirit performs his work of illumination.

85. Erickson, *Evangelical Interpretation*, 33.

interpretive process.[86] The majority of the scholars cited above recognize the effects of sin on the cognition of man and thus, the necessity of the Spirit's illuminatory work for a proper understanding of the text.[87] But what is a proper understanding of the text? Can an unbeliever attain the meaning of the text of Scripture?

Second, a distinction between meaning and understanding, and what is meant by these two words aids in our search for an explanation to this matter. More accurately, the distinctions between and the definitions of the concepts of cognitive meaning and understanding, which pertain to the unregenerate and transformative meaning and understanding, which are attained by the regenerate, are fundamental to ascertaining a proper view concerning this topic. Consequently, the purpose of this section is merely to define these concepts, the implications of which will be addressed after a full-orbed discussion regarding the doctrine of illumination.

---

86. Related to this hermeneutical issue and pertinent to the discussion is the reality of man's finitude in light of God's infinitude. Calvin, *Institutes* (2.2.19–20), 169–70, mentions that one of his contentions with man's ability to interpret the Scriptures lies in his finitude. In doing so, he recognizes the need for a special work of the Holy Spirit upon the mind of man, in order for him to fully comprehend the things of God. Similarly, Erickson, *Christian Theology*, 273, recognizes the culpability of an ontological difference between God and humanity. God is incomprehensible. He is infinite, transcendent, and as the Creator is sovereign and above all else. On the other hand, man is finite and both limited in his point of origin and knowledge. Erickson distinguishes this finitude by stating, "These limitations are inherent in being human. They are not a result of the fall or of individual human sin, but of the Creator-creature relationship. No moral connotation or stigma is attached to them" (p. 273). In addition, Smith, "The Pauline Doctrine of Illumination," 8–9, affirms, "God in His transcendence and omniscience is completely out of the reach of finite mankind. Even more, God's ways as He is revealed to us in His revelation are far more profound than human frailty can grasp. . . . The very fact of Infinity being made known to a finite recipient is an impossibility apart from a special provision made by God."

87. Also, Larkin, *Culture and Biblical Hermeneutics*, 293–8, recognizes the need for the Spirit's illumination as he asserts that the Scriptures describe the effects of sin at the "deepest level." Regarding these effects he writes, "The unregenerate mind applies reason to the Scriptures and arrives at interpretations characterized by doubt, fragmentation, and distortions "(p. 295). Doubt, he contends, manifests itself as skepticism and mockery of the Word of God (p. 296). Fragmentation introduces contrived distinctions and unnecessary separations into the biblical text (p. 297). And distortion lends itself to the reinterpretation of the text to fit human teachings (pp. 297–8).

Illumination and Interpretation

Cognitive Meaning

Based on the relationships between illumination and revelation and illumination and perspicuity as outlined above, it is this study's contention that an unregenerate person can grasp a cognitive meaning of the text of Scripture. Indeed, since God is revealing himself to mankind in the Scriptures in a special way, and since the clarity of the Scriptures is evident, a cognitive meaning is attainable by any who read the text.[88]

Simply stated cognitive meaning refers to a lexical-grammatical comprehension of the text. Therefore, a textual meaning of the Scriptures can be ascertained through a simple reading of the text or the diligent study of the text with a full arsenal of exegetical tools and proper hermeneutical methodology. For this reason, the unregenerate biblical scholar or lay person is able to read Scripture and discover its meaning cognitively. Cognitive meaning does not *require* the work of the Spirit because God has given each person certain intellectual and cognitive capabilities. As a result, the unregenerate person and the regenerate person alike can attain a cognitive meaning.[89]

However, based upon the noetic effects of sin, this cognitive meaning of the text can be deficient because of the absence of the Spirit's presence in the unregenerate life. It needs to be remembered that based upon the relationship between illumination and inspiration as previously mentioned, this is a divine book that is divinely-enabled. Consequently, despite the capability of man to intellectually arrive at a cognitive meaning of the text, his cognition remains corrupted by the power of sin.

In light of this it is helpful to refer to Vanhoozer's rubric for understanding communicative actions. He writes:

---

88. Grudem, *Systematic Theology*, 107, somewhat qualifies this statement by writing, "Scripture is able to be understood by all unbelievers *who will read it sincerely seeking salvation*, and by all believers who will read it while seeking God's help in understanding it. This is because in both cases the Holy Spirit is at work overcoming the effects of sin, which otherwise will make the truth appear foolish" (emphasis added). This statement is written in his section on the clarity of Scripture where he also writes that Scripture ". . . will not be understood rightly by those who are unwilling to receive its teachings" (ibid.). Here, Grudem emphasizes a "right" understanding of the text, but he is unclear as to the specific nature of this understanding.

89. Pinnock, *The Scripture*, 168, agrees, ". . . there is an ordinary level of comprehension. Anyone can investigate fruitfully the meaning of a text. It should be possible for Christians and others to agree on the historical meaning of the text."

Illumination and Hermeneutics

> To be precise, meaning is a three-dimensional communicative action, with form and matter (propositional content), energy and trajectory (illocutionary force), and teleology or final purpose (perlocutionary effect). This "action" model of meaning provides the best account both of the possibility of stable meaning and of the transformative capacity of texts. It also entails a view of interpretation that gives primacy to the author as communicative agent. To inquire into what the text means is to ask what the author has done in, with, and through the text. *The goal of understanding is to grasp what has been done, together with its effects; the possibility of attaining such understanding is the presupposition of communicative action.*[90]

Hence, cognitive meaning resides in the locutionary act of the text, falling short of the perlocutionary effect and at best attaining its illocutionary force in understanding. For instance, cognitive meaning that lacks perlocutionary effect of the content of the Scriptures is shown to be possible in the Gospels when Jesus converses with scribes and Pharisees (Matthew 23; John 3:9–15; 5:39–47.).[91]

Furthermore, even though Maier affirms the Spirit's indispensability for proper biblical interpretation, he asserts that not "*every* reading and *every* understanding is dependent on faith" and that there may even be circumstances when the "unregenerate make discoveries that elude the regenerate."[92] Nonetheless, Maier is quick to make clear, "The unregenerate person is thus capable of relaying tradition to others only in an insufficient fashion. And he is further disadvantaged with respect to content, because he finds acceptance of the supernatural difficult."[93] Certainly, cognitive meaning is attainable by the unregenerate, but this is an insufficient knowledge of the Scriptures.

Cognitive Understanding

As a result of the unregenerate person's ability, however deficient, to grasp a cognitive meaning of the text, it is compulsory to discuss a cognitive

90. Vanhoozer, *Meaning*, 218; emphasis in original.

91. Maier, *Biblical Hermeneutics*, 50.

92. Ibid., 51; emphasis in original. For example, a linguistically gifted Muslim that can shed light on a linguistically difficult OT passage is one of the hypothetical examples he employs to support this assertion.

93. Ibid., 53–4.

Illumination and Interpretation

understanding of that meaning, for this is the extent of his understanding. John Searle states, "The characteristic intended effect of meaning is understanding."[94] In that case, the unregenerate person's grasp of cognitive meaning will elicit some sort of effect, viz., a cognitive understanding.

In essence, cognitive meaning is delimited to "head knowledge." Man's reason and intellectual ability, although adversely affected by sin, are quite capable of grasping the cognitive meaning of the text. Osborne contends that the Scriptures do not state that an unbeliever cannot intellectually interpret the text; rather he argues that they are able to understand the meaning of the text, but will reject the implications of it.[95] To qualify Osborne's statement slightly and more precisely, the unregenerate person is able to understand the implications of the text and thus grasp its illocutionary force; however, this person is unable and unwilling to appropriate those implications, thus forgoing the text's perlocutionary effect. Jeannine Brown offers a compelling illustration of this fact using the Great Commission passage of Matt 28:17–20. She argues that anyone who reads the text may reach the conclusion that Jesus Christ desires his disciples to make other disciples; however, she continues, "Discerning this key point is not, of course, to have exhausted the meaning of this text."[96]

Moreover, in commenting on Vanhoozer's contention that perlocutionary intent regularly fails,[97] Brown argues that though this may be the case, it does not denigrate the significance of perlocutionary effect as it pertains to the communicative act. She asserts, "Although the perlocution itself is not a part of the communicative intention, the intention to elicit a certain response (i.e., perlocutionary intention) is an extension of meaning. Meaning includes perlocutionary intention as an extension of communicative intention."[98] Accordingly, since cognitive meaning and the cognitive understanding of that meaning lack the intended perlocutionary effect of the text, then a different grasp of meaning and a more holistic form of understanding is required in order to properly comprehend and interpret the Scriptures.

To be sure, the unregenerate person can grasp the cognitive meaning of the text such that it results in understanding, but without the Spirit, this

---

94. Searle, *Speech Acts*, 47.
95. Osborne, *Hermeneutical Spiral*, 437.
96. Brown, *Scripture as Communication*, 85.
97. Vanhoozer, *Meaning*, 261.
98. Brown, *Scripture as Communication*, 113.

Illumination and Hermeneutics

understanding is anemic. Ralph Herring contends, "Before a man has been born again, there are dimensions of the Bible's truth which lie beyond his perception. . . . God's wisdom requires a dimension of spirit which man in his natural state is incapable of grasping. . . . The result of this tragedy is that although the words of Scripture are intelligible to man, yet without divine aid he lacks the power to relate them to the spiritual ideas which they express."[99] Truly, cognitive understanding is not the goal of the text, but this is the only understanding that can be attained by the unregenerate.

Though it is this study's argument that the Spirit grants a proper understanding of the Word, as Saucy states:

> This does not mean that an unbeliever without the Spirit cannot comprehend what the Scripture says. Scholarly studies by unbelievers into the Bible's historical backgrounds and its languages have thrown helpful light on the meaning of Scripture. The ministry of the Spirit, however, is not so much to give intellectual understanding but to give true understanding to the heart, which enables believers to respond to the truth. The person without the ministry of the Spirit can understand the words on the pages of the Bible, but he cannot grasp their true meaning for himself, and he does not appropriate them.[100]

Pinnock comments that this lack of spiritual discernment as to the meaning of the Scriptures portrays a mundane God and offers no incentive at all to open the Bible. Subsequently, he declares that historical and linguistic tools are helpful for interpretation, but a relationship with God is paramount.[101]

Therefore, the unregenerate person's capacity to attain a cognitive meaning of the text that results in a cognitive understanding reflects a progression in the right direction. But, it still falls short of the intended perlocutionary effect of the Scriptures in cooperation with the Spirit. Indeed, the end of biblical interpretation and the Spirit's illumination is transformation.

---

99. Herring and Stagg, *How To Understand the Bible*, 40–1.

100. Saucy, *Scripture*, 241. See chapter 1, footnote 31 for examples of "scholarly studies by unbelievers."

101. Pinnock, *The Scripture*, 168.

Illumination and Interpretation

Regenerate Interpretation

In view of the previous discussion, it is necessary to distinguish biblical interpretation by the regenerate with a clear delineation between cognitive meaning and understanding and transformative meaning and understanding. There is a distinct difference between unregenerate interpretation and regenerate interpretation which centers upon the Holy Spirit's transformative work of illumination.

As mentioned above, the noetic effects of sin are an influencing factor in the pursuit of a proper biblical interpretation. However, this is not only an effect that is relegated to the unregenerate. Concerning this, Fuller speaks of the natural man's issue with pride as a deterrence to his acceptance of the truth, but he also notes that this is a continual problem with the believer who is indwelt with the Spirit of God. For this reason, the Christian is utterly dependent upon the Holy Spirit to overcome his own sinful pride so that he might accept the truth of the biblical message.[102] Although Fuller consigns the effects of sin to man's pride, and thus to his volition, it is imperative to remember this study's affirmation that sin's effects on mankind are pervasive such that the Holy Spirit is indispensable for a proper interpretation of the Scriptures; and whereas the effects of sin are evident upon the unregenerate, those same effects are indirectly proportionate to the Spirit's presence upon the regenerate.

A familiar mantra inaugurated by Augustine and carried on throughout the annals of church history is *credo ut intelligam* ("I believe in order that I may understand"). To be clear, belief is a prerequisite for understanding. Commenting on this principle, Nicholas Wolterstorff asserts that Augustine is specifically referring to the knowledge of God and that ". . . faith is the condition of knowledge and knowledge, conversely, is the *telos* of faith . . . [therefore] hostility to God makes knowledge of God impossible."[103] Additionally, Anselm constructed his theology on the tradition of *fides quaerens intellectum* ("faith seeking understanding"), in which faith is a requirement for understanding the things of God.[104] As

---

102. Fuller, "Do We Need the Holy Spirit," 47.

103. Wolterstorff, *Educating for Shalom*, 65–6.

104. Klein, Blomberg, and Hubbard, *Biblical Interpretation*, 136, are examples of modern biblical scholars who support the notion that understanding requires a framework or context in which to interpret. Particularly, they argue, "If the Bible is God's revelation to his people, then *the essential qualification for a full understanding of this book is to know the revealing God*. . . . Only the one who believes and trusts in God can truly understand what God has spoken in his Word . . . [hence] the ability

Illumination and Hermeneutics

a result, transformative meaning and understanding proves to denote a dual significance because it not only describes the transformative end of illumination through the Scriptures, but it also presupposes and requires the transformation of the unregenerate into the regenerate. This leads Vanhoozer to assert, "The Spirit's illumination of our minds is therefore dependent on his prior transformation of our hearts."[105] Subsequently, it is on these two analogous principles that the distinction between the unregenerate interpreter and the regenerate interpreter rests.

Transformative Meaning

Transformative meaning is the foundation for transformative understanding. It is not necessary to wholly separate transformative meaning from cognitive meaning because for the most part, cognitive meaning is a major component in transformative meaning. The difference is transformative meaning, instead of being constrained by cognitive meaning such that cognitive understanding is the extent of interpretation, is rather compelled by the impetus of the Holy Spirit to attain a transformative understanding of the Scriptures. Therefore, transformative meaning excels past the boundaries of cognitive meaning and understanding that enslave the unregenerate interpreter and allow the regenerate interpreter to grasp the transformative understanding of the text.

In other words, transformative meaning is cognitive meaning and understanding reaching its full illocutionary force with the potential to attain the perlocutionary effect that the Scriptures and the Spirit desire. In order to distinguish between transformative meaning and cognitive meaning, it is helpful to remember that "illocutionary efficacy is a matter of meaning."[106] Thus, illocutionary intent is a recognizable trait of all texts, not just the Scriptures. The pivotal difference in transformative meaning is the trajectory towards the appropriation of the perlocutionary effect in understanding. Brown argues, "So our reading of it [the Bible] should al-

---

to apprehend God's truth in its fullest sense belongs only to the 'spiritual person'" (emphasis in original). Moreover, Vanhoozer, *Meaning*, 30–1, uses the Augustinian approach in his work and writes, "This formula describes the critical stance of the believing reader as well as the proper epistemological stance for human beings in general. We are beings who believe, who seek to deepen and demonstrate our beliefs. To believe that there is meaning in texts is, as we shall see, an act of faith."

105. Vanhoozer, *Meaning*, 413.
106. Ibid., 427.

Illumination and Interpretation

low for the entire range of responses it envisions for readers, cognitive and otherwise. To read only for the cognitive knowledge we can get from the Bible diminishes its value and purposes. Part of allowing Scripture to shape us is submitting to it not only with our minds but also with our affections and actions. Only in this way will we truly and personally know."[107]

Transformative meaning, then, as it encompasses cognitive meaning and understanding can be viewed as preparatory to transformative understanding. Maier views this preparation as necessary for the Christian witness and declares, "Whatever is attained cognitively is worthless if it hinders or prevents this witness."[108] Nevertheless, this does not diminish the significance of cognitive meaning and understanding nor cause them to be obsolete for the faith and practice of the regenerate. On the other hand, as Maier explains, historical understanding,[109] dogmatic understanding,[110] typological understanding,[111] allegorical understanding,[112] and prophetic understanding[113] are essential ingredients for a proper cognitive under-

107. Brown, *Scripture as Communication*, 128.

108. Maier, *Biblical Hermeneutics*, 79.

109. Ibid., 80–2. To explain historical understanding, Maier offers three underlying considerations, all of which aim to construct historical understanding in such a way that contributes to a comprehensive cognitive understanding of Scripture. First, God acted in history as the creator of history in keeping with the claims of revelation. Second, the Bible itself is a historical document that came into existence throughout the course of history. Third, enscripturated revelation points back to its historical origins.

110. Ibid., 82–5. Maier refers to dogmatic understanding in the sense that the Scriptures teach doctrinal and theological matters for the purpose of comprehensive understanding. He is not referring specifically to any one system of dogmatics or dogmatic versus biblical theology for that matter, rather he is referring to "the content of the faith of Christian communities in all times" (p. 84).

111. Ibid., 85–8. Maier uses typological understanding, which also contributes to a comprehensive understanding of the text, to refer to "the doctrine latent in the history God has brought to pass . . . [which] presupposes that there are important points of analogy between what took place long ago and what takes place today . . . [and] also presupposes that God brought about the recording of what took place long ago in order to furnish later generations with information that transcends mere reminiscences. That is, he wished to point the way for subsequent generations" (p. 85).

112. Ibid., 88–90. With regard to allegorical understanding, although this likewise contributes to a comprehensive understanding of the text, Maier is quick to point out that caution is imperative as one proceeds. He describes this form of understanding as using the surface meaning of the text as a starting point for "unmasking the statement that lies behind it" (p. 88). This does not negate the surface meaning of the text; instead, it substantiates and informs it because without the surface meaning there would be no possibility for an allegorical meaning.

113. Ibid., 90–4. Maier explicates prophetic understanding in this manner: "[It]

Illumination and Hermeneutics

standing of the text that informs a transformative meaning of the text, which leads to transformative understanding.

In the end, Richard Averbeck contends that the correct interpretation of the text is dependent on the pursuit of its meaning, but ". . . we must never lose track of the goal toward which the Holy Spirit is driving us. God is concerned not only about our intellectual grasp of his word, but the grip his word has on our hearts and our lives through the effective work of his Holy Spirit in our human spirit."[114] Therefore, transformative meaning represents the initial step on the path towards transformative understanding via the Spirit's work of illumination.

Transformative Understanding

With an adequate view of transformative meaning established, it is now appropriate to introduce the concept of transformative understanding. Understanding is equated in the Bible with obedience (e.g. Luke 8:15; 11:28; Jas 1:22–25)[115] and obedience is the eventual outcome of true understanding.[116] To be more specific, Osborne asserts, "The Bible seeks not just cor-

---

uses the eschatological content of revelation to understand revelation more fully. It takes the progressive character of revelation seriously. Just as typology presupposes a salvation-historical *connection* in revelation, the prophetic understanding presupposes a salvation-historical *movement* in revelation. And just as allegorical understanding builds on the premise that God can use words as signs pointing to a still-to-be-discovered meaning, prophetic understanding assumes that God can give words of guidance into an as-yet-unrealized future. . . . Typology and allegory emphasize the presently given scriptural expression (typology), or the meaning that the expression yields (allegory). Prophetic understanding attempts to understand what will happen in and emerge from the future as God sees it" (pp. 90–1; emphasis in original).

114. Averbeck, "God, People, and the Bible," 161.

115. Luke 8:15 reads, "As for that in the good soil, they are those who, hearing the word, hold it fast in an honest and good heart, and bear fruit with patience." Luke 11:28 states, "But he [Jesus] said, "Blessed rather are those who hear the word of God and keep it!" James 1:22–25 reads, "But be doers of the word, and not hearers only, deceiving yourselves. For if anyone is a hearer of the word and not a doer, he is like a man who looks intently at his natural face in a mirror. For he looks at himself and goes away and at once forgets what he was like. But the one who looks into the perfect law, the law of liberty, and perseveres, being no hearer who forgets but a doer who acts, he will be blessed in his doing."

116. Studebaker, "Authority of the Holy Spirit," 307. Likewise, Maier, *Biblical Hermeneutics*, 76, agrees on this point when he writes about dynamic understanding. He contends, "In this dynamic encounter with the revelatory word, then, the close tie between understanding and obeying is especially impressive. If the person opens

Illumination and Interpretation

rect thinking or understanding but more the correct action that results."[117] Therefore, transformative understanding refers to the attainment of the intended perlocutionary effect of the text. That is, as Vanhoozer states, "The understanding that faith seeks is both theoretical and practical."[118] Indeed, transformative understanding represents the full, proper, and anticipated understanding of the communicative act in Scripture.

According to Vanhoozer, "The third term in speech act theory—perlocution—has a special affinity with the third person of the Trinity. The perlocutionary effect, we may recall, refers to what the speech act aims to accomplish in the reader, over and above the illocutionary effect."[119] Indeed, the Holy Spirit is the agent of the perlocutionary effect upon the reader of Scripture and is thus needed for a proper and complete interpretation. Thiselton concurs, "When the necessary conditions for interpretation become operational, an event of communication takes place *within the temporal flow of the reader's life and experience*."[120] Consequently, the Spirit's work of illumination is indispensable for a transformative understanding of the Scriptures.

As mentioned above, the Scriptures and the Spirit desire that the perlocutionary effect of the text is grasped for the purpose of transformation. However, it is imperative that the perlocutionary effect remain inherently connected to the illocutionary force and locution of the text, for these are three components of one communicative act. Vanhoozer explains, "The intended perlocutionary effect . . . is not arbitrarily related to its illocutionary act. Indeed, the trinitarian language of 'procession' is apt: as the Spirit proceeds from the Father and the Son, so the literary act proceeds from

---

himself, if he complies with what has been revealed, then he obeys, and only after that has truly understood. Understanding issues forth in new understanding. It becomes a process, and thus becomes whole."

117. Osborne, *Hermeneutical Spiral*, 455.

118. Vanhoozer, *The Drama of Doctrine*, 307–8.

119. Vanhoozer, *Meaning*, 410. Here, Vanhoozer goes on to refer to the illocutionary effect as one that produces understanding. To avoid confusion I have omitted this portion of Vanhoozer's quote because I am contrasting cognitive understanding and transformative understanding. I argue that cognitive understanding is deficient, and thus merely grasping the illocutionary force of the communicative act is likewise deficient. However, transformative understanding, being the end of the Spirit's illumination in conjunction with the text of Scripture, is the true understanding that the communicative action seeks as it takes its perlocutionary effect. Although Vanhoozer agrees that without the perlocutionary effect of the text the communicative act is incomplete, this is not explicit in the quote used above.

120. Thiselton, *New Horizons in Hermeneutics*, 31; emphasis in original.

the author, and so does the perlocution (persuading, convincing) proceed from the illocution (claiming, asserting)."[121] As a result, the concept of transformative understanding is built upon a transformative meaning of the text that encompasses cognitive meaning and understanding and constitutes the fullness of the communicative act in Scripture.

To be sure, the text of Scripture fully intends to transform the regenerate person by eliciting an appropriate response in the faith and practice of the reader.[122] Pinnock concurs, "The only proper way to read the Bible is to seek to learn its truth and to incorporate it into our lives."[123] It is then and only then that the goal of the Spirit's illuminatory work is made complete. Resultantly, the words of Brown are apt, "Reading the Bible to be fully shaped by it is a worthy goal, and one that fits the incarnational and communicative nature of Scripture. I believe the biblical writers would be disconcerted, to say the least, to think that what they had written might be used to shape only our thinking."[124]

Establishing the Holy Spirit's Role in Hermeneutics

As noted above, the Holy Spirit's role in hermeneutics is sorely neglected. To be clear, proper biblical interpretation requires the cooperation of Word *and* Spirit. With solely the Word, a cognitive meaning and understanding can be attained; but without the Spirit, transformative meaning and understanding can never be reached. Ward describes the relationship between Word and Spirit in this manner:

> Inspired Scripture—the text itself—is sufficient for simple understanding of the message of Scripture, while illuminated Scripture—the text plus the present work of the Spirit—is sufficient for a response of faith. The Spirit *is* therefore a kind of supplement to the text, but only in the sense that he brings the possibility of appropriate response to the text's illocutionary act. In the terminology of speech act theory, Scripture is sufficient for the performance of the divine illocutionary act, which includes the

---

121. Vanhoozer, *Meaning*, 410.

122. Averbeck, "God, People, and the Bible," 150, agrees, "... [T]he text of scripture intends to make something happen in the heart of the reader that will bring about the appropriate response in the reader's life. This is, in fact, the arena in which the Holy Spirit's work of illumination takes place."

123. Pinnock, *The Scripture*, 205.

124. Brown, *Scripture as Communication*, 272.

> conveying of its necessary propositional content, but insufficient to bring about the intended perlocutionary effect. For that ... the work of the Holy Spirit through the Word is required.[125]

The Spirit's indispensability for biblical interpretation is evident in the interconnectedness of the doctrine of illumination and the hermeneutical doctrines highlighted above. Ward even argues that these hermeneutical doctrines of the Word can be viewed as conjoined aspects of the doctrine of the Holy Spirit's work.[126] Illumination and revelation, inspiration, perspicuity, sufficiency, and authority are joined by the assertion that the same Spirit who worked in the past to establish these doctrines of Scripture is the same Spirit who works presently and perpetually to maintain these vital doctrines in accord with his illuminatory work.[127]

Therefore, it is necessary that the biblical interpreter is regenerate in order to properly understand the Scriptures, i.e., to arrive at a transformative understanding of the text. Ramm avowedly states, "That spiritual qualifications have an important place in the list of qualifications [of an interpreter] cannot be debated."[128] Truly, in order for the Scriptures to accomplish their intended purpose, regeneration in terms of the possession of the Holy Spirit is essential. For Vanhoozer, biblical interpretation is a form of discipleship where the text beckons the reader to witness to Scripture such that it is appropriated and applied to a transformed life that results in nothing less than the interpreter becoming both a martyr to the Word and a bearer of the Word.[129] Certainly, a proper understanding of the Scriptures requires the illumination of the Holy Spirit.

---

125. Ward, *Word and Supplement*, 202–3; emphasis in original.

126. Ward, *Words of Life*, 111.

127. Klein, Blomberg, and Hubbard, *Biblical Interpretation*, 142–53, propose several presuppositions for correct interpretation regarding the nature of the Scriptures. First, the interpreter should view the Scriptures as inspired revelation. Second, the interpreter should affirm that the Scriptures are authoritative and true. Third, the Scriptures are to be viewed as a spiritual document, in that, they operate in conjunction with the Spirit's work of illumination. Fourth, the Scriptures are to be understood as being characterized by both unity and diversity. Fifth, the affirmation that the Scriptures are understandable is vital. Sixth, an acceptance of the entire canon (all 66 books), is required. Seventh, it is necessary that the interpreter accept and employ the use of exegetical tools and proper hermeneutical methodology. Last, it is important that the ultimate goal of hermeneutics is achieved as the intended meaning of the text is understood.

128. Ramm, *Protestant Biblical Interpretation*, 12.

129. Vanhoozer, *Meaning*, 438–41.

Applying the Holy Spirit's Role in Hermeneutics

Now that the Holy Spirit's role in hermeneutics has been firmly established, an apposite understanding of the application of the doctrine of illumination and the goal of this work of the Spirit can be addressed. The relationships between illumination and the hermeneutical doctrines recounted above comprise a well-defined outline for addressing several caveats that need to be offered when applying the Holy Spirit's role in the hermeneutical enterprise.

First, it should be noted that in light of the bond between illumination and revelation, the Holy Spirit does not seek to add to the text of Scripture nor grant any new revelation to the biblical interpreter in addition to the already established text. Vanhoozer avers, "The Spirit's role . . . is not to change the meaning but to *charge* it with significance . . . not to add a new sense to the Word, but to energize and empower the sense—the speech act—that is already there. . . . Accordingly, the Spirit is most properly conceived as the *effective presence of the Word*, or as the *Word's empowering presence*."[130] More specifically, the Spirit's work does not bring about a new communicative act, rather the purpose of illumination is found in the perlocutionary effect.[131] Surely, the doctrine of illumination can be easily misconstrued to refer to new teachings from God, i.e., a new subjective revelation. However, the biblical concept of illumination refers to the already given special revelation of the Scriptures. Subsequently, John Frame emphasizes, "Word and Spirit go together, so that the Spirit is recognized in His agreement with Scripture."[132]

Also, because of the connection between illumination and inspiration, it is imperative to recognize that the Spirit's work of illumination does not guarantee a correct interpretation of the Scriptures. Both inspiration and illumination are activities of the Holy Spirit, but they should

---

130. Ibid., 421, 428–9; emphasis in original. Vanhoozer also states that the Spirit does not create new meaning, but ministers the meaning already inherent in the text (p. 413). Likewise, Zuber, "What Is Illumination," 214, states, "Illumination is a divine provision . . . of the Holy Spirit using a prior divine disclosure in some objective, intelligible form, such as the Bible. It does not involve new revelation." Also, Erickson, *Evangelical Interpretation*, 52, concurs that the Holy Spirit's role in interpretation is not to convey new information that is not already in the biblical text. In accordance, Zuck, "The Role of the Holy Spirit", 122, gives a well-formulated biblical synopsis highlighting the teaching that the Spirit works in association with the Scriptures, not beyond it or in addition to it.

131. Ward, *Word and Supplement*, 204.

132. Frame, "The Spirit and the Scriptures," 220.

Illumination and Interpretation

not be confused—the Holy Spirit's illumination provides the guide for his product of inspiration.[133] I. Howard Marshall stresses that ". . . a reliance on the Spirit will not necessarily save us from erroneous interpretations of Scripture. There are people who have claimed to be led by the Spirit who have promulgated shocking heresies."[134] The Word of God is infallible and inerrant; however, as discussed above, the mind and the heart of the fallible human being is distorted by sin. Although, the illumination of the Holy Spirit does not necessarily guarantee that a correct interpretation of the text will be achieved, it is the foundation for correct interpretation.[135]

This funnels the discussion directly into the relationship between illumination and perspicuity, and the assertion that this bond does not entail a full, unadulterated comprehension of every passage of Scripture.[136] Because of this, Marshall proposes that the entire hermeneutic process be thought of as Spirit-led, that is, "We are not to think of biblical interpretation as a human process, with the Spirit being called in to help simply at the difficult parts."[137] Undoubtedly, just as the Scriptures are a work of God with the employment of man, ". . . coming to a true understanding of the Scriptures, through which God communicates His life-giving truth, involves both God's activity and our own."[138]

Furthermore, it needs to be reemphasized that the tie between illumination and perspicuity does not counteract the necessity of the interpretive enterprise. Certainly, as stated above, the Scriptures are perspicuous, but the task of hermeneutics requires the cooperation of both Word and Spirit and both the human and the divine. Webster concurs, "Interpretation is necessary because Holy Scripture is an element in the economy of salvation, the economy whose theme is the renewal of fellowship between God and his human creatures. Interpretation is an aspect of the rebirth of our noetic fellowship with God. The history of

---

133. Heisler, *Spirit-Led Preaching*, 41. Ramm, *Protestant*, 14, also makes this assertion.

134. Marshall, "The Holy Spirit," 73.

135. Klein, Blomberg, and Hubbard, *Biblical Interpretation*, 136.

136. Zuck, "The Role of the Holy Spirit," 128–9, supports this point.

137. Marshall, "The Holy Spirit," 68.

138. Saucy, *Scripture*, 240. This is also affirmed by Brown, *Scripture as Communication*, 128. On this point, Pinnock, *The Scripture*, 198, writes, "Two things go on at the same time in interpretation. We do the reading, and God gives understanding. We attend God's Word, and the Spirit gives us discernment as to its significance. It is not as if the Spirit only comes into play on the second step."

reconciliation and revelation is not a unilateral divine history in which there is only a divine agent, with no creaturely coordinate."[139]

In addition, although there is a close tie between illumination and sufficiency, dependence on the Spirit's illumination does not entail complaisance or a disregard for the employment of hermeneutical methodology and exegetical tools. Klein, Blomberg, and Hubbard write, "This illuminating work of the Spirit does not circumvent nor allow us to dispense with the principles of hermeneutics and the techniques of exegesis."[140] Certainly, the Holy Spirit's work of illumination is vital for the interpreter in the hermeneutic process and the Scriptures are sufficient for the faith and practice of the regenerate; however, this does not present an opportunity for a slothful hermeneutic that is devoid of diligent study.[141] The Holy Spirit and the methodology of hermeneutics do not operate in isolation from one another; and instead of one being regarded as a substitute for the other as competitive players, they should be viewed as complementary counterparts of one another.[142]

Likewise, Heisler asserts that the classic disciplines of language, the principles of interpretation, and biblical studies are critical when working in conjunction with the Holy Spirit in the hermeneutic endeavor.[143] Also, the history of interpretation is a decisive component that should not be neglected in one's hermeneutical method.[144] Nevertheless, the sufficiency of the Scriptures and the need for proper hermeneutical methodology and exegetical tools does not negate the role of the Holy

---

139. Webster, "Biblical Theology," 375.

140. Klein, Blomberg, and Hubbard, *Biblical Interpretation*, 139. Zuck, "The Role of the Holy Spirit," 125–6, also makes clear that "the role of the Spirit in interpretation is no substitute for diligent study . . . [and] the Spirit's work in biblical interpretation does not rule out the use of study helps such as commentaries and Bible dictionaries." Also, Pinnock, *The Scripture*, 169, supports this assertion.

141. Ward, *Words of Life*, 114, is in accord with this point and Dockery and Nelson, "Special Revelation," 163, comment, "The believer is not lacking adequate revelation since the inspired Bible itself provides all the revelation necessary for knowing and living as God intends. The doctrine of sufficiency does not indicate that scriptural revelation is exhaustive, or that it contains all knowledge about the subjects taught therein, but the Bible is sufficient such that further revelation is not necessary beyond the scope of Scripture for faithfully living the Christian life. Since Scripture is sufficient, there is no warrant to add to or take away from the Word of God we know as the Bible (Prov 30:5–6)."

142. Erickson, *Christian Theology*, 283; Klein, Blomberg, and Hubbard, *Biblical Interpretation*, 139.

143. Heisler, *Spirit-Led Preaching*, 47.

144. Klein, Blomberg, Hubbard, *Biblical Interpretation*, 141.

Illumination and Interpretation

Spirit and replace it with an inordinate fixation for the mechanical study of the Scriptures.[145] Thus, the skilled exegete/interpreter who seeks the correct and proper interpretation of the text will use all of the exegetical and theological tools that are at his disposal, abiding by the principles of sound hermeneutical method, while simultaneously depending upon the illuminating work of the Holy Spirit to guide, convict, and grant understanding that leads to a transformed life.

Finally, in light of the close relation of illumination and authority, and the aforementioned hermeneutical doctrines and authority, it needs to be noted that one's interpretation of the Scriptures is not automatically authoritative because of an illuminatory claim, especially if the interpretation is in conflict with orthodoxy, the interpretive community, and the very Scripture itself. If an aberrant interpretation is proposed that stands in contradistinction with the Scriptures, then the loss of interpretive authority is clear and present.[146] Pinnock argues, "The key to hermeneutics is to recognize that God has given us the Bible, his written Word, and enables it to function by giving the Spirit, who brings a comprehension of its truth and a certainty of its divine origin."[147] Consequently, it is only when the Word and the Spirit are in cooperation, that illumination and authority can maintain their proper relationship.

In sum, the words of Packer are *a propos*:

> [The biblical interpreter] will . . . bring *a concept of divine communication that correlates the Spirit and the Word*. He will affirm the *coherence* of the sixty-six books of Scripture against any form of the fashionable idea that substance of one Bible writer's teaching is inconsistent with the substance of another's . . . he will affirm their God-given *sufficiency* as a guide for faith and life and a judge of any proposed supplementary guide . . . and he will affirm their *clarity*, in the sense that everything essential to salvation is stated in them so fully, in so many mutually illuminating ways, that every serious reader will see it, without any need of a supposedly infallible church to interpret it to him. With this he will affirm the ministry of the Holy Spirit, the divine

---

145. Ward, *Words of Life*, 114.

146. In accord with this, Kaiser and Silva, *Biblical Hermeneutics*, 45, assert, "Focusing on the significance of a text should never lead to proposing a new meaning of the text that is not actually taught in Scripture. To do otherwise is to risk the loss of authority, for such inferences would have no part in the written nature of the text and thus would not be authoritative for us today."

147. Pinnock, *The Scripture*, 199.

author of the books, who authenticates them to us as the Word of God; interprets them to us so that we see what they mean and know that the divine realities spoken of truly exist; applies to us the principles of believing and living that the Scriptures teach and illustrate; and animates us to respond to what we know in faith, worship, and obedience. He will underline again and again the incapacity of the fallen human mind to think rightly of God apart from the guidance of Scripture, and he will constantly emphasize that it is only as one who is himself the beneficiary of the Spirit's illuminating and interpreting ministry that he has any knowledge of divine things to share with others. Anything that looks to him like reliance on self-generated human speculation (going beyond Scripture) or supposed private revelation (going against Scripture) or uncriticized church tradition (overlaying and obscuring Scripture) will earn his special hostility.[148]

Applying the Holy Spirit's role in hermeneutics is a delicate task. However, it is a practice that is indispensable for the interpreter as he seeks the truth of the Word of God and the transformation that it demands.

---

148. Packer, "The Holy Spirit and His Work," 58; emphasis in original.

3

Initial Illumination

THE ILLUMINATION OF THE Holy Spirit is a multi-faceted work that is easily misconstrued if the proper definitions are lacking. In order to adequately distinguish the different aspects of the illuminating process, a discussion concerning the relationship between the doctrine of illumination and salvation is essential. Furthermore, the inner testimony of the Holy Spirit contributes to a formal comprehension of the doctrine of illumination. This aspect of the Spirit's work is often misunderstood and blindly included in the Spirit's work of illumination thus contributing to the convolution of the doctrine as a whole. As a result, after a thorough explication of these matters, the primary act of the Spirit's illumination will be explained and defined.

Illumination and Salvation

Though the Spirit's illuminating work is generally associated with a proper understanding of the Scriptures, it is of the essence to be mindful of the primary stage in the process of illumination, viz., initial illumination. Often, attention to this stage of the Spirit's work is bypassed, which results in an underdeveloped view of the doctrine as a whole. Nevertheless, Klooster recognizes the similitude of these two doctrines as he maintains, "The Holy Spirit's regeneration brings about a radical redirection that manifests itself in repentance and faith. The illumination of the Spirit is involved in that regeneration because the radical beginning of the interpretative process has now begun; the basic message of the gospel has been understood."[1] Hence, through a brief exegesis of the following passages, a more informed understanding of the Spirit's work of illumination will ensue by its correlation with the doctrine of salvation.[2] Truly, just as the Spirit plays a vital role in illumination, the Spirit has a major role in salvation.

2 Corinthians 3:12–4:6

Beginning in chapter 3 of the second epistle to the Corinthian believers, the Apostle Paul highlights the theme of divine illumination and the inherent necessity of the Spirit of God for a proper understanding of the things of God. To set the context, Paul declares that they are now ministers of the new covenant (2 Cor 3:6). In doing so, he highlights the glory and status of this covenant, as it is written on human hearts and not tablets of stone (2 Cor 3:3), by comparing and contrasting it with the glory of the Mosaic covenant (2 Cor 3:7–11). His basic argument is that if the glory of the Mosaic covenant which was ephemeral, exacting condemnation and death, was such that the Israelites could not gaze upon the face of Moses without the covering of a veil, much more so is the glory of the ministry of the Spirit which is of permanence, bringing righteousness and life.

Moreover, Paul declares, the unbelieving Israelites, and truly any who do not believe, have retained the same veil, which covers their hearts, such that when they read the Scriptures, their understanding is obscured (2 Cor 3:12–15).[3] For this reason, J. Rodman Williams argues, "Accordingly, there is first need for *illumination* in order to apprehend the gospel of salvation. . . . This darkness, this blindness, can be overcome only by interior illumination."[4] As the Apostle highlights in 2 Cor 3:14, the minds of unbelievers have been hardened. Here, he uses the noun *noēma* for "mind," which refers to the faculty of thought and understanding.[5] Subsequently, in 2 Cor 3:15, the Apostle states that the *hearts* of

---

1. Klooster, "The Role of the Holy Spirit," 457.

2. See footnote 17 in chapter 1 for an explanation concerning the selection of the biblical texts regarding initial illumination.

3. Furnish, *II Corinthians*, 210, 234, 239 comments that the Apostle deliberately broadens his perspective from unbelieving Israel to any unbeliever. He takes his cue from the assumption that there is an unexpressed *tis* that is the subject of the verb *epistrephō*.

4. Williams, *Renewal Theology*, 40; emphasis in original.

5. Harris, *Corinthians*, 301.

Illumination and Interpretation

unbelievers are veiled, and it should be noted that especially in light of the hardening of the mind, that this veiling is comprehensive. The noun *kardia* is used for "heart" and signifies the entirety of a person's inner life, emotion, and will, as well as the intellect.[6] The verb *pōroō* in 2 Cor 3:14, which is properly translated as "hardened," reinforces the idea that the issue is not simply one of incomprehension as a result of darkened perception; rather, it alludes to an ontological problem that needs to be remedied.[7] For this reason, Paul refers to this veil as *auto kalumma*, i.e., "the same veil" from days past because it retains the same effect in the present day.[8] Certainly, the veil does impede comprehension, but that is merely a symptom of the underlying problem of unregeneracy.[9]

Subsequently, the Apostle offers hope; and that hope is found in the Lord Jesus Christ. For when one turns to the Lord in faith with a repentant heart, the veil is removed by the power of the Holy Spirit (2 Cor 3:16–18). Garland avers, "One of the foundations of Paul's faith was his conviction that in Christ, and only in Christ, the veil is abolished ... [and] when that veil is removed, freedom from the law of sin and death results."[10] In 2 Cor 3:16, the verb *periaireō*, which means to remove or take away,[11] is used in the passive voice which alludes to the divine agency of the veil's removal.[12] To be sure, without Christ, the veil remains; and it is only through the sacrifice of Christ Jesus, that is, through salvation in Christ Jesus which is accompanied by the indwelling of the Holy Spirit, that the veil is removed.

Afterwards, Paul qualifies his ministry of the new covenant by setting himself apart from those who would resort to guile and deception to achieve their goals (2 Cor 4:1–2). And he emphasizes that even if the gospel of the Lord Jesus Christ is veiled, it is veiled solely to those who are perishing (2 Cor 4:3). Following is 2 Cor 4:4, which is of significance for the doctrine of illumination: "In their case the god of this world has blinded the minds of the unbelievers, to keep them from seeing the light of the gospel of the glory of Christ, who is the image of God." Regarding

---

6. Ibid., 305.
7. Garland, *2 Corinthians*, 191.
8. Harris, *Corinthians*, 301.
9. Palmer, *The Person and Ministry of the Holy Spirit*, 54.
10. Garland, *2 Corinthians*, 192, 197.
11. BDAG, 799.
12. Harris, *Corinthians*, 309.

this verse, Erickson argues that there is a vast difference between the believer and the unbeliever, as the unbeliever inherently possesses "an inability to see, even though the light is there. There is a veiling, a blinding. This is more than just understanding but rejecting something because it does not comport with one's self-interest. This is an inability even to understand the truth."[13] Additionally, 2 Cor 4:6 makes plain that in reference to believers, their hearts have been given "the light of the knowledge of the glory of God in the face of Jesus Christ." Erickson affirms, "These statements constitute a strong indication that there is both a veiling or blinding and an unveiling or illumination" that takes place.[14]

It is vital to recognize that this veiling is not of the gospel of Jesus Christ. To be clear, it is the gospel that is the conduit for God's glory. After Paul's description of the veiling in 2 Cor 4:3, he goes on to clarify that it is not the gospel that is veiled, but those who are unbelieving. Similarly, it is not the gospel or the Scripture that is the Holy Spirit's object of illumination; it is the person whose mind and heart have been corrupted by sin. Zuber agrees that the problem is not with the light of the gospel, as if its capacity for illumination is dimmed; no, the problem is in the hearts of the unbelievers who are incapacitated to receive and understand the Word of God.[15] Kistemaker summarizes, "God illumines us *in* our inner beings, so that we (all believers) may spread the light. While Satan blinds the human mind (v. 4), God illumines the heart, which is the wellspring of life (Prov 4:23). Satan prevents illumination, but God provides it."[16]

It is readily apparent in this passage that there is an inherent connection between the Spirit's work of illumination and the power of salvation. The gospel of Jesus Christ is the power of God to salvation, which is communicated through the Scriptures by the illuminating work of the Holy Spirit such that those who are perishing with veiled hearts might turn to the Lord for salvation.

Ephesians 1:18

Paul opens this epistle by expounding upon the spiritual blessings that are made available in Christ Jesus (Eph 1:3–14). This is important because,

13. Erickson, *Evangelical Interpretation*, 43.
14. Ibid.
15. Zuber, "What Is Illumination," 86–7.
16. Kistemaker, *Second Epistle to the Corinthians*, 144.

Illumination and Interpretation

in doing so, it is necessary to recognize that Paul is writing to those who are believers, as opposed to unbelievers who are not in Christ and thus cannot receive the spiritual blessings that are only found *in him* (Eph 1:4, 7, 10, 11, 13), i.e., in Christ (Eph 1:3, 5, 9, 12) and in the Beloved (Eph 1:6). Subsequent to this, in Eph 1:15–23, the Apostle makes intercession for the Ephesian believers and prays, ". . . that the God of our Lord Jesus Christ, the Father of glory, may give you a spirit of wisdom and of revelation in the knowledge of him, having the eyes of your hearts enlightened, that you may know what is the hope to which he has called you, what are the riches of his glorious inheritance in the saints" (Eph 1:17–18). These two verses serve to inform our understanding of the doctrine of illumination as a whole; however, it is the latter verse that is of significance for the connection between the doctrines of illumination and salvation.[17]

In Eph 1:18, the use of the participle *pephōtismenous* is of particular interest. This participle comes from the verb *phōtizō*, which in this context means "to make known in reference to the inner life or transcendent matters and thus enlighten."[18] According to Andrew Lincoln, this is specific to the illumination of conversion, such that "a decisive transformation has taken place and saving illumination has been brought by the Spirit through the gospel."[19] Indeed, this enlightening is the result of the same Spirit who grants the gift of wisdom and revelation mentioned in Eph 1:17.[20] This interpretation is bolstered by the passive voice of the verb, indicating the performance of an action completed upon the subject, which means that the work of illumination is an action of the Holy Spirit upon his recipients.

It is true that a progressive illumination might be in the author's purview, which will be discussed in greater detail later, but as Glenn Graham points out, the perfect tense of the verb *phōtizō* does not carry this meaning as it refers to a one time event that was completed in the past, and is also perpetually effective.[21] Hoehner asserts, "It is best to think that since the Ephesian believers were chosen, redeemed, and sealed, they were enlightened the moment they heard and believed (vv. 3–14). This makes good sense of the perfect passive participle, for they had

---

17. Eph 1:17 will be treated in light of Eph 1:18 in chapter 4.
18. BDAG, 1074.
19. Lincoln, *Ephesians*, 58.
20. Westcott, *Ephesians*, 24. This issue will be discussed in further detail in chapter 4.
21. Graham, *Ephesians*, 76.

once been enlightened with continuing results of enlightenment."[22] This understanding also coheres with the remainder of the epistle when the Apostle Paul contrasts his readers's old lives of darkness that were indicative of ignorance as the result of a darkened understanding and their new lives in the likeness of God as children of light (Eph 4:18; 5:8).

Moreover, the verb *phōtizō* is employed here in reference to the eyes of the heart, which represent the avenue through which the illumination of the Holy Spirit flows to the center of one's being.[23] Here, *kardia* is employed as a distributive singular which indicates the individual heart of each reader, rather than an abstract reference to the collective heart of the group.[24] Thus, the pairing of the words *ophthalmos* and *kardia* is constructed in the figurative sense and denotes an individual's capacity for understanding, i.e., a capacity for understanding which has been illuminated by the Spirit.[25] In essence, it is because of their conversion, that Paul's readers have the capacity for further understanding. Calvin states it this way, ". . . [Paul] does not consider that the eyes of our understanding are enlightened unless we know what is the hope of the eternal inheritance to which we are called."[26] In other words, because of their initial illumination they have the potential to undergo the Spirit's work of progressive illumination.

It is important to note that in Eph 1:17 the Apostle is not praying that the Ephesian believers be indwelt with the Holy Spirit, for this has already been accomplished; rather he is interceding on their behalf for a specific manifestation of the Spirit.[27] To be sure, the Apostle is asking that his read-

22. Hoehner, *Ephesians*, 263.
23. Ibid., 260.
24. Graham, *Ephesians*, 77.
25. Ibid., 76–7.
26. Calvin, *Institutes*, (3.2.16), 366.
27. Hoehner, *Ephesians*, 258. Also, Hoehner presents two major alternatives for the translation of Eph 1:18 (pp. 261–2). The first alternative takes the illumination of the Spirit as part of the intercessory request of the author meaning he is asking that his readers be given a spirit of wisdom and revelation *and* the enlightenment of the eyes of their hearts. Furthermore, a tangential translation to this major alternative indicates that the illuminatory act is the result of the gift of the Spirit of wisdom and revelation. Hoehner maintains that both of these views in the first alternative are highly unlikely given the perfect passive participle. The second major alternative is the one espoused in this study and treats this clause, not as a part of the request, but as an ancillary thought to the request. Hoehner sums up, "The point being made is that Paul is praying that God may give them the Spirit of insight and revelation, not an impossible request because the believers in Ephesus already have had their understanding enlightened" (p. 262).

Illumination and Interpretation

ers be given further insight and understanding, *since* they have already encountered the initial illumination of the Spirit, i.e., their conversion.[28] Certainly, it is only because of this truth that the Apostle can legitimately make this request.[29] This distinction between an initial illumination by the Spirit that leads to conversion and a progressive illumination by the Spirit that grants understanding is crucial for the proper comprehension of this passage and the doctrine of illumination as a whole.

Hebrews 6:4

Hebrews 6:4 is one of the most difficult verses to interpret in the entire biblical corpus and it sits in one of the most difficult passages in all of Scripture. With that said, it needs to be remembered that our task here is not to answer the many questions surrounding this passage, but that it is concerned with ascertaining the link between illumination and salvation, nothing more and nothing less. In order to accomplish this, a thorough knowledge of the context of this verse needs to be established.

The author of Hebrews begins his epistle with recognizing the Son of God as the supreme and salvific special revelation of the Father (Heb 1:1–14). After doing this, he continues with an exposition of the greatness and magnitude of this salvation that is only found in the Son, and issues a warning to his readers against neglecting so great a salvation that has indeed already been communicated to them (Heb 2:1–18). Subsequently, the author offers a comparison of Jesus Christ and Moses, in which Jesus is demonstrated to be greater than Moses in all things

---

28. The Apostle Paul, in Eph 5:18, builds upon this premise by urging his readers to "... be filled with the Spirit." Regarding this passage, Hoehner, *Ephesians*, 704, writes, "It must be noted that the present imperative passive verb [*plērousthe*], "be filled," probably indicates an iterative force, a repeated action of filling by the Spirit. The imperative mood places the responsibility on the believers. The passive voice suggests that believers cannot fill themselves. Rather, believers are to be filled by the Spirit. Thus, believers are exhorted to be filled repeatedly by the Holy Spirit." Therefore, it is only because of the Spirit's work of initial illumination that this perpetual filling can occur.

29. Ibid., 263. Hoehner agrees on this point when he argues, "Paul prays that God might give them the Spirit to procure the insight and revelation of their knowledge of God. This was possible because their understanding had already been enlightened at the moment of belief." Also, Goodwin, *Ephesians*, 283, agrees, "The things he [the author of Ephesians] prayeth for here were things that befitted the state of grown Christians. He doth not pray for them as for men to be converted. No; for it is a prayer he framed for them 'since he heard of their faith and love,' of whom he said, they were 'sealed' too 'with the Spirit of promise;' as in the former verses."

because of his divine nature and position in the Godhead (Heb 3:1–6). Again, the author admonishes his readers, whom he calls "brothers," against an unbelieving heart and the hardening effect of the deceitfulness of sin, so that they would be able to stand firm until the end, lest they fall away from the faith (Heb 3:12–14). In doing so, he utilizes the example of the Israelites's unbelief and resultant disobedience during the exodus. Certainly, because of their unbelief, they were unable to enter the rest of God (Heb 3:16–19; 4:6, 11). On the other hand though, those who have believed and remain steadfast are able to enter that promised Sabbath rest through confidence in Christ Jesus, the Son of God and the Great High Priest (Heb 4:1–5:10).

Now, directly leading up to chapter 6, the author of Hebrews initiates his warning against apostasy (Heb 5:11–14). As he does this, he awakens his readers to the reality of the dullness of their present spiritual state as children who live off of milk, and places this actuality in juxtaposition to their failed potentiality, i.e., to be mature believers and teachers who feed off of the meat of the faith exercising their powers of discernment to distinguish between good and evil. As a result, the author suggests that they progress from the previously taught elementary doctrines of Christ, ". . . for it is impossible to restore again to repentance those who have once been enlightened, who have tasted the heavenly gift, and have shared in the Holy Spirit" (Heb 6:4) if they then fall away. As a result the author is urging his readers to grasp the fullness of Christian doctrine and progress in their faith and practice, that they may guard themselves against the grave danger of apostasy.[30]

Just as in Ephesians 1:18, the key word in this verse for our present purposes is *phōtizō* and the meaning it conveys is vital for our understanding of illumination and salvation. William Lane argues, "In the NT the term is used metaphorically to refer to spiritual or intellectual illumination that removes ignorance through the action of God or the preaching of the gospel. . . . What is signified is not simply instruction for salvation but the renewal of the mind and of life."[31] Therefore, those that are mentioned in this verse must possess some sort of initial revelation of Jesus Christ.[32]

It is also of significance that *phōtizō* is used in the aorist tense denoting an antecedent action, which is especially appropriate in referring

---

30. Hagner, *Hebrews*, 90.
31. Lane, *Hebrews 1–8*, 141.
32. Guthrie, *Hebrews*, 141.

Illumination and Interpretation

to an initial conversion experience.[33] Consistent with this assessment, the subsequent clauses in Heb 6:4 also appear to refer to conversion.[34] Hagner notes that the verb *geuomai*, literally meaning to taste, ". . . does not imply a less-than-complete experience of conversion," especially in light of its previous usage where the same verb is utilized by the author to speak of the death of Jesus (Heb 2:9).[35] Delitzsch furthers this argument by directing attention towards the emphasis that the author places on this verb by its *usus loquendi*.[36] This emphasis speaks to the fact that an initial illuminatory experience to salvation has indeed occurred.

Likewise, the final clause of Heb 6:4, mentions a sharing of the Holy Spirit which is also indicative of conversion.[37] These two clauses combine to support the idea that *phōtizō* is referring to a personal salvation that is described as a gift from above which includes the reception of the Holy Spirit.[38] Westcott notes that these two clauses represent ". . . two fundamental aspects of the reception of the Christian Faith, illumination in respect to the divine action, and experience in respect to the human appropriation. The Christian is illuminated by the conscious sense of the gift of life, and by participation in the Spirit."[39] Resultantly, this twofold soteriological blessing is the substance of a spiritual act of illumination that describes the conversion event.

Despite the aforementioned evidence for taking the meaning of *phōtizō* as referring to salvation, there is a prominent argument that suggests the meaning of this verb indicates baptism. This line of reasoning extends from both the usage of this verb by Justin to describe the baptismal practice (*First Apology* 61.12; 65:1) and the sense of baptism that the translation of this verb carries in the Syriac Peshitta.[40] However, it should be recognized that prior to the second century there is no clear evidence that this verb denotes baptism and also that other Syriac versions exclude this interpretation.[41] In fact, Owen grants the

---

33. Hagner, *Hebrews*, 90, maintains that the language of "having been enlightened" (*phōtisthentas*) indicates an initial conversion experience.

34. Ibid., 90–1.

35. Ibid., 91.

36. Delitzsch, *Hebrews*, 284.

37. Hagner, *Hebrews*, 91.

38. Lane, *Hebrews 1–8*, 141–2, and Westcott, *Hebrews*, 147, support this idea.

39. Westcott, *Hebrews*, 147.

40. Bruce, *Hebrews*, 145.

41. Lane, *Hebrews 1–8*, 141.

argument for the baptismal interpretation and even acknowledges the probability of it to the point of acceptance:

> . . . if the word itself, as used here, did not require another interpretation. For it was a good while after the writing of this Epistle, and all other parts of the New Testament, at least an age or two, if not more, before this word was used mystically to express baptism. In the whole Scripture it hath another sense, denoting an inward operation of the Spirit, and not the outward administration of an ordinance. And it is too much boldness to take a word in a peculiar sense in one single place, diverse from its proper signification and constant use, if there be no circumstances in the text forcing us thereunto, as here are not.[42]

In a similar vein, Kistemaker notes that besides the two occurrences in Hebrews, this verb appears nine times within the NT corpus (Luke 11:36; John 1:9; 1 Cor 4:5; Eph 1:18; 3:9; 2 Tim 1:10; Rev 18:1; 21:23; 22:5) and in all of these instances it maintains a broader meaning than that of baptism.[43] Nevertheless, even after this idea of baptism is introduced in the early church writings, the interpretation of an initial illumination by the Spirit is not discarded, but rather the baptismal event is subsequently connected to the Spirit's illumination.[44] David Ewert explains, "Conversion is thought of as illumination, and since baptism attended conversion in the early church, baptism came to be called 'illumination.'"[45] Consequently, the distinction remains that the work of illumination as mentioned in this text refers to a salvific action of the Holy Spirit. This work is an initial act of illumination that enlightens the recipient to the saving work of the triune God.

Hebrews 10:32

As the author of Hebrews moves the reader to chapter 10 of his treatise, he once again draws the reader's attention back to the issue of apostasy. He begins by reminding them of the sufficiency of Christ's sacrifice for the atonement of sin and the Spirit-filled new covenant that he establishes (Heb 10:1–18). Based upon this, the author urges them to draw near to

---

42. Owen, *Hebrews*, 211.
43. Kistemaker, *Hebrews*, 158.
44. Lane, *Hebrews 1–8*, 141.
45. Ewert, *The Holy Spirit*, 172.

Illumination and Interpretation

God by holding fast to the hope that is set before them in Christ Jesus and living according to his purposes (Heb 10:19–25). Subsequently, the author issues another warning concerning judgment for apostasy (Heb 10:26–31) and exhorts his readers to remember their faith in the glorious light of the faithfulness of God (Heb 10:32–39).

It is evident upon a cursory examination of the text that there are distinct parallels between this passage and the passage previously discussed.[46] Lane comments, "In a parallel passage in Hebrews, the statement that corresponds to *phōtisthentas* in v 4 [of chapter 6] is 'we have received knowledge of the truth' (10:26)."[47] Here, Lane recognizes that the reception of the truth is equivalent to some form of illumination in the understanding of the text. Furthermore, regarding this illumination, Lane writes, "The reference is not to baptism . . . but to the saving illumination of the heart and mind."[48] Thus, it appears that a proper view of the doctrine of illumination serves well to inform a full-orbed understanding of the doctrine of salvation.

More specifically, what concerns this conversation is the parallel between the use of the verb *phōtizō*, which is utilized again by the author in Heb 10:32 which states, "But recall the former days when, after you were enlightened, you endured a hard struggle with sufferings." Just as in Hebrews 6, this verb has the connotation of an initial illumination unto salvation in Hebrews 10.[49] To be clear, both instances of illumination refer to a conversion experience.[50] Hence, the process of illumination begins with the initial event of salvation. Calvin describes it in this manner: "It was through God's favour that they believed, and not through their own strength; they were enlightened when immersed in darkness, and without eyes to see, except light from above had shone upon them."[51] This appeal to a contrast between pre-conversion darkness and post-conversion light

---

46. Lane, *Hebrews 9–13*, 296–7, offers a chart that notes the degree of parallelism between Heb 6:4–12 and Heb 10:26–36.

47. Lane, *Hebrews 1–8*, 141.

48. Lane, *Hebrews 9–13*, 298.

49. Westcott, *Hebrews*, 148, agrees at this point. He writes, "The word *phōtizesthai* occurs again [here]. . . . The illumination both here and there [in Heb 6:4] . . . is referred to the decisive moment when the light was apprehended in its glory. . . . Inwardly this crisis of illumination was marked by a reception of *the knowledge of the truth* (c. x. 26); and outwardly by the admission to Christian fellowship" (emphasis in original).

50. Guthrie, *Hebrews*, 221.

51. Calvin, *Hebrews*, 253.

is borrowed from the example of Scripture (e.g., Eph 5:7–14) and used in such a way to convey the essential link between the illuminating work of the Spirit and salvation. Additionally, Owen describes this illumination as ". . . the light of the knowledge of God shining into their hearts . . . the saving, sanctifying light which they received at their first effectual call, and conversion to God . . . [that is] spiritual light in its first communication."[52]

In each of the aforementioned passages, the relationship between illumination and salvation is made evident by the author's usage of particular language and imagery. The Holy Spirit is at work in both categories; hence, the recognition of this inherent connection is a necessary step towards a proper understanding of the doctrine of illumination.

Testimonium Spiritus Sancti Internum

Similar to the doctrine of illumination as a whole, the *testimonium Spiritus Sancti internum* (internal testimony of the Holy Spirit) is a doctrine that is sorely neglected and, thus, shrouded in an enigmatic veneer of complexity. Contributing to this is the fact that it was not properly formulated as a doctrine until the Reformation.[53] However, this assertion should not relegate the *testimonium* to a place of subservience in which the theological development in the life of the believer is hampered. Oftentimes though, this contention does contribute to an intermingling of the doctrines of the inner witness and the illumination of the Holy Spirit. To provide clarity on this matter, Ingle argues:

> First, all relate the inner witness as a function of the Holy Spirit. Second, this function is related to the Scriptures. So the inner testimony is basically the work of the Holy Spirit where He confirms the truth of Scripture to the believer. There is some aspect

---

52. Owen, *Hebrews*, 328–9.

53. Ramm, *The Witness of the Spirit*, 22–7, includes a brief historical development of the *testimonium*. Although Ramm states that the *testimonium* is not formally developed until the Reformation beginning with Martin Luther, he does find traces of the doctrine in the Church Fathers. For example, concerning Augustine, he writes, "Although he did not develop the doctrine of the *testimonium* in so many words, his doctrines of the knowledge of God and of divine illumination add up to the *testimonium*" (p. 23). Elsewhere, Ramm, *The God*, 38, notes, "There is no clear doctrine of the witness of the Holy Spirit in the history of theology until the time of the Reformation. Augustine's theory of illumination with reference to salvation and revelation is an anticipation of the doctrine. Thomas Aquinas' light of faith (which has become part of Roman Catholic theology) is another anticipation."

Illumination and Interpretation

of illumination or enlightenment involved, but this is not the same as the doctrine of illumination. . . . In one sense there is some overlap between these two phases or facets of the Spirit's personal enlightenment activity.[54]

This overlap between the two doctrines occurs in the realm of salvation as the *testimonium* grants certainty for both the authoritative nature of the Scriptures and for one's salvation.[55] Indeed, a well-rounded understanding of this doctrine is imperative as we seek to comprehend fully the doctrine of illumination.[56]

Martin Luther

Martin Luther should be one of the first theologians that come to mind when dealing with the *testimonium*. According to Mueller, "To Luther the written Word of the Scriptures is always indissolubly joined with the power of the Holy Spirit, who has made it for all times the means by which he operates on and in the hearts and minds of those who properly hear and read it."[57] Therefore, it is essential to begin with Luther because he lays the foundation for the proper formulation of this doctrine—the same foundation upon which Calvin constructs his edifice of the *testimonium*.

---

54. Ingle, "A Historical and Scriptural Survey of the Doctrine of Illumination," 23.

55. In accord with this point, Sawyer, "The Witness of the Spirit," 72, comments, "The doctrine of the Spirit's witness as it has developed historically has a two-pronged application: first, witness to the divine origin and veracity of the scriptures, and second, witness to the reality of the individual believer's experience of salvation."

56. The classic texts for the *testimonium Spiritus Sancti internum* vary from theologian to theologian because of a lack of distinction between the *testimonium* and illumination as a whole. Historically, theologians have recognized the fact that the *testimonium* is a doctrine that is not explicitly formulated in the Scriptures, but is nonetheless implicitly pervasive in the NT. The two classic passages regarding the inner witness are Gal 4:6 which reads, "And because you are sons, God has sent the Spirit of his Son into our hearts, crying, 'Abba! Father!'" and Rom 8:15–16 which reads, "For you did not receive the spirit of slavery to fall back into fear, but you have received the Spirit of adoption as sons, by whom we cry, 'Abba! Father!' The Spirit himself bears witness with our spirit that we are children of God." However, often passages concerning illumination are lumped together with the *testimonium* as in Sproul, *Scripture Alone*, 115–17, where he cites 1 Cor 2:4–11 and 2 Cor 3:1–11, and Ramm, *The God*, 39, where he cites 1 Cor 1–2; 2 Cor 3:3; 4:6; and 1 John 5:20.

57. Mueller, "The Holy Spirit and the Scriptures," 276.

Initial Illumination

In speaking of the power of the Holy Spirit, it is appropriate to begin with the context in which the *testimonium* was originally invoked. Frame writes:

> The Protestant Reformation contended for the gospel of justification by faith alone. But this doctrine contradicted the church tradition, or so it was said. So the Reformers argued intensively, not only about justification, but also about biblical authority and its relation to tradition. A crucial weapon in the discussion was the Reformers' doctrine of the 'internal testimony of the Holy Spirit.' Rome was willing to grant the authority of Scripture; but, she insisted, we cannot even know that Scripture is authoritative except by the testimony of the church. Thus, church tradition became, at that point at least, a more basic authority than Scripture. No, said Luther . . . our final assurance of biblical authority is, not human tradition, but the witness of God's own Spirit within us.[58]

In accord with this, George Hendry asserts that the formulation of this doctrine was a direct result of the church's desire to remain the disseminator of salvation and thus control the power of the gospel, inevitably dispelling the Word of its inherent power.[59] Luther did not maintain that the representation of Christ solely belonged to the church, but that by the sacrifice of Christ Jesus, the power of the Spirit through the living Word is able to encounter the believer thereby producing saving faith.[60] Hence, the witness of the Spirit, although directly connected with the Scriptures, for Luther, necessarily testified to the person of Christ Jesus. Luther writes in his *Small Catechism*, "I believe that by my own understanding or strength I cannot believe in Jesus Christ my Lord or come to him, but instead the Holy Spirit has called me through the gospel, enlightened me with his gifts, made me holy and kept me in true faith."[61]

In accord with this, Luther maintains that the certainty and assurance of *salvation* rests not in the Church, but with the inner witness of the Holy Spirit.[62] This is an aspect of the *testimonium* that is seldom treated when considering the doctrine of illumination; but in view of the previous discussion regarding the bond between illumination and salvation, it serves to further the conversation. In Luther's writings, Ramm asserts, "It is the

---

58. Frame, "The Spirit and the Scriptures," 220.
59. Hendry, *The Holy Spirit*, 73
60. Ibid.
61. Luther, *Basic Theological Writings*, 323.
62. Ramm, *Witness*, 21.

Illumination and Interpretation

Holy Spirit who makes Christ a reality to the believer. The center of the *testimonium* is Christ . . . [and] this action of the Spirit in making Christ really present to the believer is always in connection with the Word of God."[63]

Furthermore, Luther binds the *testimonium* to the previous discussion concerning the internal perspicuity of the Scriptures.[64] In Luther's nascent consideration of the *testimonium*, he connects the internal perspicuity of the Scriptures, the enlightening ministry of the Holy Spirit, and the internal testimony of the Holy Spirit.[65] For this reason, Luther was convinced that the inner working of the Spirit was required for a proper understanding of the Scriptures.[66] For Luther though, this proper understanding of the Scriptures is attained as the *testimonium* works primarily in conjunction with the Word that is proclaimed.[67] Hendry argues that in Luther's awareness, "the witness of the Spirit is connected with the effect or efficacy of the Word in use; it has no bearing on the character of the Word antecedent to use. . . . The testimony of the Spirit is associated primarily with its power to create faith in the hearts of men."[68]

The inner testimony of the Holy Spirit underlies Luther's conception of salvation and his understanding of the utilization of the Word of God. The *testimonium* represents an indissoluble bond between Word and Spirit that bears witness to not only the certainty of the Scripture's authoritative nature, but also to the certainty of one's salvation as found in Jesus Christ through the working of the Spirit.[69]

---

63. Ibid., 20.

64. See the section on illumination and perspicuity in chapter 2 of this work for a discussion pertaining to Luther's distinction between the internal and external perspicuity of the Scriptures.

65. Luther, *The Bondage of the Will*, 124. Although Luther rightly connects these doctrines with each other, he fails to properly delineate between them, such that these terms are used interchangeably to refer to the same concept in his mind. For our purposes this does not present a problem, rather it serves to contribute to the developing discussion regarding the inner workings of the Holy Spirit. Ramm, *The God*, 38–9, affirms, "Luther did not develop this doctrine of the Holy Spirit in any significant way apart from his special use of it in *The Bondage of the Will*."

66. Congar, *The Word and the Spirit*, 31.

67. Hendry, *The Holy Spirit*, 74–5.

68. Ibid., 75.

69. Cf. Luther, *Galatians*, 451–9.

John Calvin

Although Calvin never wrote a full-fledged systematic treatise on the Holy Spirit, he is often considered the "theologian of the Holy Spirit." B. B. Warfield writes, "In the same sense in which we may say that the doctrine of sin and grace dates from Augustine, the doctrine of satisfaction from Anselm, the doctrine of justification by faith from Luther—we must say that the doctrine of the work of the Holy Spirit is a gift from Calvin to the church."[70] During the Reformation age, in which Calvin was a leading thinker, theologian, and biblical exegete, the concept of illumination began to formally emerge as a theological doctrine. As Carl F. H. Henry notes, "In the theology of Calvin, the role of the Holy Spirit in the illumination of human beings, particularly God's elect, is highly important."[71]

In the *Institutes of the Christian Religion*, the doctrine of illumination is especially prevalent. Concerning illumination, Calvin declares, "Flesh has no capacity for such sublime wisdom as to apprehend God, and the things of God, unless illumined by his Spirit."[72] Calvin's first contention with man's ability to interpret the Scriptures lies in his finitude. He recognizes the need for a special work of the Holy Spirit upon the mind of man, in order for him to fully comprehend the things of God.[73] Thus, in Calvin's view, the illumination of the Holy Spirit works in vital conjunction with the comprehension of the Word of God; and without the Spirit, humans can neither accept nor understand the things of God.

For Calvin, the Word and the Spirit are inseparable entities. He avers, "It is no less reasonable to boast of the Spirit without the Word, than it would be an absurd thing to bring forward the same Word without the Spirit."[74] As the Scriptures are the Spirit-inspired Word of God, so the believer has need of the Spirit's power of illumination in order to fully comprehend his Word. Calvin declares, "[The Holy Spirit] wishes us to recognize him by the image which he has stamped on the Scriptures. The author of the Scriptures cannot vary, and change his likeness. Such as he there appeared at first, such he will perpetually remain."[75]

---

70. Warfield, *Calvin and Augustine*, 485.
71. Henry, *God, Revelation and Authority*, 290.
72. Calvin, *Institutes*, (2.2.19), 169.
73. Ibid., (2.2.19-20), 169–70.
74. Calvin, *Joannis Calvini Opera Selecta*, 466, "[N]on minus importunum esse, spiritum iactare sine verbo, quam futurum sit insulsum, sine spiritu verbum ipsum obtendere."
75. Calvin, *Institutes*, (1.9.2), 44.

Illumination and Interpretation

Calvin's idea of illumination then, necessarily involves the Spirit working in conjunction with the Word, so as to produce understanding in the reader. To sum up this emphasis on the cooperation between the Word and the Spirit, Calvin writes, "We have no great certainty of the word itself, until it be confirmed by the testimony of the Spirit. . . . For the Lord has so knit together the certainty of his word and his Spirit, that our minds are duly imbued with reverence for the word when the Spirit shining upon it enables us there to behold the face of God; and, on the other hand, we embrace the Spirit with no danger of delusion when we recognize him in his image, that is, in his word."[76]

In particular, Calvin refers to two aspects of the doctrine of illumination. The first is commonly designated the *testimonium Spiritus Sancti internum*, i.e., the inner testimony of the Holy Spirit. The second aspect, which is often confused with the *testimonium*, but ought to be properly distinguished, Calvin deems a progressive act, and will be treated in the next chapter.[77] Namely, the *testimonium* in Calvin's thought refers to the inward act of the Holy Spirit to confirm the authority of the Word of God by bringing about confidence in its truthfulness for those who believe. Calvin affirms, "The testimony of the Spirit is superior to reason. For as God alone can properly bear witness to his own words, so these words will not obtain full credit in the hearts of men, until they are sealed by the inward testimony of the Spirit."[78] As a result, the *testimonium* allows the believer to trust in the Word of God, so that it might penetrate his heart and his life. Calvin continues, "The highest proof of Scripture is uniformly taken from the character of him whose word it is. . . . Our conviction of the truth of Scripture must be derived from a higher source than human conjectures, judgments, or reasons; namely, the secret testimony of the Spirit."[79]

Nevertheless, the *testimonium* is not identical to the Spirit's work of illumination; rather it is corollary to it as can be noted in its link with salvation. According to Calvin, both the *testimonium* and salvation are specific acts of the Spirit's power. He writes, "In order that the word of God may gain full credit, the mind must be enlightened, and the heart confirmed, from some other quarter. . . . Faith . . . is a firm and sure knowledge of the

---

76. Ibid., (1.9.3), 45.

77. Bartholomew, "Calvin's Doctrine," 13–18, presents a good synopsis of Calvin's view of the distinction between the *testimonium* and the progressive act of illumination, which Bartholomew terms "applicative illumination."

78. Calvin, *Institutes*, (1.7.4), 33.

79. Ibid., 32–3.

divine favor toward us, founded on the truth of a free promise in Christ, and revealed to our minds, and sealed on our hearts, by the Holy Spirit."[80] Since the Holy Spirit is active in both venues, the effects of the *testimonium* are not merely constrained to a confidence regarding the Scriptures, but also project to an assurance of salvation. Kenneth Kantzer writes, concerning Calvin's articulation of this point, "Not only does the witness of the Spirit enable man to know the truth of the gospel but it also enables him to know with certainty that his own response to the gospel has been satisfactory.... The Spirit, in short, witnesses to the sinner the fact of his own forgiveness and adoption into the family of God."[81]

Therefore, similar to Luther, Calvin's doctrine of the inner testimony of the Holy Spirit is centered upon the indissoluble bond between Word and Spirit. In addition, Calvin emphasizes an important qualification of this bond, i.e., the Holy Spirit works in conjunction with the objective revelation of the Word, not in addition to it. Preiss summarizes:

> Calvin replied that the same Spirit who speaks to us in the Scriptures speaks also in our hearts. The exterior testimony which we read in black and white is confirmed to us and sealed in our hearts by the secret testimony of the Spirit. And the secret testimony of the Holy Spirit does not lift us proudly above the letter of the Word, but, on the contrary . . . the inner testimony then sends the believer back to the external testimony, which alone is normative. It adds nothing to the written revelation. . . . The Spirit only attests, seals, and confirms to the heart of man that such and such a page in the act of being read or explained . . . is truly the Word of God. The work of the Spirit then consists in making the exterior testimony speak in the inner testimony.[82]

The point of this is that the inner testimony of the Holy Spirit is not to be understood as a further revelation of God. If an internal *revelation* is necessary in order to validate the revelation of Scripture, then another revelation from God would be required in order to substantiate the inner revelation *ad infinitum*.[83] In light of Calvin's qualification, this circular argument is gratuitous.

80. Ibid., (3.2.7), 360.
81. Kantzer, "Calvin and the Holy Scriptures," 134. Also, Preiss, "The Inner Witness," 263, states, "On the part of Calvin the inner testimony of the Holy Spirit occurred at two points: it made the believer know, on the one hand, the authority of Scripture, and on the other hand the certainty of his own personal salvation."
82. Preiss, "The Inner Witness," 261–2.
83. Kantzer, *Calvin*, 129.

Illumination and Interpretation

In Calvin's understanding, "The conclusion, then, is that in the Christian religion our certainty is not derived from the rational powers of the human mind, nor from the word of the imperial church, nor from the direct delivery of a revelation within the heart. Rather, it comes only from the *testimonium spiritus sancti*."[84] This assessment results in two complementary aspects of the *testimonium*: the internal witness that assures the believer of the truth and certainty of the Word and the internal witness that assures the believer of his faith.

John Owen

John Owen, a British theologian in the seventeenth century, is one of the foremost theologians concerning the doctrine of illumination. In his influential work[85] on the subject, Owen's treatment of the doctrine is separated into two sections. The first of these handles the acceptance of the Scriptures as the Word of God and the second section considers the role of the Holy Spirit in the process of interpretation.[86]

To begin with, Owen establishes the autonomy of the individual believer in the process of biblical interpretation. Indeed, this does not preclude the ministry of the church or other believers to aid in interpretation, but Owen's primary concern is that the believer understands that the authoritative interpretation of Scripture does not depend on any ministry of the church or of a person, but on the Spirit of God himself.[87] Owen remarks:

> Although ordinary believers are obliged to make diligent and conscientious use of the *ministry of the church*, among other things, as a means appointed of God to lead, guide, and instruct them in the knowledge of his mind and will revealed in the Scripture, which is the principal end of that ordinance, yet it is not their understanding of the truth, their apprehension of it and faith in it, to rest upon or to be resolved into their authority, who are not appointed of God to be *lords of their faith*, but *helpers of their joy*. And thereon depends all our interest in that great promise, that we *shall be all taught of God*; for we are not

---

84. Ramm, *Witness*, 16.
85. Owen, *Works*, vol. 4.
86. Cf. Ibid., "Causes" (4.0.120).
87. Ibid., 122–3.

> so unless we do learn from him and by him the things he hath revealed in his word.[88]

For Owen, this assurance of the truth of the Scriptures that is arrived at by the individual believer is vital for the life and faith of the Christian, so that their spiritual judgments depend not on the authority of man, but on the authority of God alone.[89] Nevertheless, it is important to note that Owen does not believe in the sufficiency of human reason alone to interpret Scripture, but in the sufficiency of human reason as enlightened by the work of the Holy Spirit.[90]

As a result of this premise, Owen states that his "present inquiry" entails:

> How believers, or any men whatever, may attain a right understanding in their own minds of the meaning and sense of the Scriptures, as to the doctrine or truths contained in them, in answer unto the design of God, as unto what he would have us know or believe or,— How they may attain a right perception of the mind of God in the Scripture, and what he intends in the revelation of it, in opposition unto ignorance, errors, mistakes, and all false apprehensions, and so in a right manner to perform the duties which by it we are instructed in.[91]

Subsequently, he proceeds to recognize "the principal efficient cause" that allows believers to grasp a knowledge and understanding of the Word of God, viz., "the Holy Spirit of God himself alone."[92] Illumination is a ministry exclusive of the Holy Spirit as he is a member of the triune Godhead, and being the author of the Word of God, it is imperative that the Spirit of God accomplish his work in the interpretive process. Owen explains, "There is an especial work of the Spirit of God in the minds of men, communicating spiritual wisdom, light, and understanding unto them, necessary unto their discerning and apprehending aright the mind of God in his word, and the understanding of the mysteries of heavenly

---

88. Ibid., 123; emphasis in original.

89. Ibid.

90. Cf. Ibid., 125–6. Also Owen, *Works*, "The Reason" (4.4.54), states, "There is required unto such an apprehension both the spiritual elevation of the mind by supernatural illumination, and a divine assent unto the authority of the revelation thereon, before reason can be so much as satisfied in the truth and excellency of such doctrines."

91. Ibid., 124.

92. Ibid.

truth contained therein."[93] Moreover, Owen argues for the indispensability of this role of the Holy Spirit when he writes that there was never a more "false or foolish" idea in the Christian religion than the faulty assertion that the Scriptures can be interpreted apart from "the effectual aid and assistance of the Spirit of God."[94] Thus, the Holy Spirit's work of illumination is essential for a proper interpretation of the Scriptures in Owen's framework.

To be clear though, this special work of the Spirit does not operate apart from the Word of God. Similar to the stances of Luther and Calvin, Owen sees the Spirit and the Word as working cooperatively with one another. He states:

> The only unique, public, authentic, and infallible interpreter of Scripture is none other than the Author of Scripture Himself, by whose inspiration they are the truth, and by whom they possess their perspicuity and authority, that is, God the Holy Spirit. This He does partly through the express words of Scripture and partly by revelation of God's will contained in the wider context, which may be understood by a comparison of text with text, so that which seems to have been more obscurely spoken may be illuminated by what is plainer until an overall understanding of the divine will is gained. In all of the Spiritual light is afforded the interpreter, so that he may be led into all necessary truths contained in the Word. In fact, this is the appointed task of the Spirit, given Him by Christ, so that no pretended human arbiter (however much praised of men) could have any possible value without Him.[95]

Clearly, in Owen's understanding of the doctrine of illumination, the Spirit does not operate independently of the Word.

In order to arrive at this point in his theology though, Owen builds upon the *testimonium Spiritus Sancti internum*, as well as, the Spirit's vital illuminatory role in salvation. Accordingly, Owen argues that Scripture is only received as the Word of God based upon the twofold work of the *testimonium* in witnessing to the authority of the Scriptures and the assurance of one's salvation.[96] Regarding the former aspect, Owen avers,

---

93. Ibid., 125.

94. Ibid.

95. Owen, *A Defense*, 797.

96. Owen, *Works*, "The Reason" (4.4.56–7; emphasis in original), contends, "That the *faith* whereby we believe the Scripture to be the word of God is *wrought in us by the*

"There are two things considerable with respect unto our believing the Scriptures to be the word of God in a due manner, or according to our duty. The first respects the *subject*, or the *mind of man*, how it is enabled thereunto; the other, the *object* to be believed, with the true reason why we do believe the Scripture with faith divine and supernatural."[97]

For that reason, Sebastian Rehnman observes in Owen's writings that the formal reason of faith is not solely based upon fallible and human arguments; rather it is a divine and supernatural faith, based upon the veracity and authority of God.[98] To qualify this, Owen points out, that it is important we recognize that the Holy Spirit "is not the *reason* why we believe the Scriptures, but the *power* whereby we are enabled so to do."[99] The *testimonium* is a witness to the authority of the Scriptures and an enablement by the Spirit that is required because of mankind's aforementioned finitude and sinful nature.[100] Moreover, the *testimonium* is not a compelling force that necessitates the acceptance of the authority of the Word of God. On the contrary, the inner witness of the Holy Spirit is the proper outworking of the Spirit's work of regeneration. Owen declares:

> The work of the Holy Ghost unto this purpose consists in the saving *illumination* of the mind; and the effect of it is a *supernatural light*, whereby the mind is renewed. . . . Hereby we are enabled to discern the evidences of the divine original and authority of the Scripture that are in itself, as well as assent unto the truth contained in it; and without it we cannot do so. . . . [That there are] express characters of divine excellencies upon it . . . we cannot discern, be they in themselves never so illustrious, without

---

Holy Ghost can be denied only on two principles or suppositions:—(1.) That it is not *faith divine and supernatural* whereby we believe them so to be, but only we have other moral assurance thereof. (2.) That this *faith divine and supernatural* is of ourselves, and is not wrought in us by the Holy Ghost. The first of these hath been already disproved, and shall be farther evicted afterward. . . . And as to the second, what is so, it is of the operation of the Spirit of God; for to say it is *divine and supernatural* is to say that it is *not of ourselves*, but that it is the grace and gift of the Spirit of God, wrought in us by his divine and supernatural power. . . . We do not, therefore, assert any such divine formal reason of believing, as that the mind should not stand in need of supernatural assistance enabling it to assent thereunto; nay, we affirm that without this there is in no man any true faith at all."

97. Ibid., 55; emphasis in original.
98. Rehnman, *Divine Discourse*, 140.
99. Owen, *Works*, "The Reason" (4.4.56; emphasis in original).
100. Cf. chapter 2, footnote 83, regarding Owen's view on this matter.

Illumination and Interpretation

the effectual communication of the light mentioned unto our minds,—that is, without divine, supernatural illumination.[101]

Consequently, because the *testimonium* presupposes the regenerating power of the Holy Spirit, the inner witness not only serves as a testament to the authority of the Word of God, but also to the assurance of faith.[102] To be clear, Owen states, ". . . if I believe whatever is contained in the Scripture with faith divine and supernatural, I cannot but by the same faith believe the Scripture itself. . . . And the reason of this is, that we must believe the revelation and the things revealed with the same kind of faith, or we bring confusion on the whole work of believing."[103] In Owen's view, belief in the Scriptures as the Word of God is necessarily conjoined with belief in Christ Jesus as the Word of God. Indeed, this relationship is symbiotic such that, "The faith whereby we believe Jesus Christ to be the

---

101. Owen, *Works*, "The Reason" (4.4.57; emphasis in original).

102. Ibid., 62–3. Here Owen argues, "But this *internal testimony of the Spirit* is by others explained quite another way; for they say that besides the work of the Holy Ghost before insisted on, whereby he takes away our *natural blindness*, and, enlightening our minds, enables us to discern the divine excellencies that are in the Scripture, there is another internal efficiency of his, whereby we are moved, persuaded, and enabled to believe. Hereby we are taught of God, so as that, finding the glory and majesty of God in the word, our hearts do, by an ineffable power, assent unto the truth without any hesitation. And this work of the Spirit carrieth its own evidence in itself, producing an assurance above all human judgment, and such as stands in need of no farther arguments or testimonies. This faith rests on and is resolved into. And this some learned men seem to embrace, because they supposed that the *objective evidence* which is given in the Scripture itself is only moral, or such as can give only a moral assurance. Whereas, therefore, faith ought to be divine and supernatural, so must that be whereinto it is resolved; yea, it is so alone from the *formal reason* of it. And they can apprehend nothing in this work that is immediately divine but only this *internal testimony of the Spirit*, wherein God himself speaks unto our hearts" (emphasis in original).

103. Ibid., 51. Owen continues, "No man living can distinguish in his experience between that faith wherewith he believes the Scripture and that wherewith he believes the doctrine of it, or the things contained in it, nor is there any such distinction or difference intimated in the Scripture itself; but all our believing is absolutely resolved into the authority of God revealing. Nor can it be rationally apprehended that our assent unto the things revealed should be of a kind and nature superior unto that which we yield unto the revelation itself; for let the arguments which it is resolved into be never so evident and cogent, let the assent itself be as firm and certain as can be imagined, yet is it human still and natural, and therein is inferior unto that which is divine and supernatural. And yet, on this supposition, that which is of superior kind and nature is wholly resolved into that which is of an inferior, and betake itself on all occasions thereunto for relief and confirmation" (p. 51–2).

Son of God is on all occasions absolutely melted down into that whereby we believe the Scriptures to be the word of God."[104]

Echoing Owen and Calvin, Rehnman concludes:

> The work of the Spirit is not the reason of faith, nor the objective cause of faith but the efficient cause, which presents the believer with a conviction higher than human reasons, judgments, or conjectures, that Scripture is from God. However, this accentuation of the internal certainty in the Scriptures was not to the exclusion of external marks, nor of rational arguments. There are manifest marks or signs of God speaking in Scripture together with arguments, which subdue and compel those of pure eyes and upright senses to obey. *These, though, are only valid on the presupposition of Christian commitment.*"[105]

Clearly, for Owen, a formal understanding of the *testimonium Spiritus Sancti internum* is crucial to the development of a well-articulated theology of illumination. This twofold operation of the Holy Spirit rests assured on the faith of the believer as it inclines the regenerate towards the authority of the Word of God.[106]

Contemporary Theologians

For the most part, the developmental work on the *testimonium Spiritus Sancti internum* has been accomplished by the aforementioned theological predecessors. Resultantly, theologians within the past one hundred years have merely regurgitated and at times emphasized different aspects of the *testimonium* according to their contemporary milieu. Nevertheless, there are a few notions that are worthwhile contributions to the matter at hand.

---

104. Ibid., 52.

105. Rehnman, *Divine Discourse*, 154; emphasis added.

106. Owen, *Works*, "The Reason" (4.2.20; emphasis in original), confirms, "*How, or on what grounds*, for *what reasons*, do we believe the Scripture to be a divine revelation, proceeding immediately from God, or to be that word of God which is truth divine and infallible? Whereunto we answer, It is *solely* in the evidence that the Spirit of God, in and by Scripture itself, gives unto us that it was given by immediate inspiration from God; or the ground and reason whereon we believe the Scripture to be the word of God are the authority and truth of God evidencing themselves in and by it unto the minds and consciences of men. Hereon, as, whatever we assent unto as proposed in the Scripture, our faith rests on and is resolved into the veracity and faithfulness of God, so is it also in this of believing the Scripture itself to be the infallible word of God, seeing we do it on *no other* grounds but its *own evidence* that so it is."

Illumination and Interpretation

To begin with, there is a necessary distinction that should be recognized between the *testimonium* and the doctrine of illumination as a whole. Building off of Calvin, David Berry offers a helpful construct in which to view this distinction. He concludes that since both ministries of the Spirit concern faith, this demarcation does not need to be one of chronology, nor should it be; rather it is measured in reference to the effects of the Spirit's work.[107] The *testimonium* is a witness to the authority of the Word of God and the Spirit's illumination encompasses both the initial act of salvation and a progressive act that grants understanding of the Word of God. As a result, though these ministries of the Spirit are connected, they remain distinct. Ramm contributes, "The apprehension of salvation is possible only by the work of the Spirit, and therefore the apprehension of Christ by the sinner is possible only by the inner work of the Spirit. Christ is apprehended only in the illumination granted to men by the Holy Spirit. And the *testimonium* is (in part) this work of the Spirit enabling the sinner to see Christ."[108] To be clear, on one hand, the Spirit's work of illumination would be incomplete without the *testimonium*; but on the other hand, the Spirit's work of illumination is not by any means exhausted by the *testimonium*.[109]

One aspect of the *testimonium* that is present in the thought of historical theology, but should also be concretely recognized in contemporary thought as well is the inherent connection between the *testimonium* to the Word and the *testimonium* to personal salvation. Preiss serves to reify this concept as he states, ". . . it is remarkable that never in the New Testament is it a question of a testimony of the Spirit *in abstracto*: the Spirit always testifies of something precise; more exactly, he always testifies in some manner of Jesus Christ and of his work of salvation."[110] This is a crucial point in Priess' thought because of the subjective element of religious experience. The twofold testimony of the Spirit combats this tendency, as it establishes the *testimonium* in the objective Word of God,

---

107. Berry, "The Knowledge of God," 80–6, offers helpful commentary on Calvin's attempt or lack thereof to properly delineate between these two concepts. According to Berry, on the one hand, Calvin's lack of concrete distinction contributes ambiguity to the matter; but on the other hand, Calvin's attempt at delineation offers a helpful foundation for progression in this matter. Although Berry's discussion of the matter is not comprehensive and the differing effects of the Spirit's *testimonium* and his illumination are unclear, he does move the discussion in the right direction.

108. Ramm, *Witness*, 34.

109. Ibid., 49.

110. Preiss, "The Inner Witness," 263–4.

both in the Scriptures and in the person of Christ Jesus. Preiss continues, "Therefore it is important in the highest degree, to recognize that the testimony which tells us that we are sons of God and that which tells us that the Bible is truly the word of God are to be distinguished only for reason of formal clarity of thought."[111]

Moreover, the bond between the witness of the *testimonium* to the Scriptures and to salvation is well taken by Ramm, since he observes the Reformers' emphasis on the matter as they are bound up in the same event.[112] Similar to Preiss, the establishment of this concept is highly important in order to guard against the subjective tendency of religious experience. Ramm unequivocally states, "The witness in the Word means that the first message of Holy Scripture is Jesus Christ and his gospel. . . . [T]he gospel facts represent the external fulcrum of the witness of the Spirit in which the Spirit gives a persuasion in the spirit of the believer witnessing to the reality of his salvation."[113] As the *testimonium* witnesses to the authority of the Scriptures, it likewise witnesses to the assurance of salvation.[114]

Additionally, a novel aspect of the *testimonium* that has yet to be developed is mentioned by Preiss. He declares that because of Protestantism's individualistic proclivities, the application of the *testimonium* is divorced from the unity of the church body. Indeed, if the Spirit grants the individual believer the authoritative certainty of the Word of God, then "this testimony and this certainty are given to him and renewed only if he lives in the communion of the church."[115] In essence, Preiss is alluding to a renewal and restatement of a *testimonium ecclesiae*, one that is wholly

---

111. Ibid., 264.

112. Ramm, *The God*, 41.

113. Ibid., 41. Ramm sums up his understanding of the *testimonium* accordingly, "(1) Every Christian has the witness of the Spirit which persuades him that his faith is in the truth; (2) this persuasion has external anchorage in the Word of God and the redemptive acts of Christ; (3) it functions verificationally in that it is a witness of a revealed Word and a redemptive history and the persuasion that both are true; (4) it is a spiritual verification in that the primary verification of religion must be of this order else the case is deeded away to a method of verification alien to religion" (p. 44). Also, Berkouwer, "The Testimony of the Spirit," 165, declares, "The powerful operation of the testimony of the Spirit centers in the salvation that has appeared in Christ."

114. Cole, *He Who Gives Life*, 268–73, also makes this connection as he includes sections in his work on "The Witness of the Spirit and Assurance of Adoption" and "The Witness of the Spirit and the Scriptural Word."

115. Preiss, "The Inner Witness," 279, fn.

Illumination and Interpretation

other than that which incited the Protestant Reformation.[116] Rather than the authority lying with the church and its declarations, the *testimonium Spiritus* is the vessel of authority that testifies to the Word of God and the *testimonium ecclesiae* is the revitalizing and propagating agent through which the Spirit ministers.

The *testimonium Spiritus Sancti internum* is an aspect of the Spirit's work that is often misunderstood. In fact, it is a doctrine of which many Christians are not even conscious. However, it is a doctrine which concerns the faith and practice of the believer and a doctrine that can be properly comprehended. In sum, Kantzer writes:

> The witness is not a nebulous awareness of the divine presence nor an unintelligible religious idea. It is neither a blind faith by which man desperately wills to believe what he does not know nor a rationally grounded faith terminating upon objective evidence.... The witness of the Spirit conveys an immediate sight or awareness of precise propositional truth and at the same time an overt appreciation of and acquaintance with the divine person. Above all it is an act of God upon the whole soul by which man secures all the ultimate benefits of both general and special revelation, of God and His Word, of Christ and His salvation.[117]

To be sure, the Spirit's ministry of initial illumination is distinct from the *testimonium*, but is vital to the proper outworking of the inner witness of the Holy Spirit for the faith and practice of the believer.

Defining Initial Illumination

As noted above, it is evident that there is a relationship between initial illumination and the *testimonium Spiritus Sancti internum*. However, this bond merely connects the two concepts, it does not equate them. Hodge avers, "The Witness of the Holy Spirit to the Bible, then, is not something standing apart and isolated from the life of faith; it is a part of the inward enlightening work of the Spirit . . . and of precisely the same nature."[118] The *testimonium* is the Spirit's witness to the authority of the Word of God, both as the Scriptures and as the person of Christ Jesus. Therefore, the

---

116. Sproul, *Scripture*, 93–4, utilizes this language to refer to Rome's appeal to "the church's role in the formation of the canon as a basis for establishing the priority of church authority."

117. Kantzer, *Calvin*, 136–7.

118. Hodge, "The Witness of the Holy Spirit," 52.

testimonium is not effective towards salvation; rather, it is the outworking of the Spirit's indwelling presence as a result of salvation, i.e., as a result of initial illumination. Emil Brunner states it this way, "When the Holy Spirit testifies within me that the Word *Christ* is the Truth, I know, *myself*, that it is true. I do not need any further human guarantee. And since it is the Word of *God* which I know thus as the Truth, I know and recognize that I possess the truth, not by my own efforts, or in virtue of my own reason, but because I receive it from God."[119] Indeed, these two theological concepts are very closely tied, but it needs to be recognized that the *testimonium* is part of the Spirit's work of initial illumination, not exhaustive of it.[120]

Furthermore, there is an inherent connection between the doctrine of illumination and the doctrine of salvation. Klooster acknowledges, "When the Holy Spirit's regeneration occurs . . . illumination, internal testimony, and enlightenment are all present to some degree. During the lifelong process of sanctification, the need for the Spirit's illumination continues . . . , but rebirth, renewal of the heart in regeneration is the most radical form of illumination one experiences."[121] The Scriptures testify to this bond, as the Holy Spirit's enlightening activity to salvation is necessary because of man's sinful nature and finitude. Hence, this work of the Spirit is termed initial illumination. Again, this is the broader work of the Spirit, which serves as the foundation for his more specific work, e.g., the *testimonium*. In accordance, Mueller writes, "[Illumination] designates the transfer of man from his natural state of spiritual darkness into a new state of spiritual light. . . . Illumination, in its strict sense, therefore is synonymous with conversion. . . . Both illumination and conversion occur through faith in the Gospel of Christ; both have the same *terminus a quo*, namely, darkness, and the same *terminus ad quem*, namely, faith."[122] Therefore, the initial illumination of the Spirit is necessary for the sight of the spiritually blind in order that they may be able to recognize the authoritative nature of the Word of God.[123]

---

119. Brunner, *Revelation and Reason*, 178; emphasis in original.

120. Hodge, "The Witness of the Holy Spirit," 70, comments, "[T]his Witness of the Holy Spirit to the Bible . . . is a part of the entire saving work of the Holy Spirit in the heart of the sinner [i.e. initial illumination]. . . . [T]hough closely connected with all this, [the *testimonium*] is additional to this."

121. Klooster, "The Role of the Holy Spirit," 457.

122. Mueller, *Christian Dogmatics*, 364.

123. Saucy, *Scripture*, 46, comments on this point, "Until a person is brought back to God through a personal relationship with Jesus Christ, he or she cannot view the

Illumination and Interpretation

A concise definition of initial illumination follows: Initial illumination is the redeeming act of the Spirit on the heart of the unregenerate such that he recognizes the verity of Scripture's teaching. In other words, this is the primary work of the Holy Spirit that enlightens the heart and mind of the unregenerate to salvation. Without this ministry of the Spirit, all other aspects of the doctrine of illumination are null and void. Ingle states, "All those who are true believers have received the initial illumination of the Holy Spirit, [and now] the indwelling of the Holy Spirit provides the source from which all believers can obtain the *progressive* illumination."[124]

---

world from God's perspective. Only the illuminating work of God can open eyes blinded by sin."

124. Ingle, "A Historical and Scriptural Survey of the Doctrine of Illumination," 99–100; emphasis in original. Likewise, Hodge, "The Witness of the Holy Spirit," 51, maintains, "The Holy Spirit in regeneration, therefore, must enlighten the mind, renew man's whole nature, and give him spiritual light, thus enabling and moving him to recognize the marks of God in His Word. This action of the Spirit is therefore internal, supernatural and hence objective to man's consciousness. But it communicates no new truth; it simply enables us to exercise saving faith in God, in Christ, and in God's Word. It therefore give us not only an ability to believe, but also a certitude of faith, not only in our own sonship, as Paul teaches (Rom. viii. 16), but in the deity of Jesus and the divine origin of His Gospel and of God's Word."

4

Progressive Illumination

A FORMAL UNDERSTANDING OF progressive illumination is imperative for the development of our discussion concerning the indispensability of the Holy Spirit for biblical interpretation. Cursorily speaking, progressive illumination is the continuing act of the Holy Spirit in the life of the believer that enables the regenerate to understand the text, thus serving as the impetus for transformation. The function of this chapter is to present a biblical-theological model of progressive illumination that reflects the necessity of the Holy Spirit for hermeneutics. Based upon this, the purpose of progressive illumination will be clarified as we work toward a proper definition of this vital work of the Spirit that fits into the concept of transformative illumination.

The Biblical Foundation

In the course of a thorough reading of the Scriptures the progressive illumination of the Spirit is witnessed to in the biblical record. Therefore, this section will evaluate both the witness of the OT and the NT for the purpose of constructing a biblical theology of the doctrine of illumination.[1] In the words of Owen, "The work itself is variously expressed in the Scripture. . . . And the variety of expression serves both unto the confirmation of its truth and illustration of its nature."[2] As previously

---

1. See footnote 17 in chapter 1 for an explanation concerning the selection of the biblical texts regarding progressive illumination.
2. Owen, *Works*, "Causes," (4.4.162).

Illumination and Interpretation

mentioned, because of the role of the Holy Spirit in the process of illumination and the post-ascension dispensation of the Spirit of God, the NT and its representative texts will be evaluated to a greater extent. It is through this construction of a biblical theology of the doctrine of progressive illumination that the viability and indispensability of the Holy Spirit's illumination as a biblical theme for the faith and practice of the believer will be demonstrated.

Old Testament Texts

As mentioned above, the OT has less to say about the doctrine of illumination. Nevertheless, it would be a great disservice to neglect its witness to the Holy Spirit's work. Certainly, the role of the Holy Spirit is further developed in the witness of the NT, but the individualized instances of the empowerment of the Holy Spirit and the proleptic pronouncements of his pouring out in the OT serve to contribute to a well-informed doctrine of illumination.[3] Therefore, this section will examine select passages from the book of Psalms and the book of Ezekiel.

The Witness of the Psalter

PSALM 119:18

In Ps 119:18, the Psalmist requests: "Open my eyes, that I may behold wondrous things out of your law."[4] The *Gimel* refrain that encompasses Ps 119:18 and is constituted by Ps 119:17–24 is dominated by both lament

---

3. Hamilton, *God's Indwelling Presence*, 9–23, presents a discussion and a chart summarizing the different views of the capacity of the Holy Spirit's presence and activity in the OT and the NT. The different views are as follows: 1) Continuity: Old and New Covenant believers are regenerated and indwelt, 2) More Continuity than Discontinuity: differences between the Old and New Covenant eras are acknowledged, but are not viewed as fundamental differences, 3) Some Continuity, Some Discontinuity: Old and New Covenant believers are regenerated, but not indwelt, 4) More Discontinuity than Continuity: Old Covenant believers are operated upon by God, and by inference His Spirit, but not indwelt, 5) Discontinuity: The Spirit had nothing to do with the faithfulness of Old Covenant believers, and 6) Vague Discontinuity: Old Covenant believers were not indwelt, but the issue of regeneration is not raised.

4. In his seminal work on the doctrine of illumination, Owen, *Works*, "Causes," (4.2.127), considers Ps 119:18 to be a key text. He asserts, "The whole of our assertion is comprised in the prayer of the psalmist, Ps. cxix. 18."

and petition.[5] This section is a "... prayer for divine grace that God's word may be observed, that the understanding may be quickened, so that the ethical beauty, the *wonder-works*, of his Law may be apprehended."[6] The author is also praying for revitalization, and in Ps. 119:17 he describes obedience to God's word as an act of thanksgiving.[7] As Charles Augustus Briggs emphasizes, this is because, "This writer evidently thinks that the only true life is in knowing and obeying the divine Law."[8] Here, the connection to the wise man of Psalm 1 is evident, as the psalmist finds his pleasure in the Law of the Lord.

Naturally, Ps 119:18 follows as the psalmist petitions Yahweh to open his eyes for the sake of insight into the *tôrāh*. The request that the psalmist makes to Yahweh in this verse is in the piel imperative form of the root word *gālāh* which means to uncover or remove.[9] This form expresses an intensive action, as the psalmist reveals his imperative need for divine intervention. Truly, the psalmist is emphasizing that "... our discerning, our understanding, of the wonderful things of the law, is not of ourselves; it is that which is given us, that which we receive from God."[10] A similar instance of this word is used in Num 22:31 referring to the uncovering of Balaam's eyes by Yahweh as if a covering or a veil were present to obscure his sight.[11] Like in the case of Balaam however, it is important to note that the uncovering of the psalmist's eyes is not of physical significance, i.e., the psalmist is not physically blind, but it is of spiritual significance, i.e., the psalmist requires the illumination of the

---

5. Kraus, *Psalms 60–150*, 415.

6. Oesterley, *The Psalms*, 489; emphasis in original.

7. Ibid.

8. Briggs and Briggs, *Psalms*, 421.

9. BDB, 162–3.

10. Owen, *Works*, "Causes" (4.2.128). Furthermore, Owen comments, "And the expression, though in part *metaphorical*, is eminently instructive in the nature of this work; for suppose the nearest and best-disposed proposition of any object unto our bodily eyes, with an external light properly suited unto the discovery of it. Yet if our *eyes be blind*, or are closed beyond our own power to *open* them, we cannot discern it aright. Wherefore, on a supposition of the proposal unto our minds of the divine truths of supernatural revelation, and that in ways and by means suited unto the conveyance of it unto them, which is done in the Scripture and by the ministry of the church, with other outward means, yet without this work of the Spirit of God, called the 'opening of our eyes,' we cannot discern it in a due manner" (4.4.162–3; emphasis in original).

11. Ingle, "A Historical and Scriptural Survey of the Doctrine of Illumination," 48.

divine in order to behold the truths of the Word of God.[12] To be sure, the psalmist is unable to understand God's Word without the divine assistance that uncovers his spiritual eyes.[13]

Furthermore, the psalmist has a specific request to behold the wondrous things out of God's Word. He does not seek a new revelation or insight into wonders *external* to the Word of God, but he seeks divine illumination in order to understand the wonders presented *within* the Word of God.[14] The term used here to describe the wonders of God's Word is a participle coming from the root *pālā*. Clearly, what is in the psalmist's purview is not merely text written on a page, but the inspired Word of God that is living and active and profitable for faith and practice. According to Delitzsch, this is an expression that denotes "... everything supernatural and mysterious which is incomprehensible to the ordinary understanding and is left to the perception of faith."[15] Delitzsch continues, "The Tora [sic] beneath the surface of its letter contains an abundance of such 'wondrous things,' into which only eyes from which God has removed the covering of natural short-sightedness penetrate; hence the prayer in ver. 18."[16]

Additionally, Owen notes three characteristics of these "wondrous things" that are important for understanding progressive illumination.[17] First, as previously noted, these are wonders which are present within the

---

12. This allusion to the uncovering of a veil may remind the reader of the discussion in chapter 3 concerning the veil mentioned in 2 Cor 3:12–18. It is important to note that the veil in 2 Corinthians is a veil that perpetuates the hardening of the heart toward salvation. This veil is removed at initial illumination, i.e., conversion, but this does not mean that sin does not serve as a constant distraction to the interpretation of the Scriptures. Therefore, the progressive illumination of the Holy Spirit is essential for an unhindered comprehension of the Scriptures that leads to transformation in the life of the believer.

13. Briggs and Briggs, *Psalms*, 421. Concerning this, Calvin, *Psalms*, 413, writes, "The prophet's aim ... is to inform us that our illumination is to enable us to discern the light of life, that God manifests by his word."

14. Ingle, "A Historical and Scriptural Survey of the Doctrine of Illumination," 49.

15. Delitzsch, *Psalms*, 246. Owen, *Works*, "Causes" (4.2.129), agrees, "These 'wonderful things of the law' are those expressions and effects of divine wisdom in the Scripture which are above the natural reason and understandings of men to find out and comprehend. Such are the mysteries of divine truth in the Scripture ... wherefore, the 'wonderful things' of the Scripture are those mysteries of divine truth, wisdom, and grace, that revealed and contained therein, with their especial respect unto Jesus Christ."

16. Ibid., 246–7.

17. Owen, *Works*, "Causes" (4.2.129).

Scriptures, not apart from them. Owen writes, "There are wondrous things in the works of nature and providence and much of them is contained in the treasury of reason, wherein it may be discerned; but these are stored in the law only, and nowhere else."[18] Second, it is the responsibility of the believer to read, study, and meditate on the Scriptures, while imitating the psalmist in his fervent prayer. In doing so, however, the third characteristic is the inability to discern and appropriate the Scriptures without divine assistance. Indeed, Owen argues, ". . . for the psalmist, who was wiser than the wisest of us, and who had so earnest a desire after these things, yet would not trust unto his own reason, wisdom, ability, and diligence, for the understanding of them, but betakes himself unto God by prayer, acknowledging therein that it is *the especial work of God by his Spirit to enable us to understand his mind and will as revealed in the Scripture.*"[19] Thus, in Ps 119:18, the psalmist demonstrates the necessity of the illumination of the Holy Spirit in order to understand the depths of the Word of God.

Psalm 119:33–34

In Ps 119:33–34, the psalmist implores, "Teach me, O Lord, the way of your statutes; and I will keep it to the end. Give me understanding, that I may keep your law and observe it with my whole heart." The significant phrases here are the psalmist's requests to teach him and to grant him understanding. Ps 119:33 employs a hiphil imperative from the verb *yārāh* which means to direct, teach, or instruct.[20] In essence, the psalmist is petitioning the Lord for instruction, so that he might faithfully keep God's Word. H. C. Leupold suggests, "The attitude of the speaker reveals that he senses that there are hidden depths to God's revelation that cannot be searched out by man without divine aid. So he prays to be instructed and for the deeper insight which goes hand in hand with the statutes of the Lord."[21] In light of this, it appears that the psalmist recognizes his need for divine aid in order to fully comprehend the Word of God.

Also, it is of note that the psalmist is not merely asking for a cognitive knowledge of God's Word, but that this knowledge would be manifested

18. Ibid.
19. Ibid., emphasis in original.
20. BDB, 435.
21. Leupold, *Psalms*, 830–1.

in the obedience of his life. Zuber argues, "What he [the psalmist] is requesting is instruction in the Word, which will yield an appreciation for the Word that will impact his life."[22] The word employed by the psalmist for "observe" is *šāmar* which has the connotation of abiding by the Lord's instruction.[23] This is the same word that is utilized in Gen 2:15, which emphasizes man's ultimate divine purpose, viz., to serve and *obey*.[24] Hence, the psalmist is alluding to a return to his original divine purpose according to the impetus of his divinely-aided understanding. Furthermore, this obedience is not to be accomplished half-heartedly, but with the whole heart. The word used here, is the word *lēb* meaning not merely some portion of man, but that which encompasses the inner mind, will, and emotions.[25] Accordingly, Calvin, commenting on the heart and its connection with obedience, writes ". . . genuine uprightness may flourish there, whose fruits may afterwards appear in the life."[26]

In his commentary, Oesterley alludes to the parallel nature that Ps 119:34 maintains with Ps 119:33.[27] As a result of this parallel relationship, Ps 119:34 represents an intensification of the request made in Ps 119:33.[28] Likewise, the appeal made in this verse is in the hiphil imperative, but it comes from the verb *bîn* which means to give understanding, make understand, or teach.[29] This hiphil construction indicates a causative action that is enacted upon the one making the request, which suggests an inability on the part of the psalmist to attain understanding by his own faculties. Zuber makes the case that this understanding is more than merely an understanding that involves hearing or physically perceiving a certain communication; rather, it involves existential knowledge of the Word's objective content.[30] Similarly, the psalmist desires understanding in order to live a

22. Zuber, "What Is Illumination," 59.

23. BDB, 1036–7.

24. Sailhamer, "Genesis," 45, 47–8, gives a good explanation of the Hebrew terms used in this passage and the reasons for this translation and interpretation. Genesis 2:15 states, "The Lord God took the man and put him in the garden of Eden to work it and keep it" or according to the argument above, "The Lord God took the man and put him in the garden of Eden to serve and obey."

25. Ibid., 524–5.

26. Calvin, *Psalms*, 426.

27. Oesterley, *The Psalms*, 490.

28. Ingle, "A Historical and Scriptural Survey of the Doctrine of Illumination," 51.

29. BDB, 107.

30. Zuber, "What Is Illumination," 62–6. In making his case, Zuber, employs various passages of Scripture to bolster his argument that there are different levels or kinds

life of obedience to God's Word, illustrating for the reader the impact that illumination has on one's life; but again, an intensification of this request is displayed as the psalmist asks to follow God's Word with all of his being.

Although the ministry of the Holy Spirit is not explicitly mentioned in these texts, it is evident that the psalmist is cognizant of his need for divine illumination in order to properly understand and effectively apply the Word of God. In regard to this point, Calvin declares, "... it is certain that he [the psalmist] does not here treat of external teaching, but of the inward illumination of the mind, which is the gift of the Holy Spirit. The law was exhibited to all without distinction; but the prophet, well aware that unless he were enlightened by the Holy Spirit, it would be of little advantage to him, prays that he may be taught effectually by supernatural influence."[31] Indeed, it is irrelevant whether the psalmist understood divine illumination as a work of the Holy Spirit or not. What is important is that the psalmist displays a pattern of reliance upon the Lord for instruction and understanding concerning the things of the Lord, which serves to contribute to the development of the theme of progressive illumination in the Scriptures.

The Witness of the Prophet Ezekiel

As mentioned above, the role of the Holy Spirit is not a topic that is widely discussed in OT studies. In his article concerning the book of Ezekiel, Daniel Block cites several reasons why this may be the case, and summarizes his conclusions by simply stating that oftentimes in the OT, "We do not recognize the Holy Spirit when we see him at work."[32] Despite

---

of understanding, such as Neh 8:8, 12 and Isa 6:9; 31:3. Also, he argues that many times in Scripture, understanding is depicted as a divine gift in such passages as 1 Kgs 3:9; Isa 29:14; Dan 2:21. Furthermore, throughout Psalm 119, the psalmist utilizes this same verb (*bîn*), each time in reference to the Word of the Lord (Ps 119: 34, 73, 125, 130, 144, 169), which indicates an inability on the part of the psalmist to properly discern the Word of the Lord without divine aid.

31. Calvin, *Psalms*, 449.

32. Block, "The Prophet of the Spirit," 27. The reasons that Block mentions are (1) The "Holy Spirit" has emerged as a sort of slogan and since this slogan is only mentioned three times in the OT (Ps 51:11; Isa 63:10, 11), it is assumed that the OT authors have little interest in the third person of the Trinity or little information to offer on the subject; (2) A widespread neglect of the OT as a whole has been perpetuated by our theological systems, resulting in a general ignorance that permeates much of Christianity; and (3) Little effort has been made to penetrate and master the Hebrew

Illumination and Interpretation

this pervasive obduracy concerning the ministry of the Holy Spirit in OT studies, Ezekiel is often identified as "the prophet of the spirit."[33] This is because, as Block brings to our attention, the term used most often for the Holy Spirit in the OT, *rŭaḥ*, appears with greater frequency in the prophecy of Ezekiel than in any other.[34] In this section, a simultaneous examination of the virtually identical passages of Ezek 11:19–20 and Ezek 36:26–27 is in order as it pertains to the doctrine of illumination.[35]

The prophet Ezekiel conducts his prophetic ministry during the exile in Babylon. To say the least, this is a time in Israel's history when the people are downtrodden and searching for hope. Consequently, the Lord gives Ezekiel a prophetic message that proclaims a certain amount of doom and judgment, but that includes throughout it a gleaming message of hope for God's people. Included in this message is the restoration of the house of David and the pronouncement of the New Covenant. In view of this, these passages in Ezekiel are unique because they are specifically linked to the language of the New Covenant, which echo various OT passages (Deut 30:6; Jer 31:31–34; Joel 2:28–29)[36] as well as connect them to the realization of the New Covenant in the NT corpus (cf. Acts 2).

---

language and thought patterns, such that there is insufficient comprehension of the forms of expression and idioms used by the authors of the OT.

33. Ibid., 29.

34. Ibid., 28. Block explains further, "To be sure, the fifty-two occurrences of the expression are almost matched by the fifty-one in Isaiah. The contrast with Jeremiah's eighteen occurrences, however, could hardly be greater. This is especially remarkable when one takes into account the strong influence Jeremiah's ministry had on Ezekiel in other respects. . . . With his emphasis on the spirit Ezekiel is obviously going his own way."

35. Ezekiel 11:19–20 states, "And I will give them one heart, and a new spirit I will put within them. I will remove the heart of stone from their flesh and give them a heart of flesh, that they may walk in my statutes and keep my rules and obey them. And they shall be my people, and I will be their God. Ezekiel 36:26–27 states, "And I will give you a new heart, and a new spirit I will put within you. And I will remove the heart of stone from your flesh and give you a heart of flesh. And I will put my Spirit within you, and cause you to walk in my statutes and be careful to obey my rules."

36. Deuteronomy 30:6 reads, "And the Lord your God will circumcise your heart and the heart of your offspring, so that you will love the Lord your God with all your heart and with all your soul, that you may live." Jeremiah 31:31–34 states, "Behold, the days are coming, declares the Lord, when I will make a new covenant with the house of Israel and the house of Judah, not like the covenant that I made with their fathers on the day when I took them by the hand to bring them out of the land of Egypt, my covenant that they broke, though I was their husband, declares the Lord. But this is the covenant that I will make with the house of Israel after those days, declares the Lord: I

Progressive Illumination

Moreover, in these passages, the dispensation of the Spirit produces a certain verifiable result in the life of the recipient, viz., obedience to the Word of God. As noted above, the psalmist connects obedience to God's Word with an understanding of God's Word, and this understanding is not arrived at apart from divine aid. According to Calvin, "The heart of stone has no susceptibility to the impressions of the word of God and the drawing of divine grace . . ." for it is the Holy Spirit that makes the recipient accessible to the things of God.[37] Similarly, Cooke writes that this ". . . suggests the presence of a divine element in human consciousness."[38] Certainly, without divine aid, the things of the divine remain shrouded in obscurity for mankind.

Specifically, these verses in Ezekiel are reminiscent of the New Covenant prophecy in Jer 31:31–34. Cooke asserts, "Ezekiel's conception corresponds to Jeremiah's *new covenant*, in which Jahveh's law is bestowed inwardly, and written on the heart."[39] This is of significance because, as Block avers, a connection is made here between the Word of God and the activity of the Holy Spirit.[40] The Lord's endowment of the Torah in Jeremiah and the pouring out of his Holy Spirit in Ezekiel both result in a knowledge of the Lord that is manifested in a life of obedience.[41] Zuber argues, "Jeremiah's vision in parallel with Ezekiel's prevents any concept of Spirit granted insight that is something independent from the written word (the Torah). The people will be given increased understanding of

---

will put my law within them, and I will write it on their hearts. And I will be their God, and they shall be my people. And no longer shall each one teach his neighbor and each his brother, saying, 'Know the Lord,' for they shall all know me, from the least of them to the greatest, declares the Lord. For I will forgive their iniquity, and I will remember their sin no more." Joel 2:28–29 states, "And it shall come to pass afterward, that I will pour out my Spirit on all flesh; your sons and your daughters shall prophesy, your old men shall dream dreams, and your young men shall see visions. Even on the male and female servants in those days I will pour out my Spirit."

37. Calvin, *Ezekiel*, 153.
38. Cooke, *Ezekiel*, 125.
39. Ibid., 391; emphasis in original.
40. Block, "The Prophet of the Spirit," 39, argues, "Now we learn that the *rwḥ* referred to in v 26 [Ezek 36:26] is indeed Yahweh's spirit. Furthermore, the transforming effect of the infusion of this *rwḥ* is described: Yahweh thereby causes them to walk in his statutes and to observe his covenant standards. This suggests a radical spiritual revitalization of the nation."
41. Ibid., writes, "It would appear that at these points they are describing the same event. What Jeremiah attributes to the infusion of the divine Torah, Ezekiel ascribes to the infusion of the *rwḥ*. In both the result is renewal of the covenant relationship."

Illumination and Interpretation

the Torah."[42] In accordance with the psalmist, these passages affirm that the progressive illumination of the Holy Spirit does not bring a new revelation that is external to the Word of God, but a clearer understanding of the revelation that is the Holy Scriptures.

The main purpose of these two passages in Ezekiel does not concern the assertion of the illumination of the Holy Spirit, but the dispensation of the New Covenant and its resulting effects. However, divine illumination is an evident ancillary theme as the installation of the New Covenant is enacted by the pouring out of the Holy Spirit upon all believers. For it is only through the Holy Spirit's work and by his illuminating power that one can properly understand the Word of God in order to follow the Lord in obedience.

New Testament Texts

Following the lead of the OT witness, the NT authors appropriate the theme of divine illumination as it is closely aligned with the enactment of the New Covenant. As a result, the role of the Holy Spirit, as well as his person, is reified in a way that it was not in the OT. In addition, the expedited development of the doctrine of the triune Godhead serves as the impetus for the pneumatology of the early church and informs our understanding of the doctrine of illumination.

The Witness of the Gospel of Luke

Luke 24:45 states, "Then he [Jesus] opened their [the disciples'] minds to understand the Scriptures." This verse is in the context of one of Jesus Christ's post-resurrection appearances to his disciples and is constructed in a manner that speaks to the doctrine of illumination. In Luke 24:44, Jesus reminds his disciples that while he was with them before the crucifixion, everything he taught them concerning himself in the Law, the Prophets, and the Psalms would come to fruition. Certainly, the disciples were more than familiar with the Hebrew Scriptures, but it was obvious that they lacked the capacity that was needed in order to properly understand them in light of the Christ event.[43] Joel Green contends, "The

---

42. Zuber, "What Is Illumination," 73.

43. Concerning this point, Owen, *Works*, "Causes" (4.2.132–3; emphasis in original), affirms, "The truths concerning him [Jesus Christ] were revealed in the Scripture,

point of Jesus' words is not that such-and-such a verse has now come true, but that the truth to which all of the Scriptures point has now been realized!"[44] Thus, Jesus proceeds to open their minds for the expressed purpose of understanding what was written in the Scriptures and in the following verses presents a synopsis of their testimony of the Christ.

In the NT, three terms which are generally translated "understanding" are *nous* (Phil 4:7; Rev 13:18), *sunesis* (1 Cor 1:19; Eph 3:4; 2 Tim 2:7), and *dianoia* (Matt 22:37; Luke 10:27; Eph 4:18; 1 John 5:20).[45] In Luke 24:45, the author employs the word *nous*, which is typically translated as "mind," and the verb form of *sunesis*, *suniēmi*, which is rendered "to understand." The person with *sunesis* has a deeper understanding, i.e., he has a clarity of understanding that has overcome his inability to properly understand.[46]

The word that is used for "opened" is the verb *dianoigō*, which is used in the figurative sense of opening as found in the opening of the ears in Mark 7:34–35, the opening of the eyes in Luke 24:31, and the opening of the heart in Acts 16:14.[47] The form *diēnoixen* is intensive and indicates a complete opening up of the object, which in this case is the mind or the understanding for the expressed purpose of comprehending the Scriptures.[48] Therefore, it is apparent that the minds of Jesus's disciples were divinely illuminated so that they could understand what he had previously taught them concerning what was written about him in the Scriptures.[49]

---

that is, in the law, and the prophets, and the psalms, verse 44. These they [the disciples] read, these they were instructed in, these were preached unto them every Sabbath-day; and probably they were as well skilled in the *literal sense* of Scripture propositions as those who pretend highest amongst us so to be. Howbeit they could not understand those 'wonderful things' in a way of duty, and as they ought to do, until the Lord Christ 'opened their understandings.' There was needful unto them an immediate gracious act of his divine power on their minds to enable them thereunto; and I cannot yet much value those men's understanding of the Scripture whose *understandings are not opened* by the Spirit of Christ."

44. Green, *Luke*, 857.
45. Zuber, "What Is Illumination," 93.
46. Ibid., 95–6.
47. BDAG, 234.
48. Zuber, "What Is Illumination," 94.
49. Owen, *Works*, "Causes" (4.4.163; emphasis in original), commenting on Luke 24:45, states, "None, I suppose, will deny but that it is the work of the Spirit of God thus to *open our eyes*, or to *enlighten our understandings*; for this were to deny the express testimonies of the Scripture, and those frequently reiterated. . . . And this is the work of the Spirit, in that he is the *author of the Scriptures*, which he makes use of for our

Illumination and Interpretation

Accordingly, William Arndt in his commentary on this passage asserts that apart from the Holy Spirit's work of illumination upon the heart and the mind, one cannot understand the Scriptures.[50]

Again, it is of significance that divine illumination is required for understanding of the Word of God. To be sure, the illumination of the Holy Spirit works in conjunction with the written Word, not separately as to imply some sort of new revelation. Although this occurrence of divine illumination precedes the outpouring of the Holy Spirit in Acts 2 that inaugurates the New Covenant indwelling of the Spirit, it is vital to remember the previously discussed OT witness to the Spirit's empowerment for the purpose of divine aid. In his commentary on the Gospel of Luke, J. C. Ryle quotes Poole as saying, "He did not open their understanding without the Scripture; He sends them thither. He knows that Scripture would not give them a sufficient knowledge of the things of God, without the influence and illumination of His Spirit. They are truly taught by God who are taught by His Spirit to understand the Scriptures. . . . The Spirit teaches by, not without, not contrary to, the Holy Scriptures."[51] The partnership between the Spirit and the Word is of vital import. For as Calvin argues, "The heavenly teaching is of no use or effect to us unless as far as the Spirit shapes our minds to understand it, and our hearts to accept its yoke. . . . Thus is fulfilled what is written at Psalm 119.18."[52] In sum, Luke 24:45 is a vivid picture of the working of the Holy Spirit as it pertains to the activity of the progressive illumination of the Word of God.

---

illumination. And it is granted that the Scripture is the only external means of our illumination; but in these testimonies it is considered only as the object thereof. They express a work of the Spirit or grace of God *upon our minds*, with respect unto the Scripture as its object: 'Open thou mine eyes, that I may behold wondrous things out of thy law.' The law, or the Scripture, with the 'wonderful things' contained therein, are the *things to be known*, to be discovered and understood; but the means enabling us thereunto is an *internal work* upon our minds themselves, which is plainly expressed in distinction from the *things to be known*. This is the sum of what we plead: There is an efficacious work of the Spirit of God opening our eyes, enlightening our understandings or minds, to understand the things contained in the Scripture, distinct from the objective proposition of them in the Scripture itself; which the testimonies urged do fully confirm."

50. Arndt, *Luke*, 497. Similarly, regarding this passage, McGee, *Luke*, 303, affirms that the Holy Spirit is needed for a proper understanding of the Scriptures.

51. Ryle, *Luke*, 521.

52. Calvin, *A Harmony of the Gospels*, 245.

The Witness of the Gospel of John

The primary passages in the Gospel of John that concern the doctrine of the illumination of the Holy Spirit are found in the context of what is commonly referred to as Jesus Christ's Farewell Discourse.[53] The Farewell Discourse takes place during the Last Supper in the Upper Room before Jesus's arrest and crucifixion. Jesus is addressing his disciples because of their uncertainty and anxiety concerning his prophetic statements of his imminent departure from their midst. In John 14–16, Jesus introduces the *paraklētos* to the disciples as the one who will comfort, exhort, lead, and grant understanding in his physical absence.[54]

JOHN 14:26

In John 14:26, Jesus states, "But the Helper [*paraklētos*], the Holy Spirit, whom the Father will send in my name, he will teach you all things and bring to your remembrance all that I have said to you." The key verb used in this verse to describe the ministry of the Holy Spirit is the verb *didaskō*, which means to teach or to provide instruction to a person.[55] Leon Morris contends, "The particular function of the Spirit here stressed is that of teacher. . . . The Spirit is to be the guide and teacher of the church."[56] The product of the Holy Spirit's teaching and illuminating activity in the life of the believer is understanding.[57] This echoes the psalmist's cry of "teach

---

53. There are several arguments against the use of passages found within the Farewell Discourse as support/evidence for the doctrine of the illumination of the Holy Spirit. For a good synopsis of these arguments see Ingle, "A Historical and Scriptural Survey of the Doctrine of Illumination," 56–60. The main argument is based on the assertion that Jesus Christ was speaking to the Eleven, thus given this context, what is said in the Farewell Discourse cannot be applied to all believers. See Harris, *Inspiration and Canonicity of the Bible*, as a proponent of this argument as well as Carson, *John*, 505.

54. Morris, *New Testament Theology*, 263–4, presents an insightful theological explanation of the term *paraklētos*. He concludes that a transliteration of this term into English is the best for retaining the full meaning of the Greek term. In doing this, it is possible to encompass the legal background of the word, in terms of the act of coming to one's aid.

55. BDAG, 241.

56. Morris, *John*, 656.

57. Grudem, *Systematic Theology*, 645.

me, O Lord" in the aforementioned Ps 119:33–34. In addition, this verse is a reflection of the illumination that the psalmist prayed for in Ps 119:18.[58]

The Holy Spirit is to be the teacher of all things and all that the Lord Jesus taught the disciples while on earth. This includes all that Jesus taught while present upon the earth and all that he is going to communicate from heaven as the Word of the Living God.[59] To be certain, Morris declares, "The definitive Christian revelation was made in Christ, and, while the full implications of that revelation are yet to be unfolded, it is that revelation and not something else that is the proper subject of Christian teaching."[60] Hence, the teaching ministry of the Holy Spirit is specific to the Word, i.e., to the Scriptures.

Likewise, Calvin asserts that the Spirit's ministry does not consist of revealing new truths that are previously unknown and in addition to the teaching of the Word of God. Calvin, commenting on Jesus Christ's remarks concerning the Holy Spirit in John 14:25–6, states:

> Hence it follows that He [the Spirit] will not be a constructor of new revelations. By this one word we may refute all the inventions which Satan has brought into the Church from the beginning under the pretended authority of the Spirit. Mohammed and the Pope have this religious principle in common, that Scripture does not contain the perfection of doctrine, but that something higher has been revealed by the Spirit. The Anabaptists and Libertines have in our own day drawn their madness from the same ditch. But the spirit which introduces any invention foreign to the Gospel is a deceiver and not of Christ; for Christ promises the Spirit who will confirm the teaching of the Gospel, as if He were signing it.[61]

Again, Calvin stresses the connection between the Spirit and the Word, such that the Holy Spirit's ministry is connected with the written Word and the incarnate Word. This bond is crucial for the Spirit's work of illumination, as he reveals the truth of the Word of God in order to garner understanding in the heart and mind of the believer. Augustus Nicodemus Lopes summarizes, "To Calvin, the Lord Jesus' words in John 14:25 [and 26] made it clear that the Paraclete's ministry would consist not of revealing new truths which went beyond those already taught by

---

58. Ibid.
59. Hendricksen, *John*, 286.
60. Morris, *New Testament*, 260.
61. Calvin, *John: 11–21*, 88.

the Lord Jesus and his apostles, but of illuminating the minds and hearts of believers, that they might understand and believe in the truths which were now registered in the Scriptures."[62] The progressive illuminating ministry of the Holy Spirit cooperates in strict conjunction with the Word of God and operates upon the disciples of Christ Jesus.

JOHN 15:26

Next, John 15:26, which states, "But when the Helper [*paraklētos*] comes, whom I will send to you from the Father, the Spirit of truth, who proceeds from the Father, he will bear witness about me" is also of significance for the biblical theme of illumination. This verse directly follows Jesus's treatment of persecution and the hatred of the world that his disciples will inevitably experience on his behalf. Therefore, Jesus encourages his followers with a reminder of the promise of the *paraklētos* that the Father is going to send in his name. Specifically, this verse refers to the witness of the Spirit as it is concentrated on the person and testimony of the Lord Jesus Christ. Subsequently, within this verse is further evidence that the Holy Spirit always testifies in connection with the Word, i.e., the Word of Christ.[63] Köstenberger and Swain note:

> While initially focused on the Eleven (cf. 15:26), the Spirit, in a secondary sense, fulfils similar roles in believers today. He illuminates the spiritual meaning of Jesus' words and works both to believers, and, through believers, to the unbelieving world. ... [T]he Spirit is said to be 'sent' by both the Father and Jesus (14:26; 15:26) and to focus his teaching on the illumination of the spiritual significance of God's work in Jesus.[64]

In addition, Erickson asserts that the idea of the illumination of the Holy Spirit is in view in John 15:26, not only for the first generation of disciples, but also for helping succeeding generations of believers properly interpret and understand the Scriptures.[65]

62. Lopes, "Calvin, Theologian of the Holy Spirit," 42.
63. Hendricksen, *John*, 315.
64. Köstenberger and Swain, *Father, Son, and Spirit*, 98–9.
65. Erickson, *Christian Theology*, 890. Hodge, "The Witness of the Holy Spirit," 48, adds, "These promises include not only the completion of the organism of special revelation through the Apostolic revelation, but also the spiritual illumination of the Christian Church through the ages. It is, moreover, 'the things of Christ' and not new truths which are the object of the Spirit's witness. He does not speak from Himself but

Illumination and Interpretation

JOHN 16:13

The last verse that will be treated in the Farewell Discourse is John 16:13, where Jesus declares, "When the Spirit of truth comes, he will guide you into all the truth, for he will not speak on his own authority; but whatever he hears he will speak, and he will declare to you the things that are to come."[66] This verse is loaded with pneumatological insight, but two things in particular relate to the development of the doctrine of illumination.

First, Jesus says that the Spirit *odēgēsei* his disciples into all truth, which means to assist someone in acquiring information or knowledge.[67] The guiding activity of the Holy Spirit literally means that he leads the way, that is, "He exerts his influence upon the regenerated consciousness of the child of God."[68] This illuminating work of the Holy Spirit paves the way for a deeper understanding and fuller comprehension of the things of God, viz., the Word of God. Accordingly, Ingle makes a keen insight when he writes that the truth that is spoken of in John 16:13 is qualified as the revealed Word of God in John 17:17, which reads, "Sanctify them in the truth; your word is truth."[69] He explicates this further by asserting, "As Jesus had guided the disciples and others into the correct understanding of the Scriptures (Matt 5:1–7:29; 15:16–17; Mark 7:18; Luke 24:27, 32, 45), so will the Spirit guide them when He comes."[70]

Second, Jesus says that the Holy Spirit will be speaking on the authority of another. This is important because it draws attention to the fact that the Spirit is not a rogue agent communicating truth apart from Jesus Christ, but the ambassador of the trinitarian Godhead who reflects and illumines the truth that is found in Jesus. Morris aptly states, "He [the Holy Spirit] is not originating something radically new, but leading men in accordance with the teaching already given from the Father and the Son."[71] More specifically, this teaching is to be found in the Spirit-inspired Word

---

is a witness to the truth which is Christ Himself. The work of the Spirit in this respect, therefore, is a supernatural one, removing the blindness of sin, and its object or objective content is the 'things of Christ' or the Gospel."

66. See Barrett, *John*, 489–90, for an informative discussion on the textual variants found within this verse.

67. BDAG, 690.

68. Hendricksen, *John*, 328.

69. Ingle, "A Historical and Scriptural Survey of the Doctrine of Illumination," 63.

70. Ibid.

71. Morris, *John*, 700.

of God. Owen contends, "The mysteries of the gospel, of the kingdom of heaven, the counsel of God about the salvation of the church by Christ, and concerning their faith and obedience, are the truth which he [the Spirit] is promised to guide us into . . . namely, [that] which respects all the ends of our faith and obedience."[72] Thus, a proper understanding of the Scriptures is the necessary result of the illuminating work of the Holy Spirit.

The witness of the Gospel of John in reference to the doctrine of illumination is a vital one which maintains contemporary significance. Although Jesus is speaking to the Eleven in this context, this does not preclude the teachings in the Farewell Discourse from applying to His disciples today.[73] For example, the Holy Spirit's guidance of believers into truth is found elsewhere in Scripture where it is not restricted to the Eleven (Eph 3:14–19; 1 Thess 1:5).[74] Indeed, the Eleven were recipients of the promise of the Holy Spirit and his illuminating activity, but likewise, those in the present church are equal partakers of this promise.[75] Köstenberger and Swain offer an appropriate summary of this section:

---

72. Owen, *Works*, "Causes" (4.3.142). Furthermore, Owen argues, "Thus the Holy Spirit leads us into all truth, by giving us that understanding of it which of ourselves we are not able to attain. . . . It is, therefore, his work to give us a useful, saving understanding of all sacred truth, or the mind of God as revealed in the Scripture. All spiritual, *divine, supernatural truth* is revealed in the Scripture. . . . The knowledge, the *right understanding*, of this truth as so revealed, is the duty of all, according unto the means which they enjoy and the duties that are required of them. . . . Unto this end, that they may do so, the Holy Spirit is here *promised unto them that do believe*. His divine aid and assistance is, therefore, necessary hereunto. And this we are to *pray for*, as it is promised. Wherefore, of ourselves, without his especial assistance and guidance, we cannot attain a due knowledge of and understanding in the truth revealed in the Scripture" (p. 144; emphasis in original).

73. Erickson, *Christian Theology*, 276–7. Also, Owen, *Works*, "Causes" (4.3.142; emphasis added), supports this statement by writing, concerning John 16:13, ". . . for unto this end is the Holy Ghost promised unto *all believers*."

74. Ibid., 277. Eph 3:14–19 states, "For this reason I bow my knees before the Father, from whom every family in heaven and on earth is named, that according to the riches of his glory he may grant you to be strengthened with power through his Spirit in your inner being, so that Christ may dwell in your hearts through faith—that you, being rooted and grounded in love, may have strength to comprehend with all the saints what is the breadth and length and height and depth, and to know the love of Christ that surpasses knowledge, that you may be filled with all the fullness of God." First Thess 1:5 states, ". . . because our gospel came to you not only in word, but also in power and in the Holy Spirit and with full conviction. You know what kind of men we proved to be among you for your sake."

75. Owen, *Works*, "Causes" (4.3.143; emphasis in original), asserts, "The promises concerning the *mission of the Holy Spirit* in these chapters of the Gospel [by John], xiv.

Illumination and Interpretation

> The Holy Spirit is 'the Spirit of truth' (14:17; 15:26; 16:13). As the Spirit *of* truth, he will 'guide' (16:13) the disciples *in* (or *into*) the way of truth revealed in Jesus (14:6). He will enable them both to remember Jesus' enigmatic revelation (14:26; cf. 2:22) and to understand 'plainly' (16:25) the full import and meaning of that revelation (14:26; 16:12–15). The Spirit is especially equipped to play this interpretive role vis-à-vis the disciples because he too is a 'hearer' of the Father's revelation through the Son (16:13), albeit an especially privileged one, who enjoys full access to divine truth.[76]

To be clear, this ministry of the Holy Spirit is not restricted to the Eleven, rather all of Christ's disciples are in the purview of these promises of progressive illumination.[77] In light of these passages in the Farewell Discourse, it is evident that the Holy Spirit's ministry of teaching and illuminating the truth of the Word of God is an essential theme continued from the OT into the NT as it is catalyzed by the coming of the Christ and his departure from this world.

---

xv.xvi., are not to be confined unto the *apostles*, nor unto the *first age or ages of the church*. To do so is expressly contradictory unto the discourse and whole design of our Lord Jesus Christ unto that purpose; for he promiseth him in opposition unto his own temporary abode in the world, namely, that this of the Spirit should *be for ever* ... unto the *consummation* of the whole state of the church here below. And to suppose the contrary is to overthrow the foundation of all truth and comfort in the church: for their preservation in the one, and the administration of the other unto them, depend on the accomplishment of this promise alone; and so also do all the benefits of the intercession of Christ, which are not otherwise communicated unto us but by the *Holy Spirit*, as given in pursuit of this promise; for what herein he prayed for his apostles, he prayed for all them that should believe in him through their word unto the end of the world."

76. Köstenberger and Swain, *Father, Son, and Spirit*, 144–5; emphasis in original.

77. The qualification of these promises as regarding progressive illumination is vital in light of the above discussion. Kaiser, "The Single Intent of Scripture," 165, in reaction against the assertion that "... almost every cult or aberration from historical Christian doctrine has appealed at one time or another to these three texts as their grounds for adding to the inscripturated Word of God" interprets these passages as not referring to the "body of believers at large but the future writers of the New Testament." In doing so, he appeals to the physical "upper room" context of the Farewell Discourse. However, this presents problems because as Jesus spoke to his disciples, he did not single out the ones who would eventually be used in the writing of Holy Scripture, instead he spoke to the Eleven as those who follow him and seek to obey his teachings.

The Witness of the First Epistle to the Corinthians

The verses found in 1 Cor 2:6–16 are commonly held to be the key texts for the doctrine of the illumination of the Holy Spirit. Throughout the history of the church, this passage has been used to inform and develop one's view of the doctrine of illumination.[78] For the sake of brevity, this assessment will deal specifically with 1 Cor 2:10–11 and 1 Cor 2:14 after the context is set.

It is evident through a cursory reading of this epistle that the church at Corinth is a church in disarray. Nonetheless, the Apostle Paul begins his epistle with a word of thanksgiving to God for them (1 Cor 1:4–9), in recognition that they are God's people called to do God's work. Following this, and directly surrounding Paul's discussion in 1 Corinthians 2, are appeals to the Corinthians to unify as one body and dispel the divisions that are within the body of believers (1 Cor 1:10–17; 3:1–23). In doing so, the Apostle asks a pertinent question: Is Christ divided? Indeed, the question is posed to receive a negative answer, which lays the foundation for Paul's discussion of Jesus Christ in 1 Corinthians 1 and the Holy Spirit in 1 Corinthians 2.

In the latter portion of 1 Corinthians 1, Paul declares that Christ is the power and the wisdom of God (1 Cor 1:24) through which those that are perishing are being saved. He places this in direct juxtaposition to the wisdom of this world, which God has made foolish (1 Cor 1:20). Paul's emphasis here is that without Christ Jesus, a person is devoid of life, the wisdom of God, righteousness, sanctification, and redemption (1 Cor 1:30). This is because Christ Jesus is the wisdom of God. Subsequently, as Paul continues his discussion in 1 Corinthians 2, it is through the indwelling and activity of the Holy Spirit that the wisdom of God is revealed (1 Cor 2:10) and understood (1 Cor 2:12). On the other hand, those who do not possess the Spirit of God, i.e., the natural person, do not accept the things of God and are not able to understand them (1 Cor 2:14). It is only through the mind of Christ, which the believer, i.e., the spiritual person, possesses, that the things of God can be properly discerned (1 Cor 2:16).

In 1 Cor 2:10, the Apostle Paul writes, "These things God has revealed to us through the Spirit. For the Spirit searches everything, even

---

78. Thiselton, *First Corinthians*, 276–86, presents a comprehensive historical theology of the interpretation and influence of 1 Cor 2:6–16 from the Patristic Period to the Modern Period.

Illumination and Interpretation

the depths of God." This verse appropriately follows the Apostle's assertion that Jesus Christ is the wisdom of God and now he proceeds to explain that God's wisdom is only revealed to us by the Spirit of God.[79] The main force of this verse is to convey that apart from God, to be precise, the Spirit of God, we cannot even begin to comprehend the things of God, beginning with Jesus Christ. Consequently, the initial illumination of the Spirit is a necessary prerequisite for the progressive illumination of the Spirit. Garland confirms, "The believers' prior reception of the Spirit ... is foundational to Paul's argument and is taken for granted. Those who receive and experience divine revelation must have already received the Spirit (cf. Eph. 1:17). Spiritual persons are those Christians in whom the Spirit has really become the fundamental power of life."[80]

It is only through the illuminating ministry of the Spirit of the Living God that one can understand the wisdom of God in Christ Jesus and the depths of his knowledge as revealed in the Scriptures. Gordon Fee argues that without the Holy Spirit, one cannot understand the wisdom of God or the gospel of God.[81] Indeed, the trinitarian God is incomprehensible by our finite minds, which the Apostle Paul implies here, but with the Spirit of God, the depths of God can be grasped.[82] Thiselton presents the case that "the depths of God" would be more adequately translated as "the depths of God's own self" because that is what is in view here.[83] Hence, it is the knowledge of the Holy One that the Holy Spirit reveals through the revelation of Holy Scripture, for without his Spirit mankind remains incapable.

In 1 Cor 2:11, Paul explicates the truth that he just stated with an analogy. He writes, "For who knows a person's thoughts except the spirit of that person, which is in him? So also no one comprehends the thoughts of God except the Spirit of God." As Fee stresses, it is important to note that Paul is not attempting to make a definitive anthropological

---

79. There is much discussion surrounding the term *apekalupsen* which is generally translated as "revealed." The discussion is fueled by the technical use of the term to denote the giving of a divine revelation. However, as Zuber, "What Is Illumination," 128, notes there is no compelling reason for this technical force to be taken here. He presents a well-constructed argument against the technical use of the term in 1 Cor 2:10 in his work (pp. 124–30).

80. Garland, *1 Corinthians*, 99.

81. Fee, *Corinthians*, 110.

82. Grudem, *Systematic Theology*, 150.

83. Thiselton, *First Corinthians*, 257.

or pneumatological statement, lest one unnecessarily convolute Paul's argument.[84] Fee explains further, "It is analogy, pure and simple. . . . At the human level, I alone know what I am thinking, and no one else, unless I choose to reveal my thoughts in the form of words. So also only God knows what God is about. God's Spirit, therefore, who as God knows the mind of God, becomes the link to our knowing him also."[85] Therefore, without the indwelling of the Holy Spirit in the life of the believer and his critical work of illumination, it is impossible to know God as he is revealed to us in the Word of God.

Subsequently, in 1 Cor 2:14 Paul continues, "The natural person does not accept the things of the Spirit of God, for they are folly to him, and he is not able to understand them because they are spiritually discerned." There are many issues surrounding both the translation and application of various parts of this verse, but for this study, the primary impetus of the verse is what is to be discussed. Two things are of significance here: (1) the state of the natural person (*psuchikos*), and (2) the characteristics of the natural person.

First, it needs to be established that the *psuchikos* is an unspiritual person who merely functions bodily, without being touched by the Spirit of God.[86] Surely, this person does not possess the Holy Spirit. Instead, he stands in stark contradistinction to the spiritual person (*pneumatikos*), who is animated and motivated by the Spirit of God, mentioned previously in 1 Cor 2:13 and subsequently in 1 Cor 2:15.[87] Also, as Fridley puts forth, ". . . the spiritual man has experienced a subjective work of the Spirit, whereby his heart/mind is convicted of the need to engage Scripture, and he is endowed with a capacity to embrace, appreciate, and obey spiritual truth."[88] In other words, the spiritual man has experienced the initial illumination of the Holy Spirit and is therefore sufficiently prepared for the Spirit's progressive illumination. In comparing the natural man to the spiritual man, Kistemaker states, "The natural man belongs to the world, while the spiritual man belongs to God. The one is an unbeliever and the other

---

84. Fee, *Corinthians*, 112.

85. Ibid.

86. BDAG, 1100.

87. Thiselton, *First Corinthians*, 267. Moreover, when defining the word *psuchikos*, Thiselton proposes an understanding of this term in a more value-neutral manner that conveys a person who lives on an entirely human level (pp. 268–9).

88. Fridley, "Illumination," 33.

Illumination and Interpretation

a believer; the one lacks the spirit while the other has the Spirit; the one follows natural instincts . . . the other follows the Lord."[89]

Furthermore, the natural man needs to be distinguished from the stagnant believer, i.e., the believer who operates according to the flesh (*sarkikos*, 1 Cor 3:3). Garland avers, "The latter incurs censure and admonition because of his or her fleshly orientation; the former is a more neutral term referring to the natural state of a human being apart from the illuminating work of the Holy Spirit."[90] The *sarkikos* is not necessarily a wholly different group that Paul is speaking about, although it could be applied that way in the Christian life. In this context, Paul uses this term for those Corinthian believers whose lives should be indicative of the *pneumatikos*, but are not living accordingly. Fridley asserts, "Since they were not devoid of the Spirit, Paul could not address the Corinthians as [*psuchikoi*]. He was intent, however, on alerting them to the gravity of their condition. Hence, he referred to them as [*sarkinoi*]. Though technically the Corinthians were [*pneumatikoi*] they were acting like *sarkinoi*."[91] It is evident by Paul's use of these three descriptions—*psuchikos*, *sarkikos*, and *pneumatikos*—that the state of the natural man is one that is bereft of the indwelling presence of the Holy Spirit, which is indispensable for the comprehension of the things of God.

Second, there are three aspects of the *psuchikos* that are of note. To begin with, the natural person, i.e., the unspiritual person, *rejects* the things of the Spirit of God, which is in contrast to the spiritual person who has *received* the Spirit of God in 1 Cor 2:12.[92] Additionally, the unspiritual person, as a result of the distortion of their perception without the Spirit of God, has rejected the things of the Spirit because they deem them as foolish.[93] This follows the Apostle's argument developed

---

89. Kistemaker, *First Corinthians*, 91.

90. Garland, *1 Corinthians*, 100.

91. Fridley, "Illumination," 30. The difference in the spelling of the terms is attributed to the Apostle's usage of the adjective *sarkinos* in 1 Cor 3:1, and his usage of the adjective *sarkikos* in 1 Cor 3:3. According to Thiselton, *First Corinthians*, 288, "Older lexicographers suggest that whereas *sarkikos* (3:3) emphasizes a *disposition* of *sarx* (flesh), *sarkinos* denotes a *constitution* or *nature* of *sarx*, perceiving the *–ikos* ending to relate to *kata sarka einai, to live according to the flesh*, whereas the *–inos* ending reflects *en sarki einai, to live an ordinary, earthly life in this world*" (emphasis in original). However, Thiselton, maintains that this distinction is merely one of morphology rather than semantics (p. 288).

92. Fee, *Corinthians*, 116.

93. Ibid.

in 1 Cor 1:18–2:5, where the cross of Christ, the wisdom of God, is rejected as foolishness by those who are perishing.[94] In accordance, other Scripture passages bolster this statement such as when Paul is deemed a "babbler" by the Athenians (Acts 17:18), the Apostle is mocked for teaching the resurrection of the dead (Acts 17:32), and Paul is thought to be insane by Festus (Acts 26:24).

However, the unspiritual person's rejection of the things of the Spirit of God is based upon his inability to understand them because of the absence of the Spirit in his life. Fee asserts, "Without the Spirit they lack the one essential 'quality' necessary for them to know God and his ways."[95] Subsequently, the assertion that this person is unable to understand the things of the Spirit of God because they are only discerned through the guidance of the Holy Spirit is a valid one. For Klein, Blomberg, and Hubbard the belief that "the ability to apprehend God's truth in its fullest sense belongs only to the 'spiritual person'" is made clear in 1 Cor 2:14.[96]

As alluded to earlier, since this passage is such a pivotal text concerning the doctrine of illumination, it is beneficial to recount a brief history of its interpretation while focusing on the influential interpretations of Calvin and Owen. One of the key texts for Calvin in regard to the doctrine of illumination is 1 Cor 2:14. First of all, Calvin addresses the identity of the natural man, which he calls the animal man. He states, "By the *animal man* he [Paul] does not mean (as is commonly thought) the man that is given up to gross lusts, or, as they say, to his own sensuality, but any man that is endowed with nothing more than the faculties of nature."[97] Calvin believes that the animal man is one who is in a natural state, i.e., devoid of the Holy Spirit, not in a supernatural state, i.e., endowed with the Holy Spirit.[98] As a result, the things of the Spirit of God are foolishness to him and he is unable to understand them because they are spiritually discerned. Calvin asserts, "The Spirit of God, from whom the doctrine of the gospel comes, is its only true interpreter, to open it up to us. Hence in judging of it, men's minds must of necessity be in blindness until they are enlightened by the Spirit of God."[99]

---

94. Ibid., 116–7.
95. Ibid., 117.
96. Klein, Blomberg, and Hubbard, *Biblical Interpretation*, 136.
97. Calvin, *Corinthians*, 115; emphasis in original.
98. Ibid.
99. Ibid., 117.

Illumination and Interpretation

According to Calvin then, one needs to be filled with the Holy Spirit in order to properly interpret the Word of God. To be clear, the natural man who is devoid of the Spirit can comprehend nothing of God's spiritual mysteries even though he may try because they are ". . . altogether hidden from human discernment, [and] they are made known only by the revelation of the Spirit; so that they are accounted foolishness wherever the Spirit does not give light."[100] Consequently, in Calvin's understanding of 1 Cor 2:14, the Holy Spirit's work of illumination in the life of the believer is essential for a proper interpretation of the biblical text.

Next, Owen utilizes 1 Cor 2:14 to bolster his case for the necessity of the illumination of the Spirit. Similar to his theological predecessors,[101] Owen establishes a connection between 1 Cor 2:14 and Jude 19. However, he is inclined to agree with Aquinas on this matter that Jude 19 explains that the natural man is one who is devoid of the Holy Spirit, i.e., he is an unregenerate man.[102] Owen notes that some commentators interpret the natural man as a man who is given up to his senses, i.e., carnal, but he discards this interpretation because it is clear that the Apostle Paul is distributing all men into the categories of natural and spiritual, and introducing ". . . the supposition of a middle state destroys

---

100. Calvin, *Institutes*, (2.2.20), 170. Regarding Calvin's understanding of this verse, Lopes, "Calvin, Theologian of the Holy Spirit," 41–2, writes, "To him, the natural human being could not be convinced of the divinity of the Scriptures by arguments presented by the church, logical and rational as they may appear (1 Cor 2:14). It was the Spirit who persuaded the Christian to believe that God was speaking through the Scriptures, leading his heart to accept them, and giving him full assurance of this, generating faith in his heart."

101. Both Augustine and Thomas Aquinas make connections between 1 Cor 2:14 and Jude 19, which states, "It is these who cause divisions, worldly people, devoid of the Spirit." Augustine, at the beginning of section 30 of *Sermon 71*, briefly mentions Jude 19 as the text in the Scriptures that clearly states that those who are separated from the church of God do not possess the Holy Spirit. As a result of this truth, according to Augustine, the Apostle Paul writes 1 Cor 2:14 to the church at Corinth in order to address the issue of carnality within the members of the body. Augustine asserts that those who are carnal, i.e., the sensual person, are believers and are a part of the body of Christ, albeit babes or little ones in Christ. He goes on to affirm the necessity of the Holy Spirit to properly understand the things of God. See Augustine, *Sermons*, 246–75. In a similar fashion, Thomas Aquinas employs Jude 19 to make his case concerning the sensual man in his commentary on 1 Corinthians. However, based on this verse, Aquinas does not conclude that the sensual man possesses the Holy Spirit merely because he is in the church, but that he is devoid of the Spirit of God. Therefore, his conclusion is that since the sensual man lacks the Spirit of God, he cannot discern the things of God. See Aquinas, *First Corinthians*, 32–4.

102. Owen, *Pneumatologia*, 117–18.

the design of this whole discourse of the Apostle."[103] Therefore, Owen asserts, "The mind of a natural man, however excited or improved, is not able in a spiritual manner to receive and embrace spiritual things, unless it be renewed by the Holy Ghost."[104]

Furthermore, Owen contends that the consequences of the natural man's deficiency of the Holy Spirit are twofold: he can neither accept nor understand the things of the Spirit of God.[105] To be certain, Owen is not saying that the natural man cannot read the Scriptures and understand the lexical-grammatical meaning of the text; however, he is saying that he cannot comprehend the significance of that meaning in spiritual terms.[106] In addition, Owen emphasizes that the natural man's inability to understand the Scriptures is due in large part to his rejection of the things that belong to the Spirit of God as foolishness.[107] As a result, the natural man has both a natural impotence to discern spiritual things and a moral impotence to accept spiritual things.[108]

Additionally, Owen argues that the inherent nature of Scripture itself is cause for the Holy Spirit's involvement in biblical interpretation. He writes, "There are in the Scripture . . . things *deep, wonderful, mysterious*, such as in their own nature do absolutely exceed the whole compass of our understanding or reason, as unto a full comprehension of them."[109] Since Scripture is the revelation of the infinite God, man in his finitude is incapable of grasping its fullness. Consequently, Owen believes that the Holy Spirit's illumining role is indispensable in order for one to accept and understand the things that belong to the Spirit of God because of the corruption of sin and the nature of Scripture as God's revelation.

In sum, it is in 1 Cor 2:10–14 that the theme of divine illumination may be the most developed. The Apostle makes clear that without the distinctive illuminating work of the Holy Spirit it is impossible for the natural person, i.e., the unspiritual person, to accept or understand the things of God, including and beginning with the gospel of Jesus Christ. For this reason, the Holy Spirit's work of initial illumination is required in

---

103. Ibid.
104. Ibid., 117.
105. Ibid., 118.
106. Ibid.
107. Ibid., 122.
108. Ibid., 122–3.
109. Ibid., 194; emphasis in original.

order that acceptance and understanding of the Word of God may ensue. On the other hand, for the spiritual person, the things of the Spirit of God are accessible through the indwelling of the Spirit and the possession of the mind of Christ mentioned in 1 Cor 2:16 by means of the progressive illuminating ministry of the Holy Spirit. Indeed, this passage intrinsically connects both the initial illuminating ministry of the Holy Spirit and his progressive illuminating ministry. The Spirit's initial illumination is the foundation for the outworking of his progressive illumination; and it is only after an unregenerate person has been initially illuminated by the Spirit of God, that this same person now being regenerate can undergo the Spirit's progressive illumination.

The Witness of the Epistle to the Ephesians

In chapter 3, the distinction in Eph 1:17–18 between initial illumination and progressive illumination was discussed with a particular focus on the aspect of the Spirit's initial work of illumination alluded to in Eph 1:18.[110] As previously noted, God gives a "spirit of wisdom and of revelation in the knowledge of him" to believers in Eph 1:17,[111] which refers to the progressive ministry of the Spirit's illumination.

The progressive illumination of the Holy Spirit is preceded by the initial illumination of the Spirit and thus is a ministry of the Spirit that is accomplished in the life of the believer. Commenting on the two types of illumination referenced in Eph 1:17–18, Ernest Best writes, "What he [the author of Ephesians] prays for here is the enlightenment of the hearts of his readers. The hearers . . . need enlightenment . . . if they do not have it, or do not obtain it . . . they will not be able to appropriate what is being said."[112] Indeed, the Apostle is concerned about the believer's growth in the knowledge of *God*, which is unattainable without divine aid, hence his petition for the Spirit's progressive illumination. It is important to recognize that Paul is not petitioning for knowledge of the finite or any sort of human knowledge, but he is asking for divine aid for the purpose of

---

110. Cf. chapter 3, Ephesians 1:18.

111. Ephesians 1:17: ". . . that the God of our Lord Jesus Christ, the Father of glory, may give you a spirit of wisdom and of revelation in the knowledge of him."

112. Best, *Ephesians*, 165. Ingle, "A Historical and Scriptural Survey of the Doctrine of Illumination," 71, adds, "The Spirit's illuminating ministry is needed for the initial illumination unto salvation, but also the progressive illuminating ministry is needed in teaching those who have received the Spirit."

comprehending that which is infinite, uncreated, and beyond mankind's grasp. Accordingly, Owen reminds the reader of his inherent need for divine aid when accessing that which is divine:

> But if men should be allowed to suppose that our minds were no way vitiated, depraved, or darkened by the fall,—which supposition is the sole foundation of these assertions,—yet it is most irrational to imagine that we can comprehend and understand *the mysteries of the gospel* without especial *spiritual illumination;* for the original light and abilities of our minds were not suited or prepared for the receiving and understanding of them.[113]

To be sure, this knowledge (*epignōsis*) is to be attained through the Holy Spirit.[114] The word *epignōsis* is an intensification of the word *gnōsis* which signifies a more perfect knowledge of God that results in spiritual transformation in the life of the believer.[115] As a result, it is only by the Spirit that this knowledge, which is grounded in the context of faith, is attained.[116] In other words, as Zuber asserts, ". . . illumination is first the fuller, deeper, richer spiritual knowledge given by the Spirit which by the working and application of it grants a capability for even deeper realization of and personal appropriation of the knowledge of God's will and ways."[117]

In addition, the Holy Spirit is qualified as the Spirit of wisdom and revelation (*sophias kai apokalupseō*). According to Hoehner, the former

---

113. Owen, *Works*, "Causes" (4.2.137–8; emphasis in original).

114. Best, *Ephesians*, 162–3, presents a sound explanation for the anarthrous *pneuma* being taken to refer to the divine Spirit rather than the human spirit in Eph 1:17. First of all, even if the human spirit is in view, the author of Ephesians has already stated in Eph 1:13–14 that the promised Holy Spirit has been given to all believers, thus providing a divine backdrop for the human spirit. Second, *pneuma* is often anarthrous when referring to the Holy Spirit (Matt 12:28; Mark 1:8; Luke 1:15, 35, 41, 67; Rom 1:4; 1 Pet 1:2). Moreover, Hoehner, *Ephesians*, 257, argues, "Those who think that it refers to the Holy Spirit do so because the qualities of wisdom and revelation cannot be generated by humans. . . . [F]or revelation [*apokalupsis*] is not the understanding of the hidden things but the disclosing of them. The human spirit cannot disclose the hidden mysteries of God." Zuck, *Spirit-Filled Teaching*, 17–18, concurs with Hoehner, "The major objection to this view [that this verse refers to the human spirit] is that revelation cannot be thought of as a gift given to people for discerning or *understanding* spiritual mysteries. Rather, revelation means a *disclosing* of mysteries. Revelation is the work of God by which He discloses truth to people, not an ability given by God to them for comprehending truth" (emphasis in original).

115. Goodwin, *Ephesians*, 288. Also, cf. 1 Cor 13:12.

116. Lincoln, *Ephesians*, 58.

117. Zuber, "What Is Illumination," 81.

Illumination and Interpretation

term can be taken to refer to "insight into the true nature of things" and the latter term carries the meaning "to unveil [or] to disclose something that had previously been hidden."[118] This is an intriguing pair that forms a sort of hendiadys in which the Apostle is expressing a single idea in reference to the believer's increasing knowledge of God.[119] Indeed, *apokalupsis* here refers to an internal revelation "whereby no *new things* are revealed unto our minds, or are not outwardly revealed *anew*, but our minds are enabled to discern the things that are revealed already . . . in the Scriptures."[120] The Spirit, as the originator of revelation, is the dispenser of divine wisdom according to His revelation. E. K. Simpson comments, "Paul seeks for his Ephesian circle the spirit of wisdom and revelation, an open-eyed, increasing discernment of the things of God . . . [and] reminds us that the illumination he desiderates is inward, not dependent on the senses or even the mental activities, so much as on the spiritual enlightenment that assimilates divine truth as its congenial aliment."[121] This combination of wisdom and revelation is indicative of the insight and discernment into the things of God that are only available through the Spirit.[122] Hence, a believer's growth in the wisdom and revelation of God is directly proportional to the Holy Spirit's work of progressive illumination on his life.

---

118. Hoehner, *Ephesians*, 256.

119. Goodwin, *Ephesians*, 290–5, recognizes this as a common interpretation that carries weight, but he also proposes another interpretation that he has recently adopted. This other interpretation understands the Apostle to be referring to two distinct ways for gaining the knowledge of God—a way of wisdom and a way of revelation. The former way is from the human perspective and is basically defined by a solid hermeneutic. The latter way is from the divine perspective and is defined by an inward communion with God that results in some sort of divine communication.

120. Owen, *Works*, "Causes" (4.2.134; emphasis in original). Ingle, "A Historical and Scriptural Survey of the Doctrine of Illumination," 78, agrees, "The problem arises if the term [*apokalupsis*] is taken to mean a supernatural revelation, which is within the scope of meaning. The basic idea is revelation (i.e. unveiling) or disclosure of truth in general, and that general concept is applicable herein." Basically, Ingle takes the combination of wisdom and revelation to signify a spiritual disposition produced by the Holy Spirit.

121. Simpson and Bruce, *Ephesians and Colossians*, 38–9.

122. Wood, *Ephesians*, 29. Concerning this, Westcott, *Ephesians*, 22, writes, "In accordance with this usage 'the spirit of wisdom and revelation' will be that spirit, that influence and temper, through which 'wisdom and revelation,' wisdom and the materials for growth in wisdom, enter into human life. . . . Through it the Christian is at once able to test and to receive and to communicate Divine truths."

Progressive Illumination

The Witness of the First Epistle of John

There are three significant verses that pertain to the doctrine of illumination in 1 John. In essence, these verses echo the theme of divine illumination in the Gospel of John and serve to contribute to the development of the doctrine in the Scriptures. It is important to recognize that John is penning this epistle to combat the problem of Christological heresy in the church.

1 John 2:20 and 1 John 2:27

The first two verses that are of import, 1 John 2:20 and 1 John 2:27, lie in the context of those who have left the church. John distinguishes between those who have promulgated false doctrines and forsaken the brethren, calling them antichrists, and those who have truly believed in the Lord Jesus Christ.[123] Of the latter, he writes, "But you have been anointed by the Holy One and you all have knowledge" (1 John 2:20). John utilizes the word *chrisma* for "anointing," which generally refers to the anointing of the Holy Spirit.[124] Furthermore, Akin references this anointing as the indwelling of the Holy Spirit and connects it with the cohesion between the Spirit and the Word, which is essential for progressive illumination.[125]

Indeed, this language parallels the OT usage that anointing was representative of the reception of God's Spirit (1 Sam 16:13; Isa 61:1) and the NT references to Jesus's anointing being his reception of the Spirit (Acts 10:38; cf. Luke 4:18).[126] Unlike the OT references though, this anointing is a gift given to all believers. Brooke writes, "Under the new covenant, knowledge is the common possession of all. The chrism is no longer confined to kings and priests. The gift of the Spirit, of which it is the symbol and the 'effective means,' is for all Christians alike."[127]

Moreover, in 1 John 2:27, John writes, "But the anointing that you received from him abides in you, and you have no need that anyone

---

123. Akin, *1, 2, 3 John*, 117, notes an apparent play on words here in which John utilizes the terms *antichristos*, *Christos*, and *chrisma* to highlight the differences between these parties.

124. BDAG, 1090.

125. Akin, *1, 2, 3 John*, 117–8.

126. Marshall, *The Epistles of John*, 153.

127. Brooke, *The Johannine Epistles*, 57. Also, Ingle, "A Historical and Scriptural Survey of the Doctrine of Illumination," 84, maintains, "This term [*chrisma*] is then understood as a special endowment given to all believers."

Illumination and Interpretation

should teach you. But as his anointing teaches you about everything—and is true and is no lie, just as it has taught you—abide in him." The initial *kai*, attaches this verse to the previous discussion thereby introducing the result of the anointing.[128] Also, these statements concerning "the anointing" in John's epistle have definite parallels to the anointing and the promise of the Holy Spirit in the Gospel of John.[129] Specifically, John 14:26 is alluded to as the Spirit is to teach the followers of Christ all things pertaining to the Word of God.[130]

The pronoun, *humeis*, in this verse is fronted for an emphatic contrast between those who have received the anointing and those who are devoid of it.[131] Consequently, Christ's followers, i.e., those who have been anointed with the Holy Spirit, "... have no need that anyone should teach you" because the illumination of the Spirit is sufficient to guide believers in the Word of God.[132] Certainly, this does not imply that those who have been anointed have all knowledge and should not receive instruction, but that the instruction disseminated by false teachers should be rejected in favor of instruction that emanates from the Holy Spirit of God because the illumination of the Spirit is necessary for understanding. Owen describes the Spirit's dissemination of knowledge as "... his enabling us to discern, know, and understand the mind and will of God as revealed in the Scripture," and the Spirit's teaching ministry in this manner:

> All divine truths necessary to be known and to be believed, that we may live unto God in faith and obedience, or come not and abide in Christ, as also be preserved from seducers, are contained in the Scripture.... These of ourselves we cannot understand unto the ends mentioned; for if we could, there would be no need that we should be taught them by the Holy Spirit: but this is so; he teacheth us all these things, enabling us to discern comprehend, and acknowledge them.[133]

---

128. Yarbrough, *1–3 John*, 164.

129. See Rudolf Schnackenburg, *Die Johannesbrefe*, 151–4 for a discussion on this matter, as well as, the previous discussion concerning progressive illumination in John's Gospel. Also see, Owen, *Works*, "Causes" (4.3.145).

130. Bruce, *The Epistles of John*, 76–7.

131. Brooke, *The Johannine Epistles*, 79.

132. Stott, *The Letters of John*, 118–9.

133. Owen, *Works*, "Causes" (4.3.148).

Therefore, 1 John 2:20 and 1 John 2:27 offer support for the doctrine of progressive illumination already expounded in the Gospel of John and further a proper understanding of the inner workings of the Holy Spirit.

1 JOHN 5:20

Additionally, 1 John 5:20, which states, "And we know that the Son of God has come and has given us understanding, so that we may know him who is true; and we are in him who is true, in his Son Jesus Christ. He is the true God and eternal life," informs the doctrine of progressive illumination. One of the key phrases in this verse is "and has given us understanding" (*kai dedōken humin dianoian*). The word John employs for "understanding" is *dianoia*, which denotes the *faculty* of thinking, comprehending, and reasoning.[134] Hence, believers have not received all wisdom and all knowledge, but the capability of apprehending wisdom and knowledge. On the other hand, the unbeliever's mind is darkened by sin, thus he is not capable of interpreting the truths of Scripture properly.

Therefore, echoing the statement of Vanhoozer once again, "The Spirit's illumination of our minds is therefore dependent on his prior transformation of our hearts."[135] It is through the initial illumination of the Holy Spirit which leads one to the true God that ushers in the progressive illumination of the Holy Spirit needed to properly interpret and understand the Holy Scriptures. Erickson's previously noted assertion can now be qualified: "Illumination is necessary because of sin's effect on the noetic powers of human beings. Some of the countering of this blindness takes place at the point of new birth [initial illumination], but some of it is a direct spiritual work at the point of exposure to the content of Scripture [progressive illumination]."[136]

Another key phrase in this text is "so that we may know him who is true"(*hina ginōskōmen ton alēthinon*). John utilizes the verb *ginōskō* in the present tense which indicates that believers have been endowed with ". . . a power of understanding, of interpreting, of following out to their right issues, the complex facts of life; and the end of the gift is that they may know, not by one decisive act . . . but by a continuous and progressive

---

134. BDAG, 234.
135. Vanhoozer, *Meaning*, 413.
136. Erickson, *Evangelical Interpretation*, 33.

Illumination and Interpretation

apprehension."[137] The object of this progressive apprehension is none other than the Word of God, i.e., Jesus Christ, the crux of the Christian faith.

As a result, Owen interprets this passage in the light of John 17:3, which states, "And this is eternal life, that they know you the only true God, and Jesus Christ whom you have sent." Owen argues that to know Christ is to know the mind of God; and to know the mind of God is to know the things of God as revealed in the Scriptures.[138] Moreover, Owen remarks, "We are not able of ourselves to know him that is true, and the eternal life that is in him, but he hath enabled us thereunto; for this *understanding* is *given* us unto that end, that we may so know him. Wherefore, whatever is proposed unto us in the gospel, or in any divine revelation, concerning these things, we cannot *know them*, at least as we ought, unless we have the *understanding* here mentioned given unto us, for so alone do we come by it."[139] It is only with the illuminating activity of the Holy Spirit that the ability to apprehend the things of God and the realization of this apprehension can be attained.

John's first epistle has served well to inform the development of the doctrine of the Spirit's illumination in the Scriptures. It is evident that in 1 John the theme of divine illumination has been continued from the Gospel of John. According to this witness, dependence upon the progressive illuminating activity of the Holy Spirit is vital to the abundant life of the believer.

Moreover, it is plain that the illumination of the Holy Spirit is a biblical theme woven throughout the pages of Scripture. Both the OT and the NT testify to the necessity of the Spirit's illuminating activity in order to understand the things of God, and more specifically, the Word of God. It is apparent that the Holy Spirit's work of illumination consists of two forms: initial illumination which leads to salvation and progressive illumination which leads to a deeper understanding of the Scriptures. The latter ongoing ministry of the Holy Spirit is crucial in the life of the believer as it is necessary for continual development.

---

137. Westcott, *The Epistles of St. John*, 196.
138. Owen, *Works*, "Causes" (4.4.164).
139. Ibid., 164–5; emphasis in original.

The Purpose of Progressive Illumination

Now that a biblical theology of the doctrine of illumination has been sufficiently established, the purpose of the progressive action of the Holy Spirit's illuminating ministry can be discussed. According to the testimony of the Scriptures, it is clear that the Holy Spirit is indispensable for the process of biblical interpretation. However, what may be somewhat ambiguous is the manner in which the Holy Spirit exercises this role. The conversation concerning this issue primarily revolves around 1 Cor 2:10–14, which was discussed above. More specifically, the pivotal verse that is in view is 1 Cor 2:14, which states, "The natural person *does not accept* the things of the Spirit of God, for they are folly to him, and he *is not able to understand* them because they are spiritually discerned."

To be clear, the previous discussion of this passage concludes that without the illuminating work of the Holy Spirit it is impossible for the natural person, i.e., the unspiritual person, to accept or understand the things of God. For this reason, the Holy Spirit's work of initial illumination is required in order that acceptance and understanding of the Word of God may ensue. Indeed, this passage intrinsically connects both the initial illuminating ministry of the Holy Spirit and his progressive illuminating ministry. The Spirit's initial illumination is the foundation for the outworking of his progressive illumination; and it is only after an unregenerate person has been initially illuminated by the Spirit of God, that this same person now being regenerate can experience the Spirit's progressive illumination.

Nonetheless, from this passage, two schools of thought have emerged: (1) The illuminating ministry of the Holy Spirit creates the capacity for *acceptance* of the Scripture's truth, and (2) the illuminating ministry of the Holy Spirit creates the capacity for *understanding* of the Scripture's truth. Certainly, the Apostle's construction of 1 Cor 2:14 lends credence to this division of purpose; however, these two concepts are not necessarily mutually exclusive. Rather, this phantom partition, which stems from the use of imprecise language, will be dispelled as the purpose of progressive illumination seeks to reconcile and encompass this apparent duality.

Acceptance of the Scripture's Truth

The work of the Holy Spirit as acceptance of the Scripture's truth is certainly a vital aspect of the Spirit's ministry of illumination. However, this

Illumination and Interpretation

aspect of the Spirit's work is largely accomplished through his work of initial illumination rather than his work of progressive illumination. As a result, illumination to salvation is a prerequisite for the acceptance of the Scripture's truth. For this reason, because he is unregenerate and devoid of the Spirit's indwelling presence, the natural person will not, and indeed cannot, accept the things of the Spirit of God.

As mentioned above, there are two emphases of the Spirit's work of illumination that are often set against one another. The emphasis on the Spirit's work as comprising the acceptance of the Scripture's truth is championed by Daniel Fuller. In his argument, Fuller begins with the question: Do we need the Holy Spirit to understand the Bible? And he poses a follow-up question: Can an unbeliever understand God's Word? Both of these are important complementary questions that Fuller maintains can be answered with a closer look at 1 Cor 2:14. First though, with a cursory examination of 1 Cor 2:14 in the light of 1 Cor 2:13, Fuller declares that it is obvious that the Holy Spirit's role in enabling the reader to arrive at a proper interpretation of the text is indispensable because the divine message was "in words not taught by human wisdom, but taught by the Spirit" (1 Cor 2:13).[140] However, what is not clear yet, according to Fuller, is the specific purpose for the Spirit's illuminating ministry.

For the answer to this question, Fuller's argument revolves around the term *dechomai* employed by the Apostle Paul in 1 Cor 2:14 that is normally translated as 'accept' or 'receive.' When used in 1 Cor 2:14, this verb means to indicate approval or conviction by accepting.[141] Fuller argues, "Whenever the Greek word that is used for 'receive' in this verse has to do with the reception of teaching, it means that in addition to acquiring an intellectual grasp of what is said there is also a glad acceptance of what is taught as the truth. Hence, I Corinthians 2:14 is not saying that the natural man, who is devoid of the Holy Spirit, cannot understand what the Bible is saying, but that he cannot welcome its message of redemption as true."[142]

As a result, it would seem that the Spirit's work of enabling the interpreter to accept the truth of the Word of God, rather than arriving at an understanding of the Word is in his purview of illumination. He bolsters this conclusion when he writes, "The meaning [of 1 Cor 2:14] is that apart from the Holy Spirit, a person does not accept what the Bible

---

140. Fuller, "The Holy Spirit's Role, 190.
141. BDAG, 221.
142. Fuller, "Do We Need the Holy Spirit,": 22.

teaches with pleasure, willingness, and eagerness. In other words, the natural man does not *welcome* the things of the Spirit of God."[143]

Furthermore, Fuller contends that a cognitive grasp of the meaning of the Scriptures is not what is in view in this verse; rather, based on the meaning of the verb *dechomai*, an acceptance or a rejection of the truth of the Scriptures is what is at stake.[144] Nonetheless, Fuller asserts, "It would be a great mistake to think that one's acceptance or rejection of the biblical message as truth in no way affects his ability to grasp the message contained in the biblical data."[145] In this way he affirms the indispensability of the Holy Spirit in the hermeneutic process, not for understanding, but for acceptance of the Word of God as truth.[146] For Fuller, the unregenerate are fully capable of cognitively grasping an adequate understanding of the message of the Scriptures; otherwise, argues Fuller, he would not be able to reject it as foolishness.[147] What the unbeliever is unable to do is *accept* the truth of the Scriptures without the aid of the Holy Spirit.

In addition, Fuller appeals to the definitions of the terms *ginōskō* and *anakrinō* that are used subsequently in 1 Cor 2:14. Concerning *ginōskō*, Fuller asserts that mere perception or cognition is not what is in view for the natural person, but that it means "embracing things as they really are," which, closely parallels and supplements his understanding of *dechomai*.[148] As a result, when the Apostle writes that the natural person is not able to understand the things of the Spirit of God, he means that he does not embrace them as realities.[149] Now concerning *anakrinō*, Fuller contends:

---

143. Fuller, "The Holy Spirit's Role," 191. Likewise, Zuck, *Basic Bible Interpretation*, 22, concurs with this assessment, maintaining that the unregenerate have "no spiritual capacity for welcoming and appropriating spiritual truths."

144. Fuller, "Do We Need the Holy Spirit," 22.

145. Ibid., 23.

146. Ibid., 47.

147. Fuller, "The Holy Spirit's Role," 191.

148. Ibid.

149. Ibid. Tangential to Fuller's position, Stein, *Interpreting the Bible*, 66, posits concerning 1 Cor 2:14, "For what Paul is saying is not that unbelievers cannot arrive at a correct mental grasp of the things of the Spirit. They can and do, but they attribute to this understanding of the author's meaning a negative significance. They reject it as 'foolishness.'" As a result, Stein proposes that in view of the verb *dechomai*, the reader of the Scriptures should understand the term *ginōskō* to mean something other than the acquiring of a correct mental grasp of something; rather, it should be understood as referring to the embracing as true the meaning of the text (pp. 66–7). Through this, one can notice the inherent similarities between Stein's view of the Holy Spirit's role in the hermeneutic process and Fuller's position.

Illumination and Interpretation

> It represents an investigative action carried on for the purpose of rendering an appraisal or evaluation. Not being indwelt by the Holy Spirit, the natural man has no ability to see the worth, or value, of biblical teachings; and this is why he does not "know" them. One's ability to welcome spiritual things is supported more aptly by affirming that he cannot evaluate them than by affirming that he cannot even have cognition of them. Therefore, we can conclude that the words "cannot know" in 1 Cor 2:14 mean "cannot have an experiential knowledge and appreciation" of the biblical message.[150]

Hence, the natural person's rejection of the Word does not indicate a cognitive ignorance of it; on the contrary, his repudiation of it presupposes a prior cognition of the text.[151] At this point, Fuller puts forth, "A judgment that a communication is foolishness can be made only after one has some knowledge of what it says, but if absolutely nothing is communicated, then such a judgment is impossible...[therefore] Paul means that it is impossible for those devoid of the Holy Spirit to have any conviction that the Scriptures are the truth or any realization of their worth and value."[152] Therefore, Fuller maintains that the locutionary act of the text is able to be grasped by the unregenerate, even up to attaining its illocutionary force, and it is because of this comprehension that rejection of the Scripture's truth ensues.

Additionally, Fuller asserts that his actual experience with other scholars confirms his interpretation of 1 Cor 2:14. He claims that a humanist scholar by the name of Edwin A. Burtt exemplifies one who, despite his soteriological disposition, is able to understand and interpret the text in such a way that is as well as, if not better than an evangelical Christian.[153] Consequently, whether the reader of the text is a believer or an unbeliever really has no bearing on one's ability to understand the text. To be certain, Fuller declares that an agnostic or an atheist who has achieved a high degree of exegetical skill can properly interpret the text of Scripture.[154] Indeed, for Fuller, the Holy Spirit's work of illumination does not involve a comprehension of the meaning of the biblical text, for this

---

150. Ibid., 191–2.
151. Ibid., 191.
152. Fuller, "Do We Need the Holy Spirit," 22.
153. Ibid., 22–3.
154. Fuller, "The Holy Spirit's Role," 192.

can be arrived at by studying the historical and textual data alone.[155] As a matter of fact, Fuller asserts that in order to understand the text properly, the interpreter of the biblical text should work to perfect their skills of exegesis.[156] To summarize his view Fuller states, "The Holy Spirit's role in biblical interpretation does not consist in giving the interpreter cognition of what the Bible is saying, which would involve dispensing additional information, beyond the historical-grammatical data that are already there for everyone to work with. Rather, the Holy Spirit's role is to change the heart of the interpreter, so that he loves the message that is conveyed by nothing more than the historical-grammatical data."[157]

Just as the unregenerate fall short of accepting the truth of Scripture, Fuller falls short of accounting for the intended perlocutionary effect of the text. That is, Fuller neglects the transformative meaning and understanding of the text that is so vital to the Holy Spirit's work of illumination. Fuller intimates at this reality when he alludes to the unregenerate person's inability to gain experiential knowledge of and through the Scriptures; however, he never fully completes this thought. As a result, Fuller's emphasis on the Spirit's work as acceptance of the Scripture's truth is well-placed, but remains deficient because it does not encompass the transformative understanding that the Spirit and the Scriptures seek. To be sure, the acceptance of Scripture's truth is merely one facet of the Spirit's indispensable work of illumination which needs to be supplemented by the understanding of Scripture's truth.

Understanding of the Scripture's Truth

As stated throughout this study, the illuminating ministry of the Holy Spirit serves to enable understanding for biblical interpretation. In chapter 2, the concept of understanding was defined as cognitive understanding for the unregenerate and transformative understanding for the regenerate. Cognitive understanding grants that the unregenerate person can indeed attain a cognitive grasp of Scripture's meaning; however this falls vastly short of Scripture's intended perlocutionary effect. On the other hand, transformative understanding represents the full intended meaning of the Scriptures, in that it ventures beyond a mere cognitive

155. Fuller, "Do We Need the Holy Spirit, 23, and "The Holy Spirit's Role," 192.
156. Fuller, "The Holy Spirit's Role," 197–8.
157. Ibid., 192.

Illumination and Interpretation

grasp of biblical principles, and manifests itself as a life-changing comprehension that alters the faith and practice of the regenerate. Thus, the purpose of progressive illumination consists of both the acceptance and the understanding of the Scripture's truth.

In reaction to Fuller's argument, Erickson stresses the Spirit's illuminating ministry as enabling understanding of the Scripture's truth. Erickson states that the problem with views such as Fuller's is that they tend to emphasize only a single portion of Scripture, 1 Cor 2:14, in order to make their case.[158] Therefore, Erickson utilizes the surrounding context in 1 Corinthians and also brings in passages pertaining to the Holy Spirit such as John 14–16, 2 Cor 4:3–4, and Matt 16:17,[159] which in his estimation stand in complete contradistinction to Fuller's understanding of the role of the Holy Spirit in biblical interpretation.[160] Based upon this, Erickson is able to assert that there is ". . . a categorical difference between the believer and the unbeliever" because it appears that the Apostle Paul is not saying that the unspiritual person understands but does not accept the things of God; rather, he does not accept because of his lack of understanding.[161] Nonetheless, he agrees with Fuller that the Spirit creates conviction in order for one to accept that the Word of God is true, but conversely states that this in no way rejects the interpretation that the Holy Spirit also provides understanding of that truth.[162]

The key difference between these views is each theologian's definition of *understanding*. Erickson contends, "Fuller also assumes that there is basically one level of understanding of biblical meaning. The level of knowledge is that of the grammatical-exegetical meaning of the text. There is no element here of discernment as a deeper insight into the text, or of heart knowledge as contrasted with head knowledge."[163] This is precisely why, according to Erickson, Fuller is able to affirm that if the natural person

---

158. Erickson, *Christian Theology*, 281.

159. The key verses in John 14–16 are John 14:26; 15:26; 16:13, which were previously quoted. Second Cor 4:3–4 states, "And even if our gospel is veiled, it is veiled only to those who are perishing. In their case the god of this world has blinded the minds of the unbelievers, to keep them from seeing the light of the gospel of the glory of Christ, who is the image of God." Matt 16:17 states, "And Jesus answered him, 'Blessed are you, Simon Bar-Jonah! For flesh and blood has not revealed this to you, but my Father who is in heaven.'"

160. Erickson, *Evangelical Interpretation*, 41–5.

161. Erickson, *Christian Theology*, 274–5.

162. Ibid., 283.

163. Erickson, *Evangelical Interpretation*, 39.

is skilled in exegesis, then he is able to correctly discern the meaning of the text, as well as, if not better than, a regenerate person.[164] Erickson says that here, the errors that Fuller is guilty of is the assumption that exegesis is presuppositionless and the lack of recognition of the biblical truth that sin affects not only man's volition, but also his noetic powers.[165]

As a result, Erickson turns to the Scriptures to expound upon mankind's need for divine illumination. He cites numerous passages to argue for the need of the Spirit's special work to enhance human perception and understanding (Matt 13:13–15; Mark 8:18; Rom 1:21, 11:8–10; 2 Cor 4:4).[166] Each of these passages highlights the unbeliever's inability to perceive the things of God and sets up Erickson's exegesis and exposition of 1 Cor 2:14. Furthermore, Erickson cites the ontological difference between mankind and God, and human depravity as reasons for the necessity of the Holy Spirit's enablement of understanding.[167] Contra Fuller, and according to 1 Cor 2:14, Erickson avers,

---

164. Ibid., 45.

165. Ibid., 38–9. See chapter 2 (the section entitled "The Interpretation of the Scriptures—Unregenerate Interpretation) for an explanation of this position.

166. Erickson, *Christian Theology*, 274. Matt 13:13–15 states, "This is why I speak to them in parables, because seeing they do not see, and hearing they do not hear, nor do they understand. Indeed, in their case the prophecy of Isaiah is fulfilled that says: 'You will indeed hear but never understand, and you will indeed see but never perceive. For this people's heart has grown dull, and with their ears they can barely hear, and their eyes they have closed, lest they should see with their eyes and hear with their ears and understand with their heart and turn, and I would heal them.'" Mark 8:18 states, "Having eyes do you not see, and having ears do you not hear? And do you not remember?" Rom 1:21 states, "For although they knew God, they did not honor him as God or give thanks to him, but they became futile in their thinking, and their foolish hearts were darkened." Rom 11:8–10 states, ". . . as it is written, 'God gave them a spirit of stupor, eyes that would not see and ears that would not hear, down to this very day.' And David says, 'Let their table become a snare and a trap, a stumbling block and a retribution for them; let their eyes be darkened so that they cannot see, and bend their backs forever.'" Second Cor 4:4 was quoted in footnote 159.

167. Ibid., 273. Regarding the ontological distinction between God and man, Erickson affirms that God is incomprehensible. He is infinite, transcendent, and as the Creator is sovereign and above all else. On the other hand, man is finite and both limited in his point of origin and knowledge. Erickson distinguishes this finitude by stating, "These limitations are inherent in being human. They are not a result of the fall or of individual human sin, but of the Creator-creature relationship. No moral connotation or stigma is attached to them" (ibid.). Also, concerning human depravity, Erickson, *The New Evangelical Theology*, 72–3, asserts, "Indeed, he [the unbeliever] is unable to understand or grasp the true significance of Scripture because of the effect of sin upon his thinking."

Illumination and Interpretation

"The problem, then, is not merely that people in their natural state are unwilling to accept the gifts and wisdom of God, but that, without the help of the Holy Spirit, they are unable to understand them."[168]

It is important to note that Erickson does not deny that the natural person is able to attain a cognitive grasp of the grammatical-exegetical meaning of the text. He argues, "It should be noted, however, that the basic, and most crucial dimensions of Christian truth are considerably more direct and obviously on the surface of the text, so that honest and objective unbelievers can see them as well."[169] However, what he is suggesting is that the Holy Spirit's role in the hermeneutic process involves illuminating the believer's mind such that the Holy Spirit conveys insight into the meaning of the text, which results in a deeper understanding of the meaning that is there.[170] Thus, instead of the one-level understanding of biblical meaning that Fuller maintains, there is a two-level understanding in Erickson's framework that stresses both the cognitive and experiential dimensions of the truth.[171] Daniel Wallace appraises this discussion in this manner:

> In sum, 1 Cor 2:12–14 is saying that the non-Christian will not accept spiritual truths *and* cannot understand them. These are two distinct though related concepts. Non-Christians do indeed plainly understand the gospel message at times; further, unbelieving exegetes do often offer valuable insights into the text. That is not disputed here. Paul's point seems to be that the depths of God's ways and God's wisdom cannot even be touched by non-believers. There is a level to which they cannot attain.[172]

For example, an unbeliever and a believer alike can read the Gospels and deduce that Jesus was crucified at Golgotha. But, in order to properly understand the *meaning* of this event in the salvation-historical canonical framework of the Scriptures as it pertains to the life of the believer, one requires the illumination of the Holy Spirit. This involves more than mere application; this involves the transformation of the faith and practice of the regenerate.

---

168. Ibid, 274.
169. Erickson, *Evangelical Interpretation*, 54.
170. Ibid.
171. Ibid., 39, 47, 54. Also see McKinley, "John Owen's View of Illumination," 96.
172. Wallace, "The Holy Spirit and Hermeneutics," n.p., emphasis in original.

Progressive Illumination

Similarly, Poehnell argues that the understanding of *ginōskō* as referring to the gaining of cognitive knowledge that results in experiential knowledge is in line with its use in the Scriptures. He contends:

> The distinction between cognitive knowledge and experiential knowledge does not seem to be an issue in the Biblical concept of the knowledge of God. It is not that cognition is denied in favour of experience but that cognition was not considered apart from experience. Cognition and experience formed a natural pair which merged in the concept of recognition. When Paul spoke of the knowledge of God, he would not have been thinking of either cognitive or experiential knowledge to the exclusion of the other; rather he would have thought of knowledge which involved both.[173]

As a consequence, man needs the work of the Holy Spirit both to accept the Word of God as truth and to understand the meaning of that truth.

Heisler, as well as Klein, Blomberg, and Hubbard prefer to reconcile these two views by establishing a distinction between understanding the meaning of the text and the significance of the text as it pertains to the life of the believer.[174] However, this is a superficial dichotomization of the text's meaning that isolates the necessary component of applicatory significance that contributes to the unification of the concept of meaning. One is more well-informed to follow the analysis of Zuck:

> *The Spirit's ministry in interpreting the Bible is included in but not identical with illumination.* Illumination . . . is the Spirit's work on the minds and hearts of believers that enables them not only to discern the truth but also to receive it, welcome it, and apply it. In interpretation a believer is aided by the Spirit to ascertain the meaning of a passage. This is the first step in illumination. But illumination is not complete until one has appropriated it to his life. Interpretation involves perception; illumination includes it but also involves reception.[175]

Subsequently, the correct interpretation of 1 Cor 2:14 does not have to fallaciously delimit the Holy Spirit's work by precluding an understanding of the text, in exchange for an acceptance of the truth or

---

173. Poehnell, "The Relationship of Illumination to the Interpretation of Scripture," 63.

174. Heisler, *Spirit-Led Preaching*, 45–6; Klein, Blomberg, and Hubbard, *Biblical Interpretation*, 139.

175. Zuck, "The Role of the Holy Spirit," 128; emphasis in original.

Illumination and Interpretation

vice-versa; the Holy Spirit's role in the hermeneutic process encompasses both aspects. Vanhoozer aptly states, "The Sprit's role in bringing about understanding is to witness to what is other than himself (meaning accomplished) and to bring its significance to bear on the reader (meaning applied)."[176] This conception of *understanding* makes the distinction between *meaning* and *significance* nonessential, as it reveals an unnecessary dichotomy. Accordingly De Young posits, "While the first half of v. 14 [of 1 Cor 2] refers to significance, it does not seem possible to restrict the Spirit's role only to helping people accept the message as true because the second half talks about understanding. . . . [Thus] this passage supports the role of the Spirit in helping us to understand the spiritual message, not just receive it."[177] Furthermore, it is necessary for the reader of the Scriptures to possess the Holy Spirit in order to properly interpret the text that he administered. It is impossible for anyone, believer or unbeliever, to grasp the full meaning of the text apart from the illuminating work of the divine person of the Holy Spirit. According to Williams, this impossibility is highlighted and confirmed by 1 Cor 2:14.[178]

Defining Progressive Illumination

Based upon the Scripture's witness to the Spirit's work of progressive illumination it is evident that the purpose of progressive illumination includes an enablement for both the acceptance and understanding of Scripture's truth. For the most part, when scholars and theologians define the concept of illumination, their definitions reflect some understanding of the elements of progressive illumination. For instance, Heisler defines illumination as, ". . . the process whereby the Holy Spirit so impresses, convinces, and convicts the believer as to the truthfulness and significance of the author's intended meaning in the text that a change in action, attitude, or belief occurs, resulting in a more transformed, Spirit-filled life."[179] Williams presents this definition of illumination: "Illumination is that work whereby He [the Holy Spirit] produces right and helpful understanding of the words

---

176. Vanhoozer, *Meaning*, 413.

177. De Young, "The Holy Spirit," 4.

178. Williams, *The Person and Work of the Holy Spirit*, 39–40, writes, "Without the aid of the Holy Spirit, what we are asking is nothing short of impossible. That impossibility is explicitly recognized by Scripture . . . (1 Cor 2:14)."

179. Heisler, *Spirit-Led Preaching*, 43.

of Scripture in the mind and heart of the reader or hearer."[180] Furthermore, Ewert describes illumination in this manner: "It is also very important for believers who have been illumined to see the light of the glorious gospel, that they be further enlightened by the Holy Spirit in order to grasp the great truths of God's revelation more firmly and to penetrate more deeply into their meaning and see their implications for daily living."[181]

Additionally, as Calvin works through his definition of the doctrine of illumination, he likewise formulates his theology such that the initial illumination of the Spirit is preliminary to the Spirit's progressive illumination. Again, in Calvin's doctrine of illumination, the operations of the Word and the Spirit are inseparable. He expounds on this relationship when he writes, ". . . [W]ithout the Spirit of God they are utterly devoid of the light of truth, so they are not ignorant that the word is the instrument by which the illumination of the Spirit is dispensed."[182] Hence, subsequent to the Spirit's primary act of illumination that assures the believer of the truth of God's Word, the second aspect of illumination is a progressive work of the Spirit that grants understanding of the Scriptures to the believer. Calvin explains, "God works in his elect in two ways: inwardly, by his Spirit; outwardly, by his word. By his Spirit, illuminating their minds and training their hearts to the practice of righteousness, he makes them new creatures, while, by his word, he stimulates them to long and seek for this renovation."[183] This progressive act of the Spirit's continual renewal and illumination leads Calvin to declare, "That nothing more is to be expected of his Spirit than to enlighten our minds to perceive the truth of his doctrine."[184] Therefore, Calvin has put forth that the ultimate purpose of the Spirit's illumination is an understanding of the Word of God and this illumination is continually required for interpretation.

Consequently, the Holy Spirit's work of progressive illumination is that ministry of the Spirit whereby the regenerate person, having accepted the Word of God as true, is thereby continually enabled in his heart and in his mind to understand the Scriptures properly. In accordance, Larkin states, "The Holy Spirit illumines the mind at conversion not by making God's Word intelligible but by convincing sinners that

---

180. Williams, *The Person and Work of the Holy Spirit*, 39.
181. Ewert, *The Holy Spirit in the New Testament*, 175.
182. Calvin, *Institutes*, (1.9.3), 96.
183. Ibid., (2.5.5), 200.
184. Ibid., (4.8.13), 768.

Illumination and Interpretation

it is true. Throughout their life, Christians have the Spirit's presence to help them realize their spiritual resources, to aid them in application, and to assist them in distinguishing between truth and error."[185] In this way, the progressive illumination of the Holy Spirit is not a single occurrence in the life of the believer; rather the regenerate person has a constant need for the Spirit's enlightening work. The Spirit's progressive illumination enables an increasing comprehension of the Scriptures such that the regenerate person's understanding of the things of God is perpetually amplified.[186] Nevertheless, a mere cognitive understanding is not the goal of progressive illumination. Instead, as a result of the Spirit's progressive illumination, transformation in the life of the believer should ensue.

---

185. Larkin, *Culture and Biblical Hermeneutics*, 292.

186. Kwok, "Benjamin B. Warfield's Doctrine of Illumination," 71, and Koranteng-Pipim, "The Role of the Holy Spirit in Biblical Interpretation," 212–13.

5

Transformative Illumination

AN UNDERSTANDING OF THE concept of transformative illumination is essential for the continued development of this study as it regards the indispensability of the Holy Spirit for biblical interpretation. It should be remembered that this is not an attempt to introduce an entirely new type of illumination, for this would only serve to obscure the progression that has been made in the previous chapters. Rather, transformative illumination is a framework for understanding the doctrine of illumination as a whole. Hence, it is a synthesis of the doctrine which encompasses both initial and progressive illumination.

Furthermore, transformative illumination, as the name suggests, highlights the transformative aspect of the Holy Spirit's work in illumination. Inasmuch as the doctrine of illumination is neglected in hermeneutic scholarship, the goal of illumination, i.e., transformation, is disregarded as the necessary outcome of the Holy Spirit's work. It is recognized that the Holy Spirit's illumination may aid the interpreter in understanding the biblical material, but seldom is this understanding conveyed as a transformative work in the heart and life of the reader. To be clear, the goal of the Spirit's work of illumination in conjunction with the Scriptures is transformation in the faith and practice of the believer.

Consequently, this chapter serves to present a biblical-theological attestation to a transformative understanding of the doctrine of illumination that reflects the necessity of the Holy Spirit for hermeneutics. Based upon this, a well-developed definition of transformative illumination will be provided for the purpose of understanding the doctrine

Illumination and Interpretation

of illumination as a whole; and as a result, certain hermeneutical implications are necessarily treated.

Clarification of Terms

At this point, it is important to provide clarification of the terms that are being used to describe the Holy Spirit's work of illumination. Indeed, precise language is a much needed quality that serves well to combat the obduracy surrounding this doctrine. By using unambiguous terminology to describe this ministry of the Spirit, the necessary framework for a complete understanding of the concept of transformative illumination is prepared.

Illumination

Generally speaking, when the term illumination is utilized by scholars and theologians, it connotes the progressive aspect of the Spirit's illumination. Hence, the Spirit's work of initial illumination is merely assumed or sorely neglected, resulting in a misunderstanding of the doctrine of illumination at best and an abuse of the doctrine at worst. However, in order to guard against the convolution of an already complicated issue, it is of the essence that a delineation is made between the initial illumination of the Spirit and the progressive illumination of the Spirit. As shown in the previous chapters of this study, this distinction is vital to a proper understanding of illumination as it pertains to biblical interpretation and transformation in the life of the believer.

Initial Illumination

The Spirit's ministry of initial illumination is primarily a work upon the unregenerate person. Indeed, there is an intrinsic connection between initial illumination and salvation. As shown in chapter 3, the Scriptures bear witness to this bond, as the Holy Spirit's enlightening activity to salvation is necessary because of man's inherent depravity.

Initial illumination is the broader work of the Spirit, which serves as the foundation for his more specific work of the *testimonium Spiritus Sancti internum*. It is important to recognize though that this relationship between initial illumination and the *testimonium* vitally connects the two concepts, but it does not equate them. The *testimonium* is the Spirit's witness to the authority of the Word of God, both as the Scriptures and as the person of Christ Jesus. The initial illumination of the Spirit is necessary for the sight of the spiritually blind in order that they may be able to recognize the authoritative nature of the Word of God. Therefore, the *testimonium* is not effective towards salvation; rather, it is the outworking of the Spirit's indwelling presence as a result of salvation, i.e., as a result of initial illumination. Indeed, these two theological concepts are very closely tied, but it needs to be acknowledged that the *testimonium* is part of the Spirit's work of initial illumination, not exhaustive of it.

Initial illumination is the primary work of the Holy Spirit that enlightens the heart and mind of the unregenerate to salvation. Without this ministry of the Spirit, the progressive aspect of the doctrine of illumination becomes a *non sequitur*. Consequently, all who have received the Spirit's initial illumination are now prepared to engage the Spirit's progressive illumination.

Progressive Illumination

The Holy Spirit's work of progressive illumination necessarily follows his work of initial illumination. Unlike initial illumination, the progressive illumination of the Holy Spirit is not a single occurrence in the life of the believer. Rather, progressive illumination is a perpetual ministry that the Spirit offers for the understanding of the things of God.

Thus, progressive illumination is a spiritual work that is reserved for the regenerate person. In accordance with chapter 4, as a result of his sinful nature, the regenerate person maintains a constant need for the Spirit's work of illumination in order to comprehend the Scriptures. Therefore, progressive illumination is that ministry of the Spirit whereby the regenerate person, having accepted the Word of God as true, is thereby continually enabled in his heart and in his mind to understand the Scriptures properly.

Nevertheless, a mere cognitive grasp of the meaning of the text is not the goal of progressive illumination. Instead, as a result of the Spirit's progressive illumination, transformation in the life of the believer should ensue. Thus, representing the impetus for transformation, progressive illumination serves as the means and the catalyst for not merely a cognitive understanding of the text, but instead, a transformative understanding of the Scriptures. The Holy Spirit is indispensable for the interpretative endeavor such that it results in transformation in

Illumination and Interpretation

the faith and practice of the believer and it is this result that constitutes a proper understanding of the Scriptures.

Transformation

The principle of transformation has already been superficially treated in chapter 2, through the concepts of transformative meaning and understanding. It was argued there that transformation is emblematic of the type of understanding that the Scriptures and the Spirit seek in the life of the believer. An in-depth elaboration and clarification of this doctrine will ensue as the Scriptures are assessed below, but for now it is important to preemptively outline two fundamentals of this biblical notion in order to simplify the proposed concept of transformative illumination.

Transformation in the life of the believer is a work that is performed when the Spirit and the Word are in cooperation with one another. Gary Nebeker asserts, ". . . [T]he means whereby God accomplishes our transformation is through the gaze that the believer brings to bear on the christocentric witness of the Word of God. This transformation, we maintain, is attainable only through the Spirit working in conjunction with our hearing and reflection upon the scriptures."[1] Thus, genuine Christian transformation is not a rogue assignment to be governed and enacted by the believer. Rather, it is grounded in the objective Word of God and subjective working of the Spirit in the faith and practice of every believer.

To be sure, transformation manifests itself in the life of the believer in terms of an obediential response to faith. Klein, Blomberg, and Hubbard avow, "When we engage in a careful and faithful reading of the Bible, God nurtures our spiritual lives. Our minds grasp the meaning and principles, we see the examples to follow or to avoid; . . . we reflect on their implications for our lives, ministries, and relationships—all these and more provide instruction for the person who seeks to walk with God."[2] Certainly, the Christian life is a "continuing habituation" that is

---

1. Nebeker, "The Holy Spirit," 51–2.

2. Klein, Blomberg, and Hubbard, *Biblical Interpretation*, 472. Furthermore, Jones, "Formed and Transformed," 31, writes, "Yet the call of Scripture is for us to be open to the transformation of our own lives and to see the necessity of such transformation. Hence, whether in the ancient catechumenate or in the African-American church of King's day, there is a presumption that wise and faithful readings of Scripture are inextricably linked to the disciplined pursuit of holy living in other practices of Christian life."

enabled by the Spirit through the Word.[3] However, it should be noted that this is not simply an outward transformation, but an inward transformation founded upon the initial illumination of the Spirit and worked out through the Spirit's progressive illumination.

Illumination and Transformation

As stated above, this study argues that transformation is the inevitable outcome of the Spirit's illumination. The Holy Spirit's progressive illumination is an ongoing ministry in the life of the believer for the understanding of the Scriptures that serves as the avenue and catalyst for the Scripture's purpose of transformation. Nebeker comments, "The Spirit's role—or goal—in interpretation is to allow the interpreter to understand the text in such a way that the text transforms the interpreter into the image of Christ. While this may appear as a foregone conclusion, transformation as the Spirit's role in hermeneutics, surprisingly enough has not been a focal feature in the literature on this topic."[4] While this may be the case, the neglect of transformation does not merely stem from an uninformed position of the Holy Spirit's role in hermeneutics, but also from a disregard of the inherent purpose of the Spirit-inspired Scriptures. Accordingly, Jones declares, ". . . [W]e have lost a sense of the Bible as a (or the) central text in the formation of Christian character and identity . . . . [W]e have lost a clear sense of the ways in which Scripture's words (and the Word) shape both our minds and our bodies."[5] Again, the Scriptures intently seek transformation in the faith and practice of the believer through the Spirit's illumination.

Therefore, it is imperative to conduct an examination of Scripture's witness to transformation through the illuminatory process. The work of the Holy Spirit in biblical interpretation involves both aspects of the Spirit's ministry, that is, illuminating the heart and mind of the regenerate in order to aid in the understanding of the text and effecting transformation in the faith and practice of the regenerate.[6] Herring posits, "The ministry of the

---

3. Oden, *Life in the Spirit*, 219–20.

4. Nebeker, "The Holy Spirit," 47–8.

5. Jones, "Formed and Transformed," 19. Also, Vanier and Young, "Towards Transformational Reading of Scripture," 247, concur, "Scripture is the divine Word in human words—it is incarnational, and the point of Scripture is transformation: it is meant to carry conviction and change people's lives."

6. Nebeker, "The Holy Spirit," 51 agrees with this assessment.

Illumination and Interpretation

Holy Spirit in relation to the believer and the Word of God may be summed up in three words: illumination, application, and appropriation. He supplies illumination by revealing its meaning to us. He makes application by convicting us of our condition in light of its truth. He inspires appropriation by quickening its promises to challenge our faith."[7] Hence, the Spirit's role in hermeneutics involves both interpretation by means of illumination and application by means of transformation. As shown in the Scriptures below, it is only by this vital work of the Spirit that a genuine transformative understanding of the Scriptures can proceed.[8]

Romans 8:1–11

Romans 8:1–11[9] is one of the most comprehensive passages in the Scriptures that treats the life of the regenerate person as he dwells in the Spirit. This passage is couched in the Pauline theme of justification by faith and provides the framework for the necessary outcome of spiritual transformation. It is clear in the immediate context that Rom 8:1–11 is an elaboration upon Rom 7:6 which states, "But now we are released from the law, having died to that which held us captive, so that we serve not under the old written code but in the new life of the Spirit."[10] Certainly, from the beginning of Romans through chapter 8, righteousness by means of the law is jux-

---

7. Herring and Stagg, *How To Understand the Bible*, 47.

8. See footnote 17 in chapter 1 for an explanation concerning the selection of the biblical texts regarding transformative illumination.

9. Romans 8:1–11 states, "There is therefore now no condemnation for those who are in Christ Jesus. For the law of the Spirit of life has set you free in Christ Jesus from the law of sin and death. For God has done what the law weakened by the flesh, could not do. By sending his own Son in the likeness of sinful flesh and for sin, he condemned sin in the flesh, in order that the righteous requirement of the law might be fulfilled in us, who walk not according to the flesh but according to the Spirit. For those who live according to the flesh set their minds on the things of the flesh, but those who live according to the Spirit set their minds on the things of the Spirit. To set the mind on the flesh is death, but to set the mind on the Spirit is life and peace. For the mind that is set on the flesh is hostile to God, for it does not submit to God's law; indeed, it cannot. Those who are in the flesh cannot please God. You, however, are not in the flesh but in the Spirit, if in fact the Spirit of God dwells in you. Anyone who does not have the Spirit of Christ does not belong to him. But if Christ is in you, although the body is dead because of sin, the Spirit is life because of righteousness. If the Spirit of him who raised Jesus from the dead dwells in you, he who raised Christ Jesus from the dead will also give life to your mortal bodies through his Spirit who dwells in you."

10. Schreiner, *Romans*, 398.

taposed with righteousness through faith; and the latter is emphasized as sufficient while the former is shown to be grossly insufficient.[11]

As Romans 8 begins, the theme of justification by faith is continued as Paul begins by proclaiming, "There is therefore now no condemnation for those who are in Christ Jesus" (Rom 8:1). The word *katakrima* is translated as "condemnation" in Rom 8:1 and is only used two other times in the NT, in Rom 5:16 and Rom 5:18. In all three occurrences, it is used to designate ". . . the state of lostness, of estrangement from God, the state that all are born in and in which, unless Christ be embraced by faith, all will die and spend eternity."[12] For this reason, Douglas Moo highlights the parallel nature between Rom 5:12–21 and Rom 8:1–11 as he declares that in these two passages ". . . Paul assures the believer of the reality and finality of life in Christ and shows how this life is the product of righteousness."[13] Therefore, for those in Christ Jesus there is now no eternal condemnation because of the reconciliation made possible through the spiritual benefits of Christ's death and resurrection.

Immediately following Rom 8:1, the Apostle transitions to the doctrine of justificatory living, that is, he outlines the truths of the believer's life as he is in the Spirit of Christ. Ernest Best notes this crucial transition both in the text and in the life of the one who was previously unregenerate, but has now been justified by faith alone, by referring to the introduction of an entirely "new sphere of life created by the presence of the Spirit."[14] Indeed, throughout this passage, Paul introduces another significant contrast that places the truths of the unregenerate person's life in juxtaposition with the truths of the regenerate person's life. As a result, Paul begins to bring the discussion that he initiated in Romans 5 concerning righteous living to a close. The crux of his argument is that righteous living, that is, living according to the law, does not produce righteousness; rather, righteousness, that is, the imputation of Christ's righteousness, exudes righteous living as its necessary outcome. In light of this, it is interesting to note that there is not a single imperative in Rom 8:1–11 because life in the Spirit is so defined by his constant guid-

---

11. It is important to note that when Paul uses *nomos* in Rom 8:1–11 to speak of 'law,' he is referring to the Mosaic law at some points (Rom 8:3, 4) and referring to a general way of life or governing principle at other points (Rom 8:2, 7). Cf. Moo, *Romans 1–8*, 505–6, and Barrett, *Romans*, 155.

12. Moo, *Romans*, 504.

13. Ibid., 501.

14. Best, *Romans*, 88.

ance, that a string of commandments is not necessary to define righteous living.[15] Truly, Paul declares that the entire life of the believer is guided, empowered, and transformed by the Holy Spirit.

Clearly, transformation in the life of the believer is that which the Spirit seeks, and is the necessary byproduct of justification, i.e., initial illumination. Hodge comments, "It follows from the nature of this union [man and the Spirit of Christ], that it must transform the character of those who are its subjects . . . [and] the transforming power of this union with Christ is expressed by . . . the inward and outward life."[16] In this way, Rom 8:4 speaks of those "who walk not according to the flesh but according to the Spirit." The verb used for 'walk' is *peripateō* which denotes the conduct of one's life and signifies here ". . . the sphere in which one lives or ought to live, so as to be characterized by that sphere."[17] Subsequently, the use of this verb indicates a transformed life in the Spirit that is characterized by obedience—an obedience that is only possible by those in Christ Jesus.[18]

Furthermore, as Hodge progresses through his argument, he connects Rom 8:1–11 with 1 Cor 2:14–16 thus vitally connecting the Spirit's ministry of illumination with his work of transformation in the life of the believer.[19] This truth is made clear in Rom 8:5–6 especially, as the Apostle argues for a cognitive understanding of the things of God that pioneers the way to a transformative understanding, "For those who live according to the flesh set their minds on the things of the flesh, but those who live according to the Spirit set their minds on the things of the Spirit. To set the mind on the flesh is death, but to set the mind on the Spirit is life and peace." The words that are translated as 'to set the mind on' are the verb *phroneō* and the noun *phronēma*, respectively, both of which should not be relegated to signifying merely the mind, but the entirety of a person's existence.[20] Moreover, according to Brendan Byrne, Paul's use

15. Morris, *Romans*, 299.
16. Hodge, *Romans*, 249–50.
17. BDAG, 803.
18. Schreiner, *Romans*, 405–8. Moo, *Romans*, 517, concurs with this assessment as he posits, "The reference to Christian behavior in this phrase shows that Paul does not separate the fulfillment of the law from the behavior of Christians. But this does not mean that Christian behavior is how the law is fulfilled . . . . Rather, we might say, Christian behavior is the necessary mark of those in whom this fulfillment takes place. God not only provides in Christ the full completion of the law's demands for the believer, He also sends the Spirit into his or her heart to empower a new obedience to His demands."
19. Hodge, *Romans*, 250.
20. Schreiner, *Romans*, 411.

of this word ". . . goes beyond thought and aspiration to include actual achievement of the object in view—in the present case, death, on the one hand; life, on the other."[21] Consequently, it is impossible for those who are in the flesh to please God (Rom 8:8), but it is indicative of those in the Spirit to please God.

Here, Paul makes a clear contrast between those who live according to the flesh and those who live according to the Spirit as signifying the unregenerate and the regenerate, respectively. Moo avers, "To become a Christian means to be transferred from the realm dominated by the flesh to the realm dominated by the Spirit . . . [where] 'being in the flesh' . . . is *not* a possibility for the believer."[22] Therefore, Paul is not merely recognizing diverging behavioral attributes of those who profess Christ; instead, he is arguing for a positional distinctiveness between the unregenerate and the regenerate that results in disparate manners of living.[23] The Apostle reifies this understanding in Rom 8:9 when he writes, "You, however, are not in the flesh but in the Spirit, if in fact the Spirit of God dwells in you. Anyone who does not have the Spirit of Christ does not belong to him."[24] Surely, to live according to the Spirit is to be transformed by the Spirit.[25]

According to the Apostle Paul, transformation as it is defined by life in the Spirit is the necessary result of the Spirit's work of illumination. Hodge asserts, "Being thus free from the curse of the law, and from the obligation to fulfil its demands, as the condition of life . . . their [those who are in Christ] sins are gratuitously pardoned for Christ's sake; they are made partakers of the Spirit of God, are transformed more and more into his image, and God is pledged to preserve them unto eternal life."[26] Romans 8:10–11 displays this truth when the Apostle alludes to the

21. Byrne, *Romans*, 239.

22. Moo, *Romans*, 518–19; emphasis in original.

23. Ibid., 518.

24. The Apostle utilizes "the Spirit," "the Spirit of God," and "the Spirit of Christ" interchangeably here. Morris, *Romans*, 307–8, posits, "Paul clearly has the thought of a mutual indwelling; he simply varies the terminology in which he expresses it. His habit, however, is to speak of believers as in Christ (rather than Christ in them) and of the Spirit as in believers (rather than they in him). Whichever way he puts it, believers live very close to God and the constant presence of God is important. Also, Barrett, *Romans*, 159, writes, "What Paul means is that 'Spirit in you' is impossible apart from 'Christ in you.' Union with Christ is the only way into the life of the Age to Come, of which the distinguishing mark is the Spirit."

25. Byrne, *Romans*, 238.

26. Hodge, *Romans*, 251–2.

transformation of the believer's mortal body as he is transferred from the realm of death to the realm of life in the Spirit.[27] This physical transformation is externally representative and only possible through the spiritual transformation that the regenerate person has already undergone. Schreiner argues, "The fulfillment of the law by believers is the result of the Spirit's work in their heart [i.e., illumination]. New obedience is rooted in the transforming work of the Spirit, and thus is not a burden imposed from without but a delight embraced from within."[28]

Hence, Romans 8:1–11 inherently links the Spirit's work of illumination and transformation. Moo notes that in this passage, "Paul reminds his readers that the life-giving power of God's Spirit is finally effective only in those who continue to let the Spirit change their lives."[29] Thus, the initial illumination of the Spirit necessarily leads to the progressive illumination of the Spirit which inevitably results in transformation in the faith and practice of the believer.[30]

---

27. The meaning of *pneuma* in Rom 8:10 is an oft-disputed interpretive issue that some scholars interpret as the human spirit and others as the Spirit of God; although, the evidence for the latter position is heavily favored. Hodge, *Romans*, 259, is one of the few commentators that holds to the former position as he states, "By *spirit* here, is not to be understood the Holy Spirit, but the human spirit, because it stands opposed to *body* in the former clause. The *body* is dead, but the *spirit* is life. . . . The sense in which the spirit is life, is antithetical to that in which the body is dead. As the body is infected with a principle of decay which renders its dissolution inevitable, so the soul, in which the Holy Spirit dwells, is possessed of a principle of life which secures its immortal and blessed existence" (emphasis in original). In contrast, Hendriksen, *Romans*, 252, argues that this occurrence of *pneuma* should be taken to refer to the Spirit of God simply because every instance of this word in Romans 8:1–11 both before and after this particular instance refers to the Holy Spirit. Additionally, Schreiner, *Romans*, 415, asserts, "The decisive argument against a reference to the human spirit is the word *zōē*, for that word never means 'alive' but always means 'life.' It is difficult to imagine what Paul could possibly mean in saying that the human spirit is life. . . . [Instead] the reference is probably to the resurrection. The presence of the Spirit demonstrates that believers will not be saddled with their weak and corruptible bodies forever. The Spirit is a life-giving Spirit and will overcome death through the resurrection of the body."

28. Schreiner, *Romans*, 409.

29. Moo, *Romans*, 518.

30. The relationship between the Spirit's work of illumination and his work of sanctification is connected to this understanding in a dual manner. First, only a person who has been initially illuminated is capable of being sanctified by the Holy Spirit. Owen, *The Holy Spirit*, 246–53, devotes an entire chapter to this assertion. However, these two spiritual works are not wholly disparate, but inherently bound, because the person that has been initially illuminated will undoubtedly be sanctified by the same Spirit. Accordingly, Owen defines sanctification as "an immediate work of the Spirit of

Romans 12:1-2

The chapters located between Romans 8 and Romans 12 constitute one of the most difficult interpretive passages in all of Scripture. However, it should be observed that Romans 9–11, in which the Apostle gloriously recounts God's great mercies in Christ Jesus, is preceded by the powerful theological treatise of transformed Spirit-living in Romans 8 and succeeded by the fervent exhortative appeal to live a divinely-transformed life at the beginning of Romans 12. The Apostle Paul writes in Romans 12:1–2, "I appeal to you therefore, brothers, by the mercies of God, to present your bodies as a living sacrifice, holy and acceptable to God, which is your spiritual worship. Do not be conformed to this world, but be transformed by the renewal of your mind, that by testing you may discern what is the will of God, what is good and acceptable and perfect."

Consequently, the Apostle's pattern of establishing dogmatic teaching as the impetus for ethical living emerges as the pattern for Christian faith and practice. Accordingly, Barrett argues, "Paul's dogmatic teaching is misunderstood if it is not seen to require ethical action, and his ethical teaching cannot be grasped if it is not recognized that it rests at every point upon the dogmatics."[31] Surely, this directs the reader's gaze back to Rom 1:5 in which Paul establishes at the beginning of the epistle that he speaks of a faith which necessitates obedience. It is only through the knowledge of God's instruction, that is, through the knowledge of the Holy Scriptures which comes by the illumination of the Holy Spirit that genuine spiritual transformation can ensue. Calvin declares:

> After having handled those things necessary for the erection of the kingdom of God,—that righteousness is to be sought

God on the souls of believers, purifying their natures from the pollution and uncleanness of sin, renewing them in the image of God, and thereby enabling them, from a spiritual and habitual principle of grace, to yield obedience to God, according to the tenor of the new covenant, by virtue of the life and death of Jesus Christ" (p. 230). Consequently, the Spirit's sanctification of the believer enables the Spirit's inherently connected work of transformation in the faith and practice of the believer. Second, it is only by means of the Spirit's progressive illumination in regard to the Scriptures that sanctification is wrought in the life of the believer through transformation. Owen addresses the crucial nature of the understanding of Scripture for the purpose of sanctification when he writes, "Constant searching of the Scriptures . . . is the glass wherein we may take the best view of ourselves, because it represents both what we are, and what we ought to be; what we are in ourselves, and what we are by the grace of God; what are our frames, actions, and ways, and what is their defect in his sight" (p. 336).

31. Barrett, *Romans*, 230.

Illumination and Interpretation

> from God alone, that salvation is to come to us alone from his mercy, that all blessings are laid up and daily offered to us in Christ only,—Paul now passes on, according to the best order, to show how the life is to be formed . . . [that is] through the saving knowledge of God and of Christ, the soul, as it were, [is] regenerated into a celestial life, and that the life is in a manner formed and regulated by holy exhortations and precepts.[32]

In essence, the Apostle is not proposing an externally-transformed life that produces faith, but a genuine faith that produces a Spirit-transformed life.

Paul initiates his appeal in Romans 12:1 with *oun*, directing the reader back to what he has previously made evident. In the general context, the Apostle is basing his exhortation on the asseveration that justification comes by means of faith in the sacrifice of Christ Jesus and it is his righteousness alone, imputed to the sinner, which generates one who is pure, holy, and blameless before God.[33] More specifically though, Paul finds the source of his appeal in the immediately preceding declaration: "Oh, the depth of the riches and wisdom and knowledge of God! How unsearchable are his judgments and how inscrutable his ways! 'For who has known the mind of the Lord, or who has been his counselor? Or who has given a gift to him that he might be repaid?' For from him and through him and to him are all things. To him be glory forever. Amen" (Rom 11:33–36).[34] As a result of these things, Paul declares that transformation is an inevitable manifestation in the life of the believer as it is worked out of a genuine inner conversion wrought by the illumination of the Holy Spirit.

Therefore, this spiritual transformation begins with an offering of oneself. The Apostle Paul urges believers "to present your bodies as a living sacrifice, holy and acceptable to God" (Rom 12:1). This bodily sacrifice is of great significance because it not only represents the physical, material body, but also conveys a particular emphasis on a sacrificial posture toward the body's interaction and communion with the external

---

32. Calvin, *Romans*, 449.

33. Hodge, *Romans*, 383.

34. Koenig, "Vision," 309–10, emphasizes this interpretation when he asserts, "The 'therefore' of 12:1 refers primarily to the verses that immediately precede it and only secondarily to chapters 5–8. I want to make this point as forcefully as I can because the contemporary interpreters of Romans I have consulted most frequently give no attention to the 'visionary' quality of the experience Paul wants to share with his readers by means of 11:13–36. Yet it is this awe before God (11:20) that Paul presumes upon as the common experiential ground between him and the Roman congregation. It is this, he thinks, that will facilitate their assent to his hortatory statements."

Transformative Illumination

world.[35] Concerning this, Hodge remarks, "The sacrifice then which we are to make is not a transient service, like the oblation of a victim, which was in a few moments consumed upon the altar, but it is a living or perpetual sacrifice."[36] Certainly, this living sacrifice that lends itself to spiritual transformation is only possible through the initial and progressive illumination of the Holy Spirit.

Subsequently, the Apostle Paul commands nonconformity (*suschēmatizomai*) to the world and transformation (*metamorphoomai*) in the faith and practice of the regenerate, both of which are constituents of the living sacrifice.[37] It is noteworthy, that these two verbs are utilized in the present tense indicating a continual battle of nonconformity to the things of the world and a constant progression of transformation to the things of the Spirit.[38] The transformation that the Apostle speaks of is not merely an outward change in behavior, but is representative of the Spirit's illumination at work in the faith and practice of the believer. As previously indicated, this bodily sacrifice is inherently a rejection of the things of this world, thus allowing the Spirit to work in the heart and mind of the regenerate.

Resultantly, the living sacrifice does not merely pertain to the realm of the physical, but also demands a renewal of the mind. Schreiner posits, "The 'body' of verse 1 and the 'mind' of verse 2 should not be rigidly separated. Paul views human beings holistically, and thus there is an intimate connection between what one thinks and what one does."[39] Conformity to the world suggests a mind and heart that has not been illumined by

---

35. Byrne, *Romans*, 362–3.

36. Hodge, *Romans*, 384.

37. Koenig, "Vision," 313, posits that the simple *kai* ("and") connecting Rom 12:1 with Rom 12:2 suggests this interpretation.

38. Scholarship is divided as to whether the two terms *suschēmatizomai* and *metamorphoomai* are to be distinguished from one another. According to Schreiner, *Romans*, 646–7, "Older scholarship distinguished between [the two terms] . . . contending that the former term referred to outward conformity and the latter to inner and genuine transformation. This view is almost certainly mistaken . . . [and] the terms . . . are practically synonymous . . . . Thus most contemporary scholars no longer accept the attempt to distinguish between these terms." On the other hand, Hendricksen, *Romans*, 405, upholds the outward/inward distinction between the two terms. Although the side-by-side usage of these two terms is peculiar, as Hendricksen points out, Schreiner correctly argues that to distinguish between the significance of these terms is unnecessary in order to grasp the meaning of Paul's message, i.e., that genuine conversion demands a detachment from the world and its influences and assimilation to the Spirit.

39. Schreiner, *Romans*, 646.

Illumination and Interpretation

the Spirit; however, a renewed mind is indicative of both the Spirit's work of initial illumination to salvation and the Spirit's work of progressive illumination to knowledge of the things of God.[40] Regarding the regenerate, Byrne suggests, "Their 'renewed mind' creates in them the capacity to discern what is required to live according to God's will. The bodily obedience flowing from that discernment makes their lives a continual 'sacrifice' pleasing to God."[41]

The goal of the renewal of the mind, i.e., transformation, is to increase the believer's knowledge of the will of God. This transformation has been initiated at conversion by the Spirit's initial illumination and proceeds through the Spirit's progressive illumination.[42] Indeed, the Spirit's ministry is central to the process of transformation.[43] However, instruction from the Holy Spirit needs to be always coupled with the Scriptures in order that proper transformation may ensue.[44] To be sure, transformation is a work of the Holy Spirit that is inaugurated at conversion through initial illumination and perpetuated in the life of the believer through a progressive illumination of the Scriptures which grants the believer a transformative understanding of the things of God.

2 Corinthians 3:18

Second Corinthians 3:18 states, "And we all, with unveiled face, beholding the glory of the Lord, are being transformed into the same image from one degree of glory to another. For this comes from the Lord who is the Spirit." The greater context of this verse and its specific OT connections has been discussed in chapter 3 of this study as it relates to the Spirit's work of initial illumination. Now, in regards to understanding

---

40. Hodge, *Romans*, 384.

41. Byrne, *Romans*, 365. Also, Byrne writes, "The 'renewal of mind' must therefore imply the liberation of the mind from its captivity to the old, sinful age (1:21, 28; 7:23, 25) and its transformation, through the Spirit, into an apt instrument for the discernment of God's will" (p. 366).

42. Barrett, *Romans*, 233, supports this understanding when he purports, "Paul is able to speak of a radical renewal of human nature because the old age is disappearing and the new age is at hand; the renewal which is begun in conversion and baptism and advanced with every Christian decision taken ends in the glory of God."

43. Koenig, "Vision," 321–2.

44. Hendricksen, *Romans*, 406.

Transformative Illumination

illumination as a transformative process, the New Covenant ramifications of this verse need to be treated.

One of the first aspects observed in 2 Corinthians 3 is the Apostle Paul's emphasis on the Holy Spirit as the minister of the New Covenant and thus, the arbiter of transformation (2 Cor 3:3, 6, 8, 17, 18). Ralph Martin concurs, "The new covenant . . . has dawned . . . [and] believers in Christ live in a new age where 'glory' is seen in the Father's Son and shared among those who participate in that eon. It is the Spirit's work to effect this change, transforming believers into the likeness of him who is the groundplan of the new humanity."[45] Certainly, in the Apostle's understanding, the Holy Spirit is the agent of transformation.

As highlighted in chapter 3, when Paul speaks of those "with unveiled face," he is referring to those who are regenerate, i.e., those who have been initially illuminated by the Holy Spirit. The phrase that begins 2 Cor 3:18, *hēmeis de pantes*, is emphatic and contributes to the understanding that Paul is including all believers in the following statement.[46] Hence, it is only those in Christ Jesus, who are *able* to behold the glory of the Lord and more specifically, it is the *privilege* of those in Christ Jesus to behold the radiance of God's glory.[47] In light of this, the perfect participle of *anakaluptō* that is used to describe the unveiling, "stresses the permanence and irreversibility of their unveiled state . . . and refers figuratively . . . to recognition and understanding. . . . An unremoved veil prevents recognition of the glory of the new covenant. A removed veil not only guarantees recognition of that glory but also enables participation in that glory."[48] Certainly, this represents the introduction of progressive illumination in the life of the believer as he develops a more comprehensive understanding of the Scriptures.

Accordingly, the phrase *tēn doxan kuriou katoptrizomenoi* ("beholding the glory of the Lord") refers to an increasing reception of knowledge as the regenerate person is continually transformed by the Spirit.[49]

---

45. Martin, *2 Corinthians*, 71–2.

46. Furnish, *II Corinthians*, 213.

47. Harris, *The Second Epistle to the Corinthians*, 313, writes, "It was the privilege of Moses alone to glimpse Yahweh's glory when he saw his 'form' (Num. 12:8) and his 'back' (Exod. 33:23), but now all Christians without distinction are privileged to witness that glory. Moreover, although Moses' face was unveiled when he was conversing with God and was reporting God's words to the congregation, it was thereafter veiled until he returned to the Lord's presence (Exod 34:33–35). Christians, however, see the divine glory with permanently uncovered faces."

48. Ibid., 313–4.

49. Barrett, *The Second Epistle to the Corinthians*, 125. Smail, *Reflected Glory*, 25–6,

Bauer maintains that the word *katoptrizō* means to look at something as in a mirror or to contemplate something.[50] Calvin, however, asserts that this word "has a double signification . . . for it sometimes means to hold out a mirror to be looked into, and at other times to look into a mirror when presented."[51] Calvin affirms the latter option, but the issue whether this word is translated as "beholding" or "reflecting" remains among contemporary interpreters.[52] Kistemaker opts for a combination of these elements in his translation: "beholding the reflected glory of the Lord."[53] Insightfully, Kistemaker utilizes the full meaning of this word because he argues, "Even when we support the reading *beholding*, we must admit that the deeper meaning of this verb is that Christ reflects his glory in our lives . . . [and this is] an exercise that is active and coincides with the process of sanctification."[54] Thus, as the regenerate person continually beholds the glory of the Lord, he increasingly reflects this glory in his faith and practice.

Again, the image of God's glory is Jesus Christ and the instrument through which the Lord's glory is beheld is Scripture (2 Cor 4:4). Harris asserts, "The vision of God's glory accorded Christians . . . is mediated through the gospel . . . for the Christ who is proclaimed through the gospel is the exact representation (*eikōn*) of God." Therefore, transformation takes place in the life of the believer as he is under the influence of the progressive illumination of the Holy Spirit. Calvin notes:

> He [Paul] points out, however, at the same time, both the strength of the revelation [the Gospel], and our daily progress. For he has employed such a similitude to denote *three* things: *first*, That we have no occasion to fear obscurity, when we approach the gospel, for God *there* clearly discovers to us His face; *secondly*, That is not befitting, that it should be a dead contemplation, but that we should be transformed by means of it into the image of God; and, *thirdly*, that the one and the other are not accomplished in us in

---

concurs, "But as he [the believer] thus looks to Christ and opens himself to him, the knowledge of Christ that he gains is never simply objective and intellectual knowledge, it is knowledge that begins to change him, so that he begins to reflect that to which he has been exposed, and its likeness begins to be formed in him."

50. BDAG, 535.

51. Calvin, *Corinthians*, 186.

52. The NIV of the Scriptures translates this word as "reflecting" while most other versions (NKJV, NASB, ESV) opt for "beholding."

53. Kistemaker, *Second Epistle to the Corinthians*, 128.

54. Ibid.

one moment, but we must be constantly making progress both in the knowledge of God, and in conformity to His image.[55]

Moreover, the Apostle Paul directly speaks of "being transformed into the same image from one degree of glory to another." There are three aspects of this transformative illumination that are of note. First, as the passive voice of the verb *metamorphoomai* suggests, this transformation is one in which the Holy Spirit is the principal agent of change.[56] Second, this verb is utilized in the present tense, indicating a progressive action of transformation. Harris argues that the degrees of glory that Paul mentions express the nature and direction of the transformative process.[57] In other words, the transformative process finds its origination in the initial illumination of the Holy Spirit and is perpetuated by the Spirit's ministry of progressive illumination. Third, this transformation results in a greater likeness to Christ in the faith and practice of the believer. It is an inner transformation (2 Cor 4:16b) that involves the entirety of a person's being and is manifested as Christ-like behavior in the life of the believer.[58] Furnish agrees, "Transformation means conformity to the image of Christ . . . . It is a transformation that is inaugurated (though not yet completed) where by faith the believer is conformed to the image of God in God's Son . . . through the renewing power of the Spirit."[59]

The final clause of this passage emblazons the forceful stamp of the Holy Spirit's administration on the transformative undertaking.[60] In summation, Harris writes, "The new era is the era of the Spirit, for as a result of conversion to the Spirit (vv. 16, 17a), there is liberation through the Spirit (v. 17b), including the lifting of the veil of spiritual ignorance and hardheartedness, and also transformation by the Spirit (v. 18). The Spirit, his

---

55. Calvin, *Corinthians*, 187; emphasis in original.
56. Garland, *2 Corinthians*, 200.
57. Harris, *Corinthians*, 316.
58. Ibid., 315–6.
59. Furnish, *II Corinthians*, 240.
60. The Greek word ordering of this clause (*kuriou pneumatos*) is ambiguous and according to Furnish, *II Corinthians*, 216, it can be rendered in six different ways. Though this may be the case, based on the pneumatological emphasis throughout 2 Corinthians 3, Barrett, *Corinthians*, 126, proposes, "It is perhaps best to suppose that Paul wishes to affirm that the work is of God, who, whether one thinks in terms of the Father, the Son, or the Spirit, is Lord; and to add that the divine work of transformation is in fact to be ascribed to the third of these agencies."

Illumination and Interpretation

person and his work, is the hallmark of the new covenant."[61] In 2 Cor 3:18 and its immediate context, it is evident that Paul has recognized the inherent connection between the concepts of transformation and illumination and that this relationship is bound up in the Word and the Spirit.

Galatians 5:16–25

The book of Galatians consists of a series of spiritual conflicts. In Galatians 2, the battle between the understanding of justification by faith or by works of the Law ensues throughout chapter 4. Next, the conflict between legalistic Christian living and libertine Christian living is taken up by the Apostle Paul in Gal 5:1–15. Finally, in the context of the previously mentioned battles, the conflicting aims and manifestations of the flesh and the Spirit are juxtaposed in Gal 5:16–25.[62] Frank Matera asserts, "Flesh and Spirit are opposed to each other because they belong to different realms. To dwell in the realm of the Spirit is to be in Christ. To dwell in the realm of the flesh is to live in the realm of unredeemed humanity."[63] It is in the midst of this context that Paul seeks to establish the principle of transformative living for the regenerate person as a result of the illumination of the Spirit.

The Apostle seeks to confirm first that those who have been truly regenerated by the Spirit are those whose actions are indicative of the Spirit. Hendriksen affirms, "Being led by the Spirit is set forth as the indispensable characteristic of God's children. If a person is a child of God he is being led by the Spirit. If he is being led by the Spirit he is a child of God."[64] Indeed, this constitutes the transformation that Paul speaks of

---

61. Harris, *Corinthians*, 318.

62. Gal 5:16–25 states, "But I say, walk by the Spirit, and you will not gratify the desires of the flesh. For the desires of the flesh are against the Spirit, and the desires of the Spirit are against the flesh, for these are opposed to each other, to keep you from doing the things you want to do. But if you are led by the Spirit, you are not under the law. Now the works of the flesh are evident: sexual immorality, impurity, sensuality, idolatry, sorcery, enmity, strife, jealousy, fits of anger, rivalries, dissensions, divisions, envy, drunkenness, orgies, and things like these. I warn you, as I warned you before, that those who do such things will not inherit the kingdom of God. But the fruit of the Spirit is love, joy, peace, patience, kindness, goodness, faithfulness, gentleness, self-control; against such things there is no law. And those who belong to Christ Jesus have crucified the flesh with its passions and desires. If we live by the Spirit, let us also walk by the Spirit."

63. Matera, *Galatians*, 199.

64. Hendriksen, *Galatians*, 216.

which demands the exchange of the desires of the flesh for the desires of the Spirit (Gal 5:17). To be clear, this transformation is founded upon the Spirit's initial illumination to salvation and his progressive illumination in the life of the believer.[65]

Throughout Gal 5:16–25, Paul emphasizes life in the Spirit by exhorting his readers to "walk by the Spirit" (Gal 5:16), to be "led by the Spirit" (Gal 5:18), to "live by the Spirit" (Gal 5:25a), and to "keep in step with the Spirit" (Gal 5:25b). Timothy George connects the Apostle's emphasis with the discerning of God's will[66]—a transformative attribute that develops as a result of the Spirit's illumination involving the enabling of Scripture's understanding (Rom 12:1–2). Each of the aforementioned expressions, though consisting of different verbs in the Greek (*peripateō, agoō, zaō, stoicheō*, respectively) and thus different nuances, all generally refer to the practice of the believer as he is increasingly conformed to the likeness of Christ. Bruce agrees, "There is little material difference between *pneumati stoichein* [Gal 5:25], *pneumati peripatein* (v 16) and *pneumati agesthai* (v 18). Walking by the Spirit is the outward manifestation, in action and speech, of living by the Spirit. Living by the Spirit is the root; walking by the Spirit is the fruit, and that fruit is nothing less than the practical reproduction of the character (and therefore the conduct) of Christ in the lives of his people."[67]

Consequently, the Apostle Paul seeks to emphasize a life that is controlled by the Spirit such that it is revealed in the believer's faith and practice. In doing so, Paul compiles a list of the works of the flesh with the eventual outcome (Gal 5:19–21) and a list of the fruit of the Spirit with some implications (Gal 5:22–25). The former list results from the contrivances of the sinful nature, whereas the latter is the result of the Spirit's transforming presence. The list consisting of the works of the flesh is not an exhaustive compilation, as noted by Paul in Gal 5:21, but a representative list that reflects Paul's earlier admonition to abstain from abusing one's freedom in Christ (Gal 5:13).[68] Paul's warning in Gal 5:21 of disqualification from the kingdom of God demonstrates that those who

---

65. George, *Galatians*, 386, uses different terminology, but expresses the same point: "Only the Spirit of God who has made us free from sin and given us new life in regeneration can keep us truly free as we experience through walking in him the power of sanctification."

66. Ibid., 386.

67. Bruce, *Galatians*, 257.

68. George, *Galatians*, 389.

are not progressively living according to the Spirit are proving that they lack the Spirit's initial illumination. Hendriksen notes, "It should also be observed that although according to Paul's argumentation it is not possible to gain entrance to the kingdom of God by means of what were deemed to be *good* practices (law-works), it is definitely possible to shut oneself out by *evil* practices."[69]

The subsequent list outlines the *singular* fruit of the Spirit as opposed to the multitudinous renderings of the flesh contrasting the unity and harmony of the Spirit in the life of the believer with the chaotic and interminable influence of the flesh.[70] The fruit of the Spirit "is the result of his [the Spirit's] indwelling presence and the spiritual metamorphosis that dynamic reality brings about (cf. Rom 12:1–2)."[71] Therefore, the law is powerless over the believer's life in the fruit of the Spirit, not because it dispels the law, but because it fulfills it (Gal 5:23).[72] Certainly, transformation in the faith and practice of the believer is the outworking of the Spirit's work of illumination. Paul reflects this understanding when he writes, "And those who belong to Christ Jesus have crucified the flesh with its passions and desires" (Gal 5:24). With the verb *stauroō* used in the aorist tense, Paul indicates that those who are regenerate ("those who belong to Christ Jesus") have already crucified the flesh when they encountered the Spirit's initial illumination during their conversion.[73]

In another sense though, it is clear that believers need to continually crucify the flesh along with its desires as the Spirit works progressively in their lives.[74] For the Apostle writes, "If we live by the Spirit, let us also walk by the Spirit" (Gal 5:25). Both of the verbs in this verse, *zaō* and *stoicheō*, occur in the present tense, demonstrating perpetual activities in and by the Spirit. In addition, the sentence structure of this verse forms a chiasm in which "by the Spirit" receives the utmost emphasis and in which discovering one's source of life in the Spirit necessitates the continual manifestation of spiritual conduct.[75]

---

69. Hendriksen, *Galatians*, 222; emphasis in original.
70. George, *Galatians*, 391.
71. Ibid., 390.
72. Burton, *Galatians*, 318 and Calvin, *Galatians and Ephesians*, 168.
73. Fung, *Galatians*, 274.
74. Ibid., 275.
75. Hendriksen, *Galatians*, 226. Fung, *Galatians*, 275, notes concerning Gal 5:25 that the asyndeton preceding this verse further bolsters the force of Paul's statement. In addition, Fung argues, "The juxtaposition of the indicative and the imperative in

Transformative Illumination

Although this passage does not explicitly reference the witness of the Scriptures in conjunction with the work of the Spirit, it is evident that the knowledge of the things of God is a prerequisite for transformed living. Thus, the Spirit's initial illumination to salvation and the Spirit's progressive illumination that enables understanding of the Scriptures are both necessary elements for conformation to Christ's image. Hendriksen argues that Gal 5:16–25 in regards to life in the Spirit gives rise to this definition of the Spirit's working: "It is that constant, effective, and beneficent influence which the Holy Spirit exercises within the hearts of God's children whereby they are being directed and enabled more and more to crush the power of indwelling sin and to walk in the way of God's commandments, freely and cheerfully."[76] Truly, this is an apt description of the Spirit's work of transformative illumination.

Ephesians 4:17–24

In the previous two chapters of this study, it has been demonstrated that the book of Ephesians is a theological mainstay for the doctrine of illumination. Indeed, Eph 1:17–18 speaks both to the initial illumination and progressive illumination of the Holy Spirit. Therefore, it is appropriate that the Apostle Paul supplements this discussion by emphasizing the transformative effect of the Spirit's work in the life of the believer in Eph 4:17–24.[77]

As the Apostle begins this discussion on transformation, first he addresses a former way of living that is constituted by unbelief (Eph 4:17–19) and then he treats a wholly new way of living that is worthy of

---

this verse indicates once again (cf. on vv. 1, 6) the close relationship between the two: the imperative is based on the indicative, and is intended to bring about in the lives of believers the practical outworking of the reality expressed by the indicative. Its relation to the indicative is therefore basically that of consequence. Precisely because the Spirit is the source of their life, they are to keep in step continuously with the Spirit in their conduct" (p. 276).

76. Ibid., 217.

77. Eph 4:17–24 states, "Now this I say and testify in the Lord, that you must no longer walk as the Gentiles do, in the futility of their minds. They are darkened in their understanding, alienated from the life of God because of the ignorance that is in them, due to their hardness of heart. They have become callous and have given themselves up to sensuality, greedy to practice every kind of impurity. But that is not the way you learned Christ!—assuming that you have heard about him and were taught in him, as the truth is in Jesus, to put off your old self, which belongs to your former manner of life and is corrupt through deceitful desires, and to be renewed in the spirit of your minds, and to put on the new self, created after the likeness of God in true righteousness and holiness."

Christ Jesus (Eph 4:20–24). In the first portion of Paul's argument, the *oun* ("therefore") that begins Eph 4:17 refers back to Eph 4:1, in which believers are urged "to walk in a manner worthy of the calling to which you have been called."[78] In doing this, Paul is about to contrast starkly the difference between the transformed living of the regenerate and the destitute life of the unregenerate.

The description of the former life that ensues is certainly pessimistic. To illustrate the gravity of the cause and effects that Paul stresses in Eph 4:17–18, Hoehner writes, "The hardness of their hearts toward God caused their ignorance. Their ignorance concerning God and his will caused them to be alienated from the life of God. Their alienation caused their minds to be darkened, and their darkened minds caused them to walk in the futility of mind."[79] It is readily apparent that Paul is making a distinction between those who have had the eyes of their hearts enlightened by the initial illumination of the Spirit (Eph 1:18) and those who still reside in the darkness of sin.[80]

Paul argues that the full weight of this distinction is displayed in one's knowledge of God as it is manifested through one's conduct. In this context, the word *nous* ("mind") in Eph 4:17 refers not merely to the mental faculty of man, but it connotes an established connection between one's mind and one's conduct, encompassing the total person.[81] Likewise, the word *dianoia* ("understanding") utilized in Eph 4:18, represents "the whole person viewed as one who can experience knowledge, and understand and accept salvation."[82] However, this understanding has escaped those whose conduct is not becoming of a life that has been transformed by the Spirit. Instead, the unregenerate has been alienated from the life of God, that is, "the life of which the indwelling Spirit is the principle or source"[83] because of their ignorance and the hardening of themselves to the knowledge of God that was available to them.[84] This fact, the Apostle establishes in Eph 4:19 as the callousness of unbelievers is reflected in a life of impurity. Concerning this reality, Markus Barth remarks, "Just as

---

78. Hoehner, *Ephesians*, 582.
79. Ibid., 588–9.
80. Lincoln, *Ephesians*, 277.
81. Best, *Ephesians*, 417–8.
82. Ibid., 419.
83. Hodge, *Ephesians*, 252.
84. Lincoln, *Ephesians*, 278.

knowledge means participation in life and obedience to God, so ignorance equals the inability to live, to grow, to act sensibly."[85]

On the other hand, Paul emphatically states in Eph 4:20–24 that those who are truly regenerate exemplify a lifestyle that has been transformed by the Spirit.[86] In Eph 4:20, he begins by using a peculiar phrase, in which he couples the verb *manthanō* ("to learn") with the person of Christ. This unique phraseology encompasses "the tradition about him [Christ] and is brought into direct relation with Christian conduct."[87] The resulting connotation evokes a classroom of the most intimate proportions of which a cognitive understanding is deemed insufficient and a transformative understanding through the knowledge of God is not only desired, but required.[88] Calvin avers, "So here he [Paul] affirms that any knowledge of Christ, which is not accompanied by mortification of the flesh, is not true and sincere . . . . He demands from a Christian man repentance, or a new life, which he makes to consist of self-denial and the regeneration of the Holy Spirit."[89]

To be sure, regeneration by the Holy Spirit is the foundation for transformation. In fact, the aorist tense of the verb *manthanō* points back to the believer's time of conversion.[90] Since, the initial illumination of the Spirit has taken place, the regenerate person has also heard (*akouō*) about Christ and been taught (*didaskō*) in Him. Therefore, to learn Christ not only occurs at conversion, but also throughout the transformed life of the regenerate through the progressive illumination of the Spirit.[91] Additionally, Paul makes clear in Eph 4:21 that the truth (*alētheia*) is Jesus as the Christ.[92] Certainly, this points the reader to the gospel as its truth

---

85. Barth, *Ephesians*, 500.

86. Hoehner, *Ephesians*, 593, writes, "The emphatic contrast with the previous verses is noted by : (1) the adversative *de*; (2) the change from *ta ethnē* to *humeis* which is emphatically placed; and (3) the adverbial conjuction *houtōs* which applies what had been stated before (cf. 5:24, 28, 33), namely, that the conduct of Gentiles is not what believers learned regarding Christ."

87. Lincoln, *Ephesians*, 279.

88. Hoehner, *Ephesians*, 594.

89. Calvin, *Galatians and Ephesians*, 294.

90. Hoehner, *Ephesians*, 595.

91. Ibid.

92. Barth, *Ephesians*, 533, concurs that the truth here refers to the Son of God as he is "in person the full revelation of God, the totality of God's will and promise, and the sum of the fulfillment of all that is hoped for and commanded." Subsequently, the truth is that "the incarnation is the core of the gospel" (p. 534) and "all that 'Jesus'

Illumination and Interpretation

is summed up in the person of Christ Jesus (Eph 1:13; Col 1:5–6) and transmitted through the Scriptures which acts as the primary means for knowledge of the truth (cf. 1 Tim 2:3–7; 3:14–16; 6:3–5; 2 Tim 2:15–18, 22–26; 3:7, 8; 4:1–5; Titus 1:1–3).[93] Nebeker remarks, "While 'truth' certainly has to do with cognitive convictions or beliefs about God that are not false, 'truth' must also be understood as that which is *personal* and *relational* in character. With Jesus as the personification of 'truth,' as the 'truth' to whom we relate, 'truth,' we could also argue, is he who transforms us into his image."[94]

In Eph 4:17–24, the initial and progressive illumination of the Spirit are communicated in the context of transformation. This truth cannot be more evident than it is in Eph 4:22–24 which is managed by three infinitives that describe the process of this transformation: *apotithēmi* ("to put off"), *ananeoō* ("to renew"), and *enduō* ("to put on").[95] The first infinitival

---

taught during his ministry on earth is also the essence of the church's proclamation and doctrine . . . [resulting in] a conduct true and faithful to Jesus" (p. 535).

93. Lincoln, *Ephesians*, 282–3.

94. Nebeker, "The Holy Spirit," 48. Likewise, Hodge, *Ephesians*, 266, states, "Truth is spiritual knowledge, that knowledge which is eternal life, which not only illuminates the understanding but sanctifies the heart. The Holy Ghost is called the Spirit of truth as the author of this divine illumination which irradiates the whole soul." Additionally, Brunner, *Revelation and Reason*, 184, affirms, "True faith, on the other hand, the *fides viva*, is no human achievement on the basis of a human command; it is not a belief on authority, a *sacrificium intellectus*; it is not an act of servile obedience to a law; but it is a divinely effectual miracle that man, through the illumination of the Holy Spirit, becomes able to see the truth of God in Jesus Christ. Hence this faith means the effectual working of the Holy Spirit in the spirit of man, life-renewing energy, the principle of new birth and of sanctification. From faith of this kind spring spontaneously the good movements of the will. Is it not indeed simply reception of the 'love of God which is poured out in our hearts by the Holy Spirit,' [Rom 5:5] and therefore that 'faith which worketh through love' [Gal 5:6]? This faith is not merely related to the 'being' of the person; it is rather the coming to birth of a *new* person; it is rebirth, the restoration of the defaced image of God; for it is the break with man's sinful autonomy, and his return to the original 'theonomy' of the man who has been created in the image of God. It is the same as existence in the truth, because it is existence 'in Christ,' who Himself is the Truth" (emphasis in original).

95. Some scholars argue that the infinitives employed in Eph 4:22–24 refer to the ritual of baptism [Meeks, "The Image of the Androgyne," 183–9, 207; Schnackenburg, *Ephesians*, 199–201; Schlier, *Der Brief An Die Epheser*, 218–22]. Lincoln, *Ephesians*, 284–5, is a little less definitive and argues, "'Putting off' is, as we have seen, found in Rom 13:12 where it is in close juxtaposition with 'putting on the Lord Jesus Christ' in Rom 13:14. 'Putting on' is again employed in an exhortation in 1 Thess 5:8, while in Gal 3:27 to have put on Christ is equated with to have been baptized into Christ. Nowhere in the undisputed Paulines is this clothing imagery linked with the notion

phrase (Eph 4:22) suggests a completed act of inward and thus outward transformation.[96] The second infinitival phrase (Eph 4:23) indicates a process of renewal that occurs perennially in the life of the believer.[97] The "spirit of your minds" terminology alludes to the previously discussed Rom 12:2 where in both passages the innermost being of mankind is in view as the renewed foundation for a transformed life.[98] Often disputed in this verse, similar to Ephesians 1:17, is whether *pneuma* refers to the human spirit or the Holy Spirit.[99] However, Hoehner declares, "Only

---

of the old or new person. In fact, the only occurrence of that notion is in Rom 6:6 where it is said that the believer's old person was crucified with Christ. It is frequently asserted that the language of putting off the old person and putting on the new derives from the practice of the removal of clothing before entering the water in baptism and subsequent reclothing in a new garment . . . . This may have been the case, but the evidence is by no means decisive. Obviously, the clothing imagery cannot be confined to a baptismal context. In the OT there is the idea of being clothed with salvation (2 Chr 6:41) or with moral qualities (e.g., righteousness in Job 29:14; Ps 132:9) . . . . [Here] the change of clothing imagery signifies an exchange of identities, and the concepts of the old and the new persons reinforce this." On the other hand, in reference to Eph 4:22–24, Hoehner, *Ephesians*, 613, asserts, "In conclusion, believers have put on the new person. This occurred when they laid off the old person at the time of their conversion. Some want to relate this to baptism. However, one cannot know this with any certainty . . . . Even if this were a part of a water baptism ritual the ritual did not put off the old person and put on the new person. Water baptism is not the basis of the believer's experience. Rather, regeneration is the basis of the believer's experience and water baptism is only an outward symbol of an inward reality." Furthermore, Barth, *Ephesians*, 544, avers, "Indeed Eph 4:22–24 is a piece of instruction well suited for the preparation for, or the liturgy of, baptism. But its usefulness for a given service does not necessarily demonstrate the original *Sitz im Leben*. As yet there is no evidence that the exhortation to 'strip off,' to 'be renewed,' or to 'put on' is in substance to be identified with the command and promise, 'Be baptized and you shall be new men!'"

96. Hodge, *Ephesians*, 260.

97. Hoehner, *Ephesians*, 607.

98. Barth, *Ephesians*, 508.

99. See Graham, *Ephesians*, 373–4, for an outline of the different views concerning the human spirit versus the Holy Spirit. Barth, *Ephesians*, 508–9, while recognizing the legitimacy and desirability of the argument for the Holy Spirit, still affirms the translation of the lower-case spirit and simultaneously affirms the superintendence of the Holy Spirit throughout this process. He writes, "There seem to exist many reasons for capitalizing the noun 'spirit' and treating it as a reference to the 'Holy Spirit of God' who is mentioned in [Eph] 4:30. Among these reasons are: (a) The absence of the preposition 'in' (or 'by') in analogy to [Eph] 1:13; (b) the Pauline distinction between spirit (Spirit?) and mind (I Cor 14:14) or between (God's) Spirit and the (human) spirit (Rom 8:16); (c) the attribution of 'newness,' 'regeneration,' 'rebirth' to the Spirit in other NT passages and the corresponding conviction that man's spirit and mind are too corrupt to be a means of eschatological renewal. If at this point, however, Paul had

the Spirit of God can ultimately change our lives. As the Spirit of God quickens the human spirit, then believers are being renewed by that spirit which is in the mind.... It receives the truth and will of God and appropriates it in our lives."[100] Finally, the third infinitival phrase (Eph 4:24) refers back to the dispelling of the former life mentioned in Eph 4:22, but also points forward to a complete transformation that displays God in true righteousness and holiness.[101] Barth articulates the usage of the infinitives in this manner: "The first of them, in vs. 22, is in the aorist tense and denotes a once and for all, definite, concluding action: the stripping off is to be done at once, and for good and all. The second infinitive is in the present tense: the 'renewal' is to be perpetual and cannot be concluded in one act. The third is in the aorist tense again: ... a resolute, final step of 'putting on' is envisaged."[102]

Certainly, a life that has experienced the Spirit's transformational power of initial illumination will be a life that is perennially likened to Christ through the Spirit's progressive illumination. Regarding Eph 4:17–24, Calvin pronounces, "That those who have been taught in the school of Christ, and enlightened by the doctrine of salvation, should follow vanity, and in no respect differ from those unbelieving and blind nations on whom no light of truth has ever shone, would be singularly foolish."[103] Hence, believers are taught to put off their former way of living when they encounter the initial illumination of the Spirit, to be constantly renewed by the Spirit through his progressive illumination, and to be completely and perfectly transformed in true righteousness and holiness.

---

intended to say that the Spirit must exert its creative and guiding rule over the human mind, he would probably have qualified the word 'spirit' with unmistakable epithets (as he does in 1:13; 4:30) and not have spoken of (lit.) 'the spirit of your mind.' Rather he uses the words 'spirit' and 'mind' practically as synonyms ... for describing man's innermost being. It is the core, the heart, the soul of man ... that require total and ongoing renewal.... Renewal means much more than reform, reorientation, or reactivation. Since spirit and mind exert a dominating and steering function, a renewed 'spirit and mind' mean no less than a total change of the total man. His internal and external capacities and actions are equally affected.... In vs. 23 the means used by God for effecting this change are not mentioned. However, the next verse reveals that the instrument of renewal is not taken from some untapped or unspoiled resources inside man; rather it is given to him from outside."

100. Hoehner, *Ephesians*, 608–9.
101. Ibid., 609–10.
102. Barth, *Ephesians*, 505.
103. Calvin, *Galatians and Ephesians*, 289.

Colossians 1:9–10

The epistle to the Colossians parallels closely the epistle to the Ephesians and Col 1:9–10 is no exception. This passage and the previously discussed Eph 1:17–18 contain many similarities that reflect the doctrine of divine illumination. More specifically, transformative illumination is brought to the forefront as the Apostle Paul states in Col 1:9–10, "And so, from the day we heard, we have not ceased to pray for you, asking that you may be filled with the knowledge of his will in all spiritual wisdom and understanding, so as to walk in a manner worthy of the Lord, fully pleasing to him, bearing fruit in every good work and increasing in the knowledge of God."

After expressing thanksgiving to God for the church at Colossae (Col 1:3–8), the Apostle constructs a sentence beginning in Col 1:9 that extends through Col 1:20. Nevertheless, Col 1:9–14 can be considered its own unit of thought because in Col 1:15–20 Paul ventures into a Christological treatise.[104] In this study however, Col 1:9–10 is of primary relevance since it directly addresses the relationship between illumination and transformation.

These two verses constitute the beginning of a prayer for the believers to guard them against heretical teaching (cf. Col 2:4, 8, 16–23). The content of the prayer is indicated by a purpose clause (*hina plērōthēte*) and consists of an infinitive construction that communicates Paul's desire for the lives of those who are regenerate, namely, "to walk in a manner worthy of the Lord" (*peripatēsai axiōs tou kuriou*), which is defined by the two participial phrases of "bearing fruit in every good work" (*en panti ergō agathō karpophorountes*) and "increasing in the knowledge of God" (*auxanomenoi tē epignōsei tou theou*).[105] The purpose clause is written in the passive voice and is to be taken as a divine passive, signifying that the act of being filled with knowledge does not originate from man, but is indeed an act of God.[106] The word used for knowledge, *epignōsis*, can denote full or complete knowledge, but in this case the prefix added to *gnōsis* expresses a specific kind of knowledge directed towards a particular object, namely, the will of God.[107] Additionally, Richard Melick ar-

---

104. Hendriksen, *Colossians and Philemon*, 54.

105. O'Brien, *Colossians, Philemon*, 19. There are two other participial phrases that inform Paul's infinitival construction in Col 1:11–12. These are "being strengthened" (*dunamoumenoi*) and "giving thanks" (*eucharistountes*). These verses however do not directly pertain to the discussion at hand so any further treatment of them will be excluded from this study.

106. Barth and Blanke, *Colossians*, 174.

107. MacDonald, *Colossians and Ephesians*, 47.

Illumination and Interpretation

gues that this term "stressed a true knowledge of God and his will. It was also, generally, the appropriate term for personal rather than intellectual knowledge."[108] Hence, what Paul desires for believers is an experiential knowledge of God's will that amounts to a transformative understanding which is simultaneously spiritual and practical.[109]

In Col 1:9, the knowledge of God's will consists of all spiritual wisdom and understanding. The word used to qualify wisdom and understanding, *pneumatikos*, can refer to generic spiritual or supernatural influences (1 Cor 10:3–4; Eph 6:12), but in the majority of the Pauline corpus it refers to that which is derived from the Spirit of God (1 Cor 2:13, 15; 3:1; 9:11; 12:1; 14:1, 37; 15:44, 46; Gal 6:1; Eph 1:3; 5:19; Col 3:16). Consequently, to make this understanding clear, Eduard Lohse renders his translation as "in all wisdom and insight worked by the Spirit."[110] Certainly, true wisdom and understanding is only a product of the divine. Bruce concludes, "His [Paul's] prayer for them, then, is that they may attain to the full knowledge of God's will through the insight that His Spirit imparts, and thus be able to please Him in everything and live in a way that befits His children."[111]

The Spirit's illumination is the conduit for knowledge of God's will that corresponds to transformed living. This knowledge is not an abstract knowledge that is difficult to attain; rather, it is a knowledge that finds its concrete realization in the Scriptures through the progressive illumination of the Spirit. Calvin contends, "The knowledge of *the divine will*, by which expression he [Paul] sets aside all inventions of men, and all speculations that are at variance with the word of God. For his will is not to be sought anywhere else than in his word."[112] Additionally, this knowledge is not merely contained in a cognitive understanding, but is manifested in a life of obedience by means of a transformative understanding of the Scriptures.

---

108. Melick, *Philippians, Colossians, Philemon*, 201.

109. Hendriksen, *Colossians*, 57.

110. Lohse, *Colossians and Philemon*, 27. Likewise, O'Brien, *Colossians*, 22, writes, "'Spiritual' suggests that the full knowledge of God's will, for which Paul prays, comes through the insight God's Spirit imparts;" and Hendriksen, *Colossians*, 57, affirms, "Such *wisdom and understanding* . . . is the work of the Holy Spirit in human hearts" (emphasis in original). Calvin, *Philippians, Colossians, and Thessalonians*, 143, contends, "Both [wisdom and understanding] are called *spiritual* by Paul, because they are not attained in any other way than by the guidance of the Spirit. For the *animal man does not perceive the things that are of God*. (1 Cor. ii.14.)" [emphasis in original].

111. Simpson and Bruce, *Ephesians and the Colossians*, 185.

112. Calvin, *Colossians*, 142.

Therefore, a transformed faith and practice is the goal of the Christian life. In Col 1:10, *peripatēsai* ("to walk") is an infinitive of purpose that suggests that the knowledge for which Paul prays is intended to lead to a lifestyle of biblical obedience.[113] Calvin argues, "In the *first* place he [Paul] teaches, what is the end of *spiritual understanding*, and for what purpose we ought to make proficiency in God's school—that we may *walk worthy of God*, that is, that it may be manifest in our life, that we have not in vain been taught by God."[114] As mentioned above, the manner in which the believer is to live is informed by two participial phrases. The first, "bearing fruit in every good work," is to demonstrate the inward transformation that has taken place through the Spirit's illumination.[115] The second phrase, "increasing in the knowledge of God," refers to a certain progress in maturity, not only in cognitive understanding, but also in transformative understanding.[116] Accordingly, Bruce declares, "For obedience to the knowledge of God which one has already received is a necessary and certain condition for the reception of further knowledge."[117]

Col 1:9–10 then, is a passage that directly handles the concept of transformative illumination. Hendriksen agrees that the knowledge which one receives from the Spirit of God according to his will is "heart-transforming and life-renewing."[118] Through this passage, it is clear that knowledge of the things of God does not result in a mere cognitive understanding, but finds its fulfillment in the transformative understanding that only comes by the power of the Holy Spirit.

Defining Transformative Illumination

A definition of the concept of transformative illumination based on the previously examined Scripture passages is essential for the continued development of this study as it regards the indispensability of the Holy Spirit for biblical interpretation. Again, it should be remembered that this is not an attempt to introduce an entirely new type of illumination, for this would only serve to convolute the doctrine that this study has earnestly

---

113. O'Brien, *Colossians*, 22.
114. Calvin, *Colossians*, 143.
115. MacDonald, *Colossians and Ephesians*, 48.
116. O'Brien, *Colossians*, 23.
117. Simpson and Bruce, *Ephesians and Colossians*, 186.
118. Hendriksen, *Colossians*, 57.

attempted to provide with clarity. Rather, transformative illumination is a framework for understanding the doctrine of illumination as a whole. Averbeck offers this understanding of the relationship between illumination and transformation:

> Biblical transformation of the heart (mind, understanding, feelings, attitudes, motivations, etc.) takes place when we become so deeply impressed with God and his purposes in our lives that our will, our volition, becomes engaged in the ongoing process of change and growth. When what we are impressed with changes, then what we desire changes along with it. Deep and meaningful change takes place when the things that matter to us change, and that should be one of the major goals in our study of the Bible . . . . The Holy Spirit is directly involved in bringing about such encounters with God in our hearts and lives as part of his ministry of illumination.[119]

Hence, transformative illumination is a synthesis of the biblical teaching which encompasses both initial and progressive illumination.

It is evident in the Scripture passages just assessed that the concept of transformation is a genuine work of the Holy Spirit. This work is substantiated by a regenerate mindset centered upon the Spirit (Rom 8:1–11) and evidence of life in the Spirit (Gal 5:16–25). Through the renewing of the mind and the knowledge of God's will (Rom 12:1–2), the regenerate person is able to bear spiritual fruit and increase in the knowledge of God (Col 1:9–10), for the expressed purpose of being progressively and divinely changed (2 Cor 3:18) according to the true righteousness and holiness of the new self created in Christ Jesus (Eph 4:17–24).

Additionally, transformation in the life of the believer occurs through the conduit of the Spirit's illumination in conjunction with the Scriptures. In the biblical passages above, the Spirit's work of transformation is necessarily bonded to his ministry of illumination. Beginning with the Spirit's initial illumination to salvation, and employing the understanding that results from the Spirit's progressive illumination, transformation becomes a necessary element in the faith and practice of the regenerate. Bloesch contends, "Understanding happens when God's Word speaks to us anew as we submit ourselves to his authority and direction mediated through Holy Scripture. We begin to know when the text becomes transparent to its transcendent meaning through action of

---

119. Averbeck, "God, People, and the Bible," 155–6.

the Spirit in the biblical words and in the human heart."[120] The intent of illumination is to enable proper interpretation and understanding of the Scriptures for the purpose of conformity to Christ. Just as the Word and the Spirit share an indissoluble bond, the Spirit's ministries of illumination and transformation are inherently bound. Summarizing the thoughts of J. I. Packer, Koranteng-Pipim writes, "The foregoing enumeration of the effects of the Spirit's illumination on the interpreter of Scripture confirms that, indeed for Packer, illumination results in a recognition of the divinity of Scripture, cognition of its message and its contemporary relevance, and reception of its message through obediential response. Therefore, without illumination the student of the Bible cannot accept, correctly understand, and obey the message of Scripture."[121] Therefore, transformative illumination is that process whereby the Holy Spirit's initial illumination enables his ministry of progressive illumination such that his work of transformation results in the life of the believer.

Hermeneutical Implications

With this newly acquired definition of transformative illumination in mind, it is vital to revisit the discussion regarding unregenerate and regenerate biblical interpretation initiated in chapter 2. The purpose of this section is to make clear, by the light of the concept of transformative illumination, the difference between the interpretation of those who are nonbelievers and those who have dedicated their lives to Christ Jesus.

Biblical Interpretation by the Unregenerate

Based on the relationships between illumination and the hermeneutical doctrines in chapter 2, specifically revelation and perspicuity, an unregenerate person can grasp a cognitive meaning of the text of Scripture though this falls vastly short of Scripture's intended purpose of transformation. Nebeker intimates at this awareness when he argues, "Perhaps we should suggest that nonbelievers can at times 'understand' the text, but they do not regard what they understand as 'truth' that is personally relevant. Personal relevance, we submit, is something that can be achieved only through

---

120. Bloesch, *Holy Scripture*, 178.
121. Koranteng-Pipim, "The Role of the Holy Spirit," 191.

Illumination and Interpretation

the 'assessment' or 'appraisal' of the Holy Spirit."[122] This is certainly a valid consideration because those who are unregenerate are devoid of the Spirit's illuminating presence as they seek to interpret a Spirit-inspired text.

Hence, a cognitive meaning of the text is the extent of the unregenerate person's interpretive endeavor. Since cognitive meaning refers to a lexical-grammatical comprehension of the text, a cognitive meaning of the Scriptures can be ascertained through a cursory reading of the text or the diligent study of the text with a multifarious arsenal of exegetical tools and proper hermeneutical methodology. For this reason, the unregenerate person is able to read Scripture and discover its meaning cognitively. Cognitive meaning does not *require* the work of the Spirit because God has given each person certain intellectual and cognitive capabilities; nonetheless, it should be remembered that the effects of sin upon mankind are pervasive and may hinder these faculties. Owen confirms:

> There is a knowledge of spiritual things that is purely natural and disciplinary, attainable and attained without any especial aid or assistance of the Holy Ghost. . . . Some knowledge of the Scripture, and the things contained in it, is attainable at the same rate of pains and study with that of any other art or science. The illumination intended, being a gift of the Holy Ghost, differs from, and is exalted above this knowledge that is purely natural. For it makes nearer approaches to the light of spiritual things in their own nature, than the other doth. Notwithstanding the utmost improvements of scientifical notions that are purely natural, the things of the gospel in their own nature, are not only unsuited to the wills and affections of persons endued with them, but are really foolishness to their minds. . . . Moreover, the knowledge that is merely natural hath little or no power on the soul, either to keep it from sin, or to constrain it to obedience. There is not a more secure and profligate generation of sinners in the world, than those who are under the sole conduct of it.[123]

---

122. Nebeker, "The Holy Spirit," 51.

123. Owen, *Hebrews*, 213. Additionally, Fridley, "Illumination," 26–7, in reference to 1 Cor 2:14, writes, "That the natural man views the biblical teachings as foolishness does not mean they are incomprehensible to him or that he is unable to cognitively grasp the content of the message. . . . [T]his phrase should not be taken to mean that spiritual teachings are unintelligible or beyond the cognition of unregenerate man."

Transformative Illumination

Truly, the unregenerate person can grasp the cognitive meaning of the text such that it results in understanding, but without the Spirit, this understanding is anemic.[124]

Therefore, the extent of an unregenerate person's understanding is cognitive as well. Cognitive meaning resides in the locutionary act of the text, falling short of the perlocutionary effect and at best attaining its illocutionary force in understanding. Henry Virkler declares:

> According to Scripture, persons do not truly possess knowledge unless they are living in the light of that knowledge. True faith is not only knowledge about God (which even the demons possess) but knowledge acted on. The unbeliever can *know* (intellectually comprehend) many of the truths of Scripture using the same means of interpretation he would use with nonbiblical texts, but he cannot truly *know* (act on and appropriate) these truths as long as he remains in rebellion against God . . . . Thus unbelievers do not *know* the full meaning of scriptural teaching, not because that meaning is unavailable to them in the words of the text, but because they refuse to act on and appropriate spiritual truths for their own lives.[125]

Cognitive meaning and the cognitive understanding of that meaning lack the intended perlocutionary effect of the text. Thus, a different grasp of meaning and a more holistic form of understanding is required in order to properly comprehend and interpret the Scriptures. The unregenerate person's capacity to attain a cognitive meaning of the text that results in a cognitive understanding reflects a movement in the right direction, but it still falls short of the intended perlocutionary effect of the Scriptures in cooperation with the Spirit. Indeed, the end of biblical interpretation and the Spirit's illumination is transformation.

As a result, the interpreter who lacks the illumination of the Holy Spirit is at a severe disadvantage in attaining a proper understanding of the text. Jones avers, ". . . [R]eaders who attempt to remain detached and neutral in their interpretation of the Bible will typically understand it less deeply than those who discipline their lives by studying Scripture . . . . Scripture bears witness to the God of Jesus Christ so that we may be transformed by the

---

124. Maier, *Biblical Hermeneutics*, 53–4, concurs, "The unregenerate person is thus capable of relaying tradition to others only in an insufficient fashion. And he is further disadvantaged with respect to content, because he finds acceptance of the supernatural difficult."

125. Virkler, *Hermeneutics*, 30; emphasis in original.

Illumination and Interpretation

power of the Holy Spirit into the likeness of Christ."[126] Likewise, Klooster maintains that an unbeliever cannot truly understand the Scriptures because he lacks "heart-knowledge" that is enacted by faith.[127]

To be clear, what is at stake is not whether a cognitively correct interpretation of the text has the potential to be attained. As stated earlier, both believing and unbelieving exegetes can grasp this meaning of the text and subsequently arrive at a valid cognitive understanding of the Scriptures. This anthropocentric notion that focuses on the human exegete and his resultant interpretation needs to be replaced by a pneumatic perspective that concentrates on the Spirit's and the Scripture's intended effect of transformation in the life of the believer, that of which cannot be achieved by the unregenerate interpreter.[128] In their respective hermeneutic texts, both Stein and Klein, Blomberg, and Hubbard present examples that support the argument that unregenerate interpreters are able to interpret the Scriptures at a cognitive level as well as, if not at times better than those who are regenerate.[129] While this may be the case, Maier asserts:

126. Jones, "Formed and Transformed," 31.

127. Klooster, "The Role of the Holy Spirit," 455. The terminology of heart-knowledge and heart-understanding that Klooster uses is not preferred because it does not explicitly emphasize the transforming power of the Spirit's illumination. Klooster emphasizes the pairing of faith and knowledge in his terms (p. 461–3), and the process of sanctification that genuine heart-knowledge contributes to (p. 459–60), but the language of transformative meaning and understanding specifically convey the goal of biblical interpretation in light of the Spirit's illumination.

128. Maier, *Biblical Hermeneutics*, 54–5.

129. Stein, *Interpreting the Bible*, 66–71, argues through two illustrations, that an unbeliever by means of erudition and exegetical tools can arrive at a correct mental grasp of the Scriptures. In doing so, however, he relegates the Spirit's illuminatory role in interpretation to include only an acceptance of the truth that is in the Scriptures. As a result, Stein falls just short of including the Spirit's ministry of transformation in his role of illumination thus leaving the reader with a deficient understanding of the difference between regenerate and unregenerate biblical interpretation. Klein, Blomberg, and Hubbard, *Biblical Interpretation*, 136–8, begin by asserting that faith is essential for a full comprehension of the Scriptures and is indeed the foundation for a correct interpretation of the Scriptures. Nevertheless, they argue, "Unbelievers, even skeptics, can grasp much of its meaning.... Thus, a competent, unbelieving scholar may produce an outstanding technical commentary on a biblical book—perhaps even better than many believing Christian scholars could write. But that unbelieving scholar cannot understand and portray the true *significance* of the Bible's message, for he or she is not ultimately committed to the Bible as divine revelation" (p. 136; emphasis in original). Similar to Stein, Klein, Blomberg, and Hubbard appear to fall just short of describing and affirming a complete interpretation of the text that includes transformation. The authors do include a section on obedience and purport that "willingness

> It would also not be desirable to detach faith and love for God's Word from the person doing biblical research . . . . Such dislocation between thinking and believing, the researching and the practicing self, is hermeneutically the most infelicitous position thinkable. Already at the anthropological level it impairs congeniality. It makes contradiction a normal form of living, which is then consciously or unconsciously imposed on the object. And this all takes place in opposition to the devotion that revelation demands. In contrast, the renewed person endowed with the Spirit of revelation itself, who opens himself in commitment of his entire person to this revelation, who enters this encounter in trust and love—this person turns out to be better suited as an interpreter.[130]

Indeed, mere mental cognition of the meaning and understanding of the Scriptures is not what the Spirit desires. Rather, the Spirit in strict cooperation with the Scriptures desires that meaning and understanding arise out of the hermeneutical task which transforms the believer's faith and practice.[131]

Biblical Interpretation by the Regenerate

Regenerate biblical interpretation when accompanied by the Spirit and empowered by his illumination is wholly different from the interpretation of the unregenerate person. Only the regenerate interpreter aided by the Holy Spirit's illumination can attain the perlocutionary effect of the text, i.e., transformation. Marshall asserts:

> The Bible must be understood and interpreted in line with its intended function, and that function is to lead people to God

---

to put oneself 'under' the text, to submit one's will to hear the text in the way its author intended" is a "requirement" of the interpretive endeavor (p. 138–9), but again, the distinction between unregenerate and regenerate biblical interpretation in terms of the transformative ministry of the Holy Spirit is left somewhat ambiguous.

130. Maier, *Biblical Hermeneutics*, 52–3.

131. Zuck, *Spirit-Filled Teaching*, 42–3, sums it up this way, "Obviously unsaved people can mentally grasp something of the Bible's objective data. Many unbelievers have understood many of the historical facts presented in the Word of God. Some have even followed biblical logic. They have cognitively grasped certain objective biblical facts . . . yet they do not know the God of the Scriptures . . . . Even with determined and diligent research on a high scholarly level, they are unable to respond to the true divine sense of the Scriptures. The Spirit's illumination of Christians, then, must include something more than that mental apprehension of the Bible of which Christians are capable."

Illumination and Interpretation

> and a knowledge of His salvation. Put otherwise, we must recognize the intention of the author. If we believe that the author is God Himself, inspiring human instruments by His Spirit, then this does make a difference to our understanding of the book. Surely the task of the Spirit is to lead us to recognize that the Bible is the Word of God and to interpret it accordingly. The task of the Spirit in biblical interpretation is thus to enable us to recognize the true character and purpose of the Bible and then to interpret the text in the light of this fact. The Author Himself comes to our side and helps us to understand what He has written. He gives us the eyes of faith and the mind of Christ so that we receive the message that God intends for us.[132]

Truly, the communication of transformative meaning and understanding is the ultimate goal of the text of Scripture.

The Holy Spirit's initial illumination plays a foundational role in preparing the interpreter to properly understand the Scriptures. For this reason, Goldsworthy refers to initial illumination, i.e., the salvation event, as a "radical hermeneutical realignment" that reorients the regenerate person's heart and mind, such that he is primed for proper biblical interpretation.[133] Maier concurs and states, "Only spiritual regeneration, with the faith and practical obedience it brings, equips one for theology.... [T]he faith of the interpreter is a welcome, helpful, and indeed ultimately indispensable presupposition of understanding."[134] In point of fact, transformative illumination begins with the Spirit's work of initial illumination and is carried along by the Spirit's progressive illumination.

Thereby, the Spirit's continual presence in the life of the believer is necessary for a proper interpretation of Scripture. Watson contends, "... [I]n order properly to understand this revelation there must be a continuous operation of the Holy Spirit. Ye must be born again. Ye must be indwelt and taught of this Spirit. Only thus are we able to appreciate the things of God."[135] Here, Watson highlights the exigency of the Spirit's ini-

---

132. Marshall, "The Holy Spirit," 72–3.
133. Goldsworthy, *Gospel-Centered Hermeneutics*, 307–8.
134. Maier, *Biblical Hermeneutics*, 48, 51.
135. Watson, "The Holy Spirit and the Bible," 278. Additionally, Pinnock, *The Scripture*, 168, 173, declares, "First, there is the simple fact that involvement with a text like the Bible and an open receptivity to its message puts one in a position to understand it better.... But if it is true that the presence of the Spirit is essential for the work of interpretation to be effective, then it follows that the practitioners must be believers filled with the Spirit."

tial illumination as the momentum undergirding the Spirit's progressive illumination. A proper understanding of the Scriptures is only available to those who are of the Spirit and driven by faith. Dockery and Nelson stress, "The proper setting of special revelation is Christian faith. God makes himself known to those who receive his revelation in faith. Faith is the instrument by which we receive God's revelation. When faith is present, the things of God become manifest (Heb. 11:1–6). Faith is the glad recognition of truth, the reception of God's revelation without reservation or hesitation (Rom. 10:17). God is pleased to reveal himself and his majestic Word to people of faith."[136]

However, it is not necessary to separate transformative meaning from cognitive meaning because cognitive meaning is a chief constituent of transformative meaning. The difference is transformative meaning, instead of being constrained by cognitive meaning such that cognitive understanding is the extent of interpretation, is rather compelled by the impetus of the Holy Spirit to grasp a transformative understanding of the Scriptures. Pinnock explains, "Underlying our hermeneutics is a belief in the reality of the Spirit of God, who helps us to recognize God's Word for what it is, aids us in grasping the point, and assists us in applying it to our circumstances so that it speaks as a living Bible within our horizon."[137]

Therefore, transformative meaning arises beyond the confines of cognitive meaning and understanding that bind the unregenerate interpreter and allow the regenerate interpreter to grasp the transformative understanding of the text. In other words, transformative meaning is cognitive meaning and understanding reaching its full illocutionary force with the potential to attain the perlocutionary effect that the Scriptures and the Spirit desire. Vanhoozer avers:

> The text aims at producing real effects on readers: at transforming them into the image of the Word. It wants not only to be

---

136. Dockery and Nelson, "Special Revelation," 121. Similarly, Herring and Stagg, *Understand the Bible*, 38–9, write, "A first step in understanding the Scriptures is to realize that while much of it can be quite readily understood, its real wealth of meaning is a matter of spiritual insight rather than mental ability. The Bible draws a sharp distinction between truth known to man on the level of his own thinking and truth which is disclosed to him through an experience with God." Also, Veenhof, "The Holy Spirit and Hermeneutics," 116–7, states that Scripture ". . . can be discerned and accepted in its true nature only by spiritual, 'pneumatical,' people. . . . The pneumatical must be discerned, perceived pneumatically; and at the same time, the physical man does not accept what comes from the Spirit of God."

137. Pinnock, *The Scripture*, 213.

Illumination and Interpretation

followed, but to be, as it were, incarnated. The end of interpretation, I submit, is *embodiment* . . . . The Word seeks, by the Spirit, to be taken to heart, to be embodied in the life of the people of God. Scripture's warnings call for attention, its commands call for obedience, its promises call for faith. *The vocation of the biblical interpreter is not simply to point at biblical meaning, but to embody it.*[138]

As a result, the concept of transformative illumination is built upon a transformative meaning and understanding of the text that encompasses cognitive meaning and understanding and comprises the fullness of the communicative act in Scripture by means of the Holy Spirit's illumination.

---

138. Vanhoozer, *Meaning*, 440; emphasis in original. In addition, Averbeck "God, People, and the Bible," 149, emphasizes, "The goal is to describe and encourage the kind of biblical scholarship in which the Bible is not only the subject of investigation, but the investigation itself turns back upon the scholar in a transforming way."

6

Conclusion

THE APPARENT SUBJECTIVITY OF the Holy Spirit's work, especially in regard to the doctrine of illumination, has exiled this doctrine to a place of solitude that has perpetuated a negligent trepidation concerning the Holy Spirit's ministry to believers. De Young declares, "Yet wonderfully the role of the Spirit has a double edge: he not only reveals truth . . . , but he reveals only *truth*—he will not teach in contradiction to what he has already taught in Scripture . . . . We need to be less characterized by a fear of heresy and subjectivity and more by an eager expectation of communion with the living Spirit."[1] When properly paired with the Word of God, the Holy Spirit's ministry of illumination assumes an objective form that reifies the Holy Spirit's work in such a way that the regenerate person can appropriately understand the Scriptures in light of their purpose of transformation.[2]

1. De Young, "The Holy Spirit, 19.
2. Vanier and Young, "Towards Transformational Reading of Scripture", 249, assert, "So our model necessitates the recognised involvement of the reader when it comes to the interpretation of Scripture. The reader's interests and response are not to be bracketed out; but they are to be in a dynamic relationship with author and text. The reader cannot simply make the text mean anything he or she likes—he or she must respect the 'otherness' of the text. So while the scholar may still wish to be as 'objective' as possible, trying to release the text from its accumulated meanings, its multi-levelled resonances, and all the traditions of the interpretive communities which have overlaid it, at the same time the scholar will inevitably have his or her own interest, explicit or implicit, and might even admit an interest which derives from not leaving his or her faith at the door, but rather from a search for meaning that is potentially enhanced, despite the enormous cultural gap between the ancient and modern worlds, through the empathy of considerable shared perspectives, such as belief in God. On the other

Illumination and Interpretation

It is imperative to recognize that the Holy Spirit's work of illumination is necessary for biblical interpretation so that it results in transformation in the life of the believer. It is not an abstract doctrine, but one that is reified by the cooperation of Word and Spirit. Brunner comments:

> The revealing activity of the Holy Spirit in the heart and mind of man is a mystery, just as the incarnation of the Word in the historical person of Jesus Christ is a mystery. We cannot fathom it; we experience it in faith. But the fact that we cannot fathom it does not mean that we can understand nothing at all about it, that for our intellect it must always remain a "scandal" and a "folly." The intellect which has been illuminated is able not only to assert wisdom, but to perceive it.[3]

Indeed, the nebulous reputation of the doctrine of illumination can be displaced with the preceding biblical-theological framework to constitute a comprehension that is characterized by lucidity, not ambiguity. Transformative illumination, then, is not only a beneficial concept, but it is truly a necessary construct for understanding the doctrine of illumination in its entirety. It is in the light of transformative illumination that the Holy Spirit is displayed as indispensable for biblical interpretation so that the life of the believer is transformed according to the image of Christ Jesus.

Pastoral Implications

Since orthodoxy is not always manifested in orthopraxy and orthopraxy is not necessarily the result of orthodoxy, it is important to address some pastoral implications that flow out of a proper understanding of the doctrine of illumination.[4] Peifer declares, "Indeed, there can be no question that the Bible has been given to us for the *life* of the Church: the Holy

---

hand, we can discern a legitimate place for the believer approaching the texts for insight and spiritual transformation, despite the fact that his / her interests have been liable to be dismissed, as merely 'subjective' and as making the texts mean what they like; for it is new insight that the believer seeks from the texts—a mirror reflecting back his or her own prejudices is a danger, but not necessarily the outcome: rather the text itself aims at transformation and stands over against the reader, challenging and calling into a new future ... for the point of Scripture is transformation."

3. Brunner, *Revelation and Reason*, 172.

4. Marshall, "The Holy Spirit," 73–4, and Klein, Blomberg, and Hubbard, *Biblical Interpretation*, 503–4 present lists of practical applications for the Holy Spirit's ministry of illumination.

Spirit did not intend it to be solely an object of erudition, but primarily a source of nourishment for the Christian people."[5] Surely, the Holy Spirit's illumination is not a doctrine that is enslaved by the confines of the intellect. Rather, it is a practical doctrine that only finds its relevancy and purpose in the life of the believer as it is worked out through faith.

Consequently, it needs to be stated preemptively that the partnership between the interpretive endeavor and the illumination of the Holy Spirit is chiefly accomplished through prayer. Owen professes that the principal means by which the regenerate person comes to an understanding of the Scriptures is by "frequent and fervent prayers for the aid and assistance of the Holy Spirit."[6] Just as the Apostle Paul prayed for spiritual wisdom and understanding (Col 1:9) for the purpose of transformation (2 Thess 1:11–12) and Jude urged his readers to pray in the Holy Spirit (Jude 20), those who are regenerate should appeal to the Spirit for aid. It is of the essence that the believer interpreting the Spirit-inspired Scriptures be in submission to the Holy Spirit through prayer in order that he might be filled with the Holy Spirit (Eph 5:18), walk by the Holy Spirit (Gal 5:16–25), and live by the Holy Spirit (Rom 8:1–11) so that his sinful nature might not quench the Holy Spirit's work (1 Thess 5:19).

Through the illuminating work of the Holy Spirit, God applies his Word to the life of the believer as he seeks the will of God through diligent study and prayer. Klein, Blomberg, and Hubbard assert:

> Instead of being in control by seeking the author's intended meaning in the text, we let the text itself control the process—under the prayerful guidance of the Holy Spirit. More meditative, this kind of reading does not seek so much the meaning in the text as the meaning of our lives *under* the text's mastery . . . . [R]eading the Bible for 'information' is important . . . . But we dare not allow this informational approach to crowd out the Bible's 'formational' role—to allow God's Spirit to speak at the core of our being.[7]

Hence, as the Holy Spirit labors in the process of illumination, a proper understanding of the Word of God will necessarily result in a manifestation of application in the believer that leads to a life that is transformed and controlled by the power of the Spirit. Just as the illumination of the Holy Spirit is an indispensable ingredient for the proper

---

5. Peifer, "The Experience of Sin, Salvation, and the Spirit," 3; emphasis in original.
6. Owen, *Works*, "Causes," (4.4.170).
7. Klein, Blomberg, and Hubbard, *Biblical Interpretation*, 472; emphasis in original.

Illumination and Interpretation

understanding of Scripture, likewise, prayer is necessary for the strict cooperation of the Scriptures and the Spirit. To be clear, prayer is the means by which illumination is requested and it also serves as the bond between hermeneutical method and the illuminating work of the Holy Spirit. As the psalmist prays, so should the biblical interpreter: "Open my eyes, that I may behold wondrous things out of your law" (Ps 119:18).

The partnership between illumination and interpretation is accomplished mainly through prayer, but it should be noted that this is most effectively accomplished in the midst of the body of Christ. For this reason, David Power purports, "A pneuma-conscious hermeneutics . . . cannot be developed without a pneuma-conscious ecclesiology."[8] Hauerwas contends that discipleship in the context of the community of believers is directly proportional to one's ability to interpret the Scriptures.[9] In other words, it is through participation in the church that transformation in the life of the believer becomes a distinct reality. Accordingly, Stephen Fowl and Gregory Jones maintain:

> Christian communities are central for the ongoing task of enabling people to become wise readers of Scripture. To become wise readers of Scripture, we need to acquire a range of skills and virtues manifested in Christian discipleship. These skills and virtues are given their shape and form under the guidance of the Holy Spirit in and through the particular friendships and practices of Christian communities. They are both the prerequisite for, and the result of, wise readings of Scripture. These skills and virtues not only enable wise reading but faithful practice.[10]

On the one hand, it is important to make clear that the purpose of transformation is not merely an individualistic enterprise, but a corporate activity that aims at spiritual maturity in Christ Jesus.[11] On the other hand, this does not negate the power of the Spirit's transformative work and his enablement for the understanding of the Scriptures in the life of the individual believer.[12] Geoffrey Bromiley concurs, "The Spirit's ministry relates also to the understanding of scripture . . . . The church

---

8. Power, "The Holy Spirit", 161.

9. Hauerwas, *The Hauerwas Reader*, 255–66.

10. Fowl and Jones, *Reading in Communion*, 35–6. Also see Fowl, *Engaging Scripture*, 178–206, for a chapter regarding the topic of Christian formation in Christian communities.

11. Nebeker, "The Holy Spirit," 53–4.

12. Ward, *Words of Life*, 155, and Ward, *Word and Supplement*, 187–90.

alone cannot help here; only the Holy Spirit can illuminate the darkened mind through the 'inherent light' of scripture itself."[13]

Furthermore, the community of faith serves as a safeguard for biblical interpretation in two ways.[14] As the primary agent of communication in the body of believers, the pastor-teacher is responsible for the upholding of proper biblical interpretation. Again, although Spirit-gifted teachers of the Word are representative of the community's interpretation, this does not nullify the individual believer's duty in the interpretive endeavor or invalidate his hermeneutical function as part of the believing community. To be sure, the Berean attitude displayed in Acts 17:11 is a worthy principle to abide by: "They received the word with all eagerness, examining the Scriptures daily to see if these things were so." However, the pastor-teacher's responsibility is not merely one of word, but also of deed. Vanhoozer affirms, "Readers schooled in the community of faith acquire the skills to read the Bible as Scripture, that is, to follow its illocutions and perlocutions so that its meaning is both accomplished and applied. This specifically Christian understanding has as its goal knowledge of the God of Jesus Christ . . . that ultimately leads to righteousness."[15] The goal of the Scriptures and the Spirit's illumination is transformation, and the pastor-teacher is responsible for exemplifying the effects of transformative illumination in his own life in order to assist in this same process in the lives of the body of believers.[16]

Not only is the pastor-teacher responsible for the promotion of illumination and the preservation of interpretation, but also those within the community of believers serve as hermeneutical safeguards. Hunt comments:

> Through the living interaction of these three authorities, scripture, tradition, and reason, God makes his presence known today to believers through the Holy Spirit. The process in its living wholeness is what we mean by the illumination of the Holy Spirit. It is essentially a personal process, involving vastly more than the mere communication of proposition or doctrines. The Spirit brings scripture, tradition, and reason into dynamic dialogue. Out of this living confrontation the Spirit imparts the sense of God's speaking to particular situations. As a personal process, the

13. Bromiley, *Historical Theology*, 323.
14. Pinnock, *The Scripture*, 217–8.
15. Vanhoozer, *Meaning*, 406.
16. Jones, "Formed and Transformed," 32.

Illumination and Interpretation

> Spirit's illumination has particular affinities for the living Word in Christian proclamation, worship, edification, and witness.[17]

Correct doctrine leads to correct practice. The Holy Spirit is inherent to the success of both. As the Spirit is accessed through prayer and the fellowship of the body of Christ, the doctrine of illumination will necessarily and inevitably lead to transformation in the believer's faith and practice. The union of illumination and interpretation and the cooperation of Spirit and Scripture define the Holy Spirit's transformative role in hermeneutics.

---

17. Hunt, "The Holy Spirit and Revelation Today," 42.

Bibliography

Achtemeier, Paul J. *Inspiration and Authority: Nature and Function of Christian Scripture*. Peabody, Mass.: Hendrickson, 1999.
Akin, Daniel L. *1, 2, 3 John*. The New American Commentary 38. Nashville: Broadman & Holman, 2001.
Akin, Daniel L., David P. Nelson, and Peter R. Schemm, Jr. *A Theology for the Church*. Nashville: Broadman & Holman, 2007.
Alexander, T. Desmond, Brian S. Rosner, D. A. Carson, Graeme Goldsworthy, eds. *New Dictionary of Biblical Theology: Exploring the Unity & Diversity of Scripture*. Downers Grove: InterVarsity Press, 2000.
Allen, Leslie C. *Ezekiel*. 2 vols. Word Biblical Commentary 28–29. Dallas: Word Books, 1990–94.
———. *Psalms 101–150*. Word Biblical Commentary 21. Waco: Word Books, 1983.
Aquinas, Thomas. *First Corinthians*. St. Paul Center for Biblical Studies. Cited 4 May 2009. Online: http://www.aquinas.avemaria.edu/Aquinas-Corinthians.pdf.
Arndt, William F. *Luke*. Concordia Classic Commentary Series. St. Louis: Concordia, 1956.
Auerbach, Erich. *Mimesis: The Representation of Reality in Western Literature*. Princeton: Princeton University Press, 1973.
Augustine. *De Trinitate*. Edited by John E. Rotelle. Translated by Edmund Hill. Hyde Park, N.Y.: New City Press, 1991.
———. *Expositions of the Psalms*. Edited by Boniface Ramsey. Translated by Maria Boulding. Hyde Park, N.Y.: New City Press, 2003.
———. *Sermons*. Edited by John E. Rotelle. Translated by Edmund Hill. Brooklyn, N.Y.: New City Press, 1991.
Averbeck, Richard E. "God, People, and the Bible: The Relationship between Illumination and Biblical Scholarship." Pages 137–165 in *Who's Afraid of the Holy Spirit?*. Edited by Daniel B. Wallace and M. James Sawyer. Dallas: Biblical Studies Press, 2005.
Baldwin, Henry Scott. "The Perspicuity of Scripture: The Clarity of Scripture in an Age of Hermeneutical Nihilism." Paper presented at the annual meeting of the Evangelical Theological Society, Tyson's Corner, Va., November 18–20, 1993.
Barrett, C. K. *A Commentary on the Epistle to the Romans*. Harper's New Testament Commentaries. New York: Harper & Row, 1957.
———. *The Gospel According to St. John: An Introduction with Commentary and Notes on the Greek Text*. Philadelphia: The Westminster Press, 1978.

Bibliography

———. *The Second Epistle to the Corinthians.* Black's New Testament Commentary. London: A & C Black, 1973.

Barth, Markus. *Ephesians: Translation and Commentary on Chapters 4–6.* The Anchor Bible 34. Garden City, N. Y.: Doubleday & Company, 1974.

Barth, Markus and Helmut Blanke. *Colossians.* Translated by Astrid B. Beck. The Anchor Bible. New York: Doubleday, 1994.

Bartholomew, Clayton Sterling. "Calvin's Doctrine of the Cognitive Illumination of the Holy Spirit as Developed in the Institutes of the Christian Religion." MA Thesis, Western Conservative Baptist Seminary, 1977.

Basil of Caesarea. "De Spiritu Sancto." Pages 1–50 in *St. Basil: Letters and Selected Works.* Edited by Philip Schaff and Henry Wace. Vol. 8 of *Nicene and Post-Nicene Fathers.* Grand Rapids: Eerdmans, 1955.

Bauer, Walter. *A Greek-English Lexicon of the New Testament and other Early Christian Literature.* 3d edition. Edited by F. W. Danker, W. F. Arndt, and F. W. Gingrich. Chicago: The University of Chicago Press, 2000.

Berkouwer, G. C. "The Testimony of the Spirit." Pages 155–81 in *The Authoritative Word: Essays on The Nature of Scripture.* Edited by Donald K. McKim. Grand Rapids: Eerdmans, 1983.

Berry, David George. "The Knowledge of God and Faith in the Theology of John Calvin with Particular Reference to the Testimonium Internum Spiritus Sancti." ThM thesis, University of Edinburgh, 1984.

Best, Ernest. *Ephesians.* The International Critical Commentary. Edinburgh: T & T Clark, 1998.

———. *Second Corinthians.* Interpretation. Atlanta: John Knox Press, 1987.

———. *The Letter of Paul to the Romans.* The Cambridge Bible Commentary. Cambridge: Cambridge University Press, 1967.

Block, Daniel I. "The Prophet of the Spirit: The Use of RWH in the Book of Ezekiel." *Journal of the Evangelical Theological Society* 32, no. 1 (Mar. 1989): 27–49.

Bloesch, Donald G. *A Theology of Word & Spirit.* Downers Grove: InterVarsity Press, 1992.

———. *Essentials of Evangelical Theology: God, Authority, and Salvation.* Vol. 1. New York: Harper & Row, 1978.

———. *Holy Scripture: Revelation, Inspiration, & Interpretation.* Downers Grove: InterVarsity Press, 1994.

———. *The Holy Spirit: Works & Gifts.* Downers Grove: InterVarsity Press, 2000.

———. "The Primacy of Scripture." Pages 117–53 in *The Authoritative Word: Essays on The Nature of Scripture.* Edited by Donald K. McKim. Grand Rapids: Eerdmans, 1983.

Briggs, Charles Augustus and Emilie Grace Briggs. *A Critical and Exegetical Commentary on The Book of Psalms.* Vol. 2. The International Critical Commentary. New York: Charles Scribner's Sons, 1907.

Bromiley, Geoffrey W. *Historical Theology: An Introduction.* Grand Rapids: Eerdmans, 1978.

———. "The Church Fathers and the Holy Scripture." Pages 199–220 in *Scripture and Truth.* Edited by D. A. Carson and John D. Woodbridge. Grand Rapids: Baker, 1992.

Brooke, A. E. *The Johannine Epistles.* The International Critical Commentary. New York: Charles Scribner's Sons, 1912.

Brown, Francis, S. R. Driver, and Charles A. Briggs. *The Brown-Driver-Briggs Hebrew and English Lexicon*. Peabody, Mass.: Hendrickson, 2003.

Brown, Jeannine K. *Scripture as Communication: Introducing Biblical Hermeneutics*. Grand Rapids: Baker, 2007.

Brown, Paul E. *The Holy Spirit & The Bible: The Spirit's Interpreting Role in Relation to Biblical Hermeneutics*. Fearn, Scotland: Christian Focus Publications, 2002.

Brown, William P., ed. *Character and Scripture: Moral Formation, Community, and Biblical Interpretation*. Grand Rapids: Eerdmans, 2002.

Bruce, F. F. *The Epistles of John*. Old Tappan, N. J.: Fleming H. Revell Company, 1970.

———. *The Epistle to the Galatians*. The New International Greek Testament Commentary. Grand Rapids: Eerdmans, 1982.

———. *The Epistle to the Hebrews*. The New International Commentary on the New Testament. Grand Rapids: Eerdmans, 1990.

Brunner, Emil. *Revelation and Reason: The Christian Doctrine of Faith and Knowledge*. Wake Forest: Chanticleer Publishing Company, 1946.

Burton, Ernest De Witt. *The Epistle to the Galatians*. The International Critical Commentary. Edinburgh: T. & T. Clark, 1921.

Byrne, Brendan. *Romans*. Sacra Pagina 6. Collegeville, Minn.: The Liturgical Press, 1996.

Calvin, John. *A Harmony of the Gospels Matthew, Mark, and Luke and the Epistles of James and Jude*. Vol. 3. Translated by A. W. Morrison. Calvin's Commentaries. Grand Rapids: Eerdmans, 1994.

———. *Commentaries on the Epistle of Paul the Apostle to the Galatians and Ephesians*. Vol. 21. Translated by William Pringle. Calvin's Commentaries. Grand Rapids: Baker, 2009.

———. *Commentaries on the Epistle of Paul the Apostle to the Hebrews*. Vol. 22. Translated by John Owen. Calvin's Commentaries. Grand Rapids: Baker, 2009.

———. *Commentary on the Epistle of Paul the Apostle to the Philippians, Colossians, and Thessalonians*. Vol. 21. Translated by John Pringle. Calvin's Commentaries. Grand Rapids: Baker, 2009.

———. *Commentaries on the Epistle of Paul the Apostle to the Romans*. Vol. 19. Translated by John Owen. Calvin's Commentaries. Grand Rapids: Baker, 2009.

———. *Commentary on the Book of Psalms*. Vol. 4. Translated by James Anderson. Calvin's Commentaries. Grand Rapids: Eerdmans, 1949.

———. *Commentary on the Epistles of Paul to the Corinthians*. Vol. 20. Translated by John Pringle. Calvin's Commentaries. Grand Rapids: Baker, 1948.

———. *Commentary on the Gospel According to John*. 2 vols. Translated by William Pringle. Calvin's Commentaries. Grand Rapids: Eerdmans, 1956.

———. *Commentary on the Prophet Ezekiel*. 2 vols. Translated by Thomas Myers. Calvin's Commentaries. Grand Rapids: Eerdmans, 1948.

———. *Institutes of the Christian Religion*. Translated by Henry Beveridge. Peabody, Mass.: Hendrickson, 2008.

———. *Joannis Calvini Opera Selecta*. Vol. 1. Edited by Peter Barth. Monachii: C. Kaiser, 1926.

———. *The Gospel According to John: 11–21 and The First Epistle of John*. Translated by T. H. L. Parker. Calvin's Commentaries. Edinburgh: Oliver and Boyd, 1959.

Camfield, F. W. *Revelation and the Holy Spirit*. London: Elliot Stock, 1938.

Carson, D. A. *The Gospel According to John*. Grand Rapids: Eerdmans, 1991.

Bibliography

Carson, D. A. and John D. Woodbridge, eds. *Scripture and Truth*. Grand Rapids: Baker, 1992.

———. *Hermeneutics, Authority, and Canon*. Grand Rapids: Zondervan, 1986.

Cole, Graham A. *He Who Gives Life: The Doctrine of the Holy Spirit*. Wheaton: Crossway Books, 2007.

Colyer, Elmer M. "A Theology of Word and Spirit: Donald Bloesch's Theological Method." No pages. Cited 10 Febraury 2010. Online: http://www2.luthersem.edu/ctrf/JCTR/Vol01/ Colyer.htm.

———. "Thomas F. Torrance on the Holy Spirit." *Word & World* 23, no. 2 (Spring 2003): 160–67.

Congar, Yves M. J. *The Word and the Spirit*. Translated by David Smith. London: Geoffrey Chapman, 1986.

Cooke G. A. *A Critical and Exegetical Commentary on The Book Ezekiel*. The International Critical Commentary. Edinburgh: T. & T. Clark, 1951.

Corley, Bruce, Steve W. Lemke, and Grant I. Lovejoy, eds. *Biblical Hermeneutics: A Comprehensive Introduction to Interpreting Scripture*. Nashville: Broadman & Holman, 2002.

De Klerk, Peter, ed. *Calvin and the Holy Spirit: Papers and Responses presented at the Sixth Colloquium on Calvin & Calvin Studies*. Grand Rapids: Calvin Studies Society, 1989.

Delitzsch, Franz. *Biblical Commentary on the Psalms*. Vol. 3. Translated by Francis Bolton. Edinburgh: T. & T. Clark, 1871.

———. *Commentary on the Epistle to the Hebrews*. 2 vols. Translated by Thomas L. Kingsbury. Edinburgh: T. & T. Clark, 1868.

Demarest, B. "Revelation, General." Pages 1019–21 in *Evangelical Dictionary of Theology*. 2nd ed. Edited by Walter E. Elwell. Grand Rapids: Baker, 2001.

De Young, James B. "The Holy Spirit, The Divine Exegete: How Are We Able to Hear Him?" Paper presented at the annual meeting of the Evangelical Theological Society. Jackson, Miss., November 21–23, 1996.

Dockery, David S. *New Dimensions in Evangelical Thought: Essays in Honor of Millard J. Erickson*. Downers Grove: InterVarsity Press, 1998.

Dockery, David S. and David P. Nelson. "Special Revelation." Pages 118–74 in *A Theology for the Church*. Edited by Daniel L. Akin. Nashville: Broadman & Holman, 2007.

Dorman, Ted M. "Holy Spirit, History, Hermeneutics and Theology: Toward an Evangelical/Catholic Consensus." *Journal of the Evangelical Theological Society* 41, no. 3 (Sept. 1998): 427–38.

Ellingworth, Paul. *The Epistle to the Hebrews: A Commentary on the Greek Text*. Grand Rapids: Eerdmans, 1993.

Elwell, Walter A., ed. *Evangelical Dictionary of Theology*. Grand Rapids: Baker, 2001.

Erickson, Millard J. *Christian Theology*. Grand Rapids: Baker, 1983.

———. *Evangelical Interpretation: Perspectives on Hermeneutical Issues*. Grand Rapids: Baker, 1993.

———. *Introducing Christian Doctrine*. Edited by L. Arnold Hustad. Grand Rapids: Baker, 1992.

———. "Language: Human Vehicle for Divine Truth." Pages 208–16 in *Biblical Hermeneutics: A Comprehensive Introduction to Interpreting Scripture*. Edited by Bruce Corley, Steve W. Lemke, and Grant I. Lovejoy. Nashville: Broadman & Holman, 2002.

———. *The New Evangelical Theology*. Westwood, N. J.: Fleming H. Revell Company, 1968.
Evans, Eifion. "John Calvin: Theologian of the Holy Spirit." *Reformation and Revival* 10, no. 4 (Fall 2001): 83-104.
Ewert, David. *The Holy Spirit in the New Testament*. Scottdale, Pa.: Herald Press, 1983.
Fee, Gordon D. *God's Empowering Presence: The Holy Spirit in the Letters of Paul*. Peabody, Mass.: Hendrickson Publishers, 1994.
———. *Gospel and Spirit: Issues in New Testament Hermeneutics*. Peabody, Mass.: Hendrickson, 1991.
———. *The First Epistle to the Corinthians*. The New International Commentary on the New Testament. Grand Rapids: Eerdmans, 1987.
Finlayson, R. A. "Contemporary Ideas of Inspiration." Pages 221-34 in *Revelation and the Bible*. Edited by Carl F. H. Henry. Grand Rapids: Baker, 1958.
Forstman, H. Jackson. *Word and Spirit: Calvin's Doctrine of Biblical Authority*. Stanford, Calif.: Stanford University Press, 1962.
Fowl, Stephen E. *Engaging Scripture: A Model for Theological Interpretation*. Malden, Mass.: Blackwell, 1998.
Fowl, Stephen E. and L. Gregory Jones. *Reading in Communion: Scripture and Ethics in Christian Life*. Grand Rapids: Eerdmans, 1991.
Fox, Michael V. *Character and Ideology in the Book of Esther*. Columbia: University of South Carolina Press, 1991.
Frame, John M. "The Spirit and the Scriptures." Pages 217-35 in *Hermeneutics, Authority, and Canon*. Edited by D. A. Carson and John Woodbridge. Grand Rapids: Zondervan, 1986.
Frei, Hans W. *The Eclipse of Biblical Narrative: A Study in Eighteenth and Nineteenth Century Hermeneutics*. New Haven: Yale University Press, 1974.
Fridley, William Lloyd. "Illumination in 1 Corinthians 2:6-3:4 and the Paraclete Passages." ThM thesis, Grace Theological Seminary, 1991.
Fuller, Daniel P. "Do We Need the Holy Spirit To Understand the Bible?" *Eternity* (Jan. 1959): 22-23, 47.
———. "The Holy Spirit's Role in Biblical Interpretation." Pages 189-98 in *Scripture, Tradition, and Interpretation*. Edited by W. Ward Gasque and William Sanford LaSor. Grand Rapids: Eerdmans, 1977.
Fung, Ronald Y. K. *The Epistle to the Galatians*. The New International Commentary on the New Testament. Grand Rapids: Eerdmans, 1988.
Furnish, Victor Paul. *II Corinthians*. The Anchor Bible 32A. Garden City, N. Y.: Doubleday & Company, 1984.
Garland, David E. *1 Corinthians*. Baker Exegetical Commentary on the New Testament. Grand Rapids: Baker, 2003.
———. *2 Corinthians*. The New American Commentary 29. Nashville: Broadman & Holman, 1999.
Garrett, Duane A. and Richard R. Melick, Jr., eds. *Authority and Interpretation: A Baptist Perspective*. Grand Rapids: Baker, 1987.
Gasque, W. Ward and William Sanford LaSor, eds. *Scripture, Tradition, and Interpretation*. Grand Rapids: Eerdmans, 1977.
George, Timothy. *Galatians*. The New American Commentary 30. Nashville: Broadman & Holman, 1994.
———. *Theology of the Reformers*. Nashville: Broadman Press, 1988.

Bibliography

Gleason, Randall C. "'Letter' and 'Spirit' in Luther's Hermeneutics." *Bibliotheca Sacra* 157, no. 628 (Oct/Dec 2000): 468–85.

Goldsworthy, Graeme. *Gospel-Centered Hermeneutics: Foundations and Principles of Evangelical Biblical Interpretation.* Downers Grove: InterVarsity Press, 2006.

Goodwin, Thomas. *An Exposition of Ephesians: Chapter 1 to 2:10.* Grand Rapids: Zondervan, 1958.

Graham, Glenn H. *An Exegetical Summary of Ephesians.* Dallas: Summer Institute of Linguistics, 1997.

Green, Joel B. *The Gospel of Luke.* The New International Commentary on the New Testament. Grand Rapids: Eerdmans, 1997.

Grenz, Stanley J. "The Spirit and the Word: The World-Creating Function of the Text." *Theology Today* 57 (2000): 357–74.

Grudem, Wayne. *Systematic Theology.* Grand Rapids: Zondervan, 1994.

Guthrie, Donald. *The Letter to the Hebrews.* The Tyndale New Testament Commentaries. Grand Rapids: Eerdmans, 1983.

Hagner, Donald A. *Hebrews.* New International Biblical Commentary. Peabody, Mass.: Hendrikson, 1990.

Hamilton, James M. Jr. *God's Indwelling Presence: The Holy Spirit in the Old & New Testaments.* Nashville: Broadman & Holman, 2006.

Harris, Murray J. *The Second Epistle to the Corinthians: A Commentary on the Greek Text.* The New International Greek Testament Commentary. Grand Rapids: Eerdmans, 2005.

Harris, R. Laird. *Inspiration and Canonicity of the Bible.* Grand Rapids: Zondervan, 1957.

Harris, R. Laird, Gleason L. Archer, Jr., Bruce K. Waltke. *Theological Wordbook of the Old Testament.* 2 vols. Chicago: Moody Press, 1980.

Hart, Larry. "Hermeneutics, Theology, and the Holy Spirit." *Perspectives in Religious Studies* 14, no. 4 (Wint. 1987): 53–64.

Hascup, JohnDavid Michael. "The Doctrine of Word and Spirit in John Calvin." ThD diss., Dallas Theological Seminary, 1992.

Hatchett, R. L. "The Authority of the Bible." Pages 194–207 in *Biblical Hermeneutics: A Comprehensive Introduction to Interpreting Scripture.* Edited by Bruce Corley, Steve W. Lemke, and Grant I. Lovejoy. Nashville: Broadman & Holman, 2002.

Hauerwas, Stanley. *The Hauerwas Reader.* Edited by John Berkman and Michael Cartwright. Durham, N. C.: Duke University Press, 2001.

Heisler, Greg. *Spirit-Led Preaching: The Holy Spirit's Role in Sermon Preparation and Delivery.* Nashville: Broadman & Holman, 2007.

Hendriksen, William. *Exposition of Colossians and Philemon.* New Testament Commentary. Grand Rapids: Baker, 1964.

———. *Exposition of Galatians.* New Testament Commentary. Grand Rapids, Baker, 1968.

———. *Exposition of Paul's Epistle to the Romans.* New Testament Commentary. Grand Rapids: Baker, 1980.

———. *Exposition of the Gospel According to John.* Vol. 2. New Testament Commentary. Grand Rapids: Baker, 1954.

Hendry, George S. *The Holy Spirit in Christian Theology.* Rev. and enl. ed. Philadelphia: The Westminster Press, 1965.

Henry, Carl F. H. *God, Revelation and Authority.* Vol. 4. Waco: Word, 1979.

Bibliography

———, ed. *Revelation and the Bible*. Grand Rapids: Baker, 1958.
———. "Revelation, Special." Pages 1021–23 in *Evangelical Dictionary of Theology*. 2nd ed. Edited by Walter E. Elwell. Grand Rapids: Baker, 2001.
Herring, Ralph and Frank Stagg. *How To Understand the Bible*. Nashville: Broadman Press, 1974.
Hodge, Charles. *A Commentary on the Epistle to the Ephesians*. Grand Rapids: Eerdmans, 1950.
———. *A Commentary on the Epistle to the Romans*. Grand Rapids: Eerdmans, 1950.
———. *An Exposition of the First Epistle to the Corinthians*. Grand Rapids: Eerdmans, 1950.
———. *Systematic Theology*. Vol. 1. Grand Rapids: Eerdmans, 1986.
———. "The Witness of the Holy Spirit to the Bible." *Princeton Theological Review* 11 (Jan. 1913): 41–84.
Hoehner, Harold W. *Ephesians: An Exegetical Commentary*. Grand Rapids: Baker, 2002.
House, H. Wayne and Gordon Carle. *Doctrine Twisting: How Core Biblical Truths Are Distorted*. Downers Grove: InterVarsity Press, 2003.
Hunt, W. Boyd. "The Holy Spirit and Revelation Today." *Southwestern Journal of Theology* 16 (Spring 1974): 31–46.
Ingle, Jeff. "A Historical and Scriptural Survey of the Doctrine of Illumination With Application to Hermeneutics." ThM thesis, Grace Theological Seminary, 1987.
Johnson, Dale. "Time, Scripture and Tradition: A Historical Survey of the Sufficiency of Scripture." Pages 31–50 in *Written for Our Instruction: The Sufficiency of Scripture for All of Life*. Edited by Joseph A. Pipa, Jr. and J. Andrew Wortman. Taylors, S. C.: Southern Presbyterian Press, 2001.
Jones, L. Gregory. "Formed and Transformed by Scripture: Character, Community, and Authority in Biblical Interpretation." Pages 18–33 in *Character and Scripture: Moral Formation, Community, and Biblical Interpretation*. Edited by William P. Brown. Grand Rapids: Eerdmans, 2002.
Kaiser, Walter C. Jr. "A Neglected Text in Bibliology Discussions: I Corinthians 2:6–16." *Westminster Theological Journal* 43, no. 2 (Spring 1981): 301–19.
———. "Legitimate Hermeneutics." Pages 117–47 in *Inerrancy*. Edited by Norman L. Geisler. Grand Rapids: Zondervan, 1979.
———. "The Single Intent of Scripture." Pages 158–70 in *Rightly Divided: Readings in Biblical Hermeneutics*. Edited by Roy B. Zuck. Grand Rapids: Kregel Publications, 1996.
Kaiser, Walter C. Jr. and Moises Silva. *An Introduction to Biblical Hermeneutics: The Search For Meaning*. Grand Rapids: Zondervan, 1994.
Kantzer, Kenneth S., ed. *Applying the Scriptures: Papers from ICBI Summit III*. Grand Rapids: Zondervan, 1987.
———. "Calvin and the Holy Scriptures." Pages 115–55 in *Inspiration and Interpretation*. Edited by John F. Walvoord. Grand Rapids: Eerdmans, 1957.
Keil, Carl Friedrich. *Biblical Commentary on the Prophecies of Ezekiel*. 2 vols. Translated by James Martin. Edinburgh: T. & T. Clark, 1876.
Kistemaker, Simon J. *Exposition of the Epistle to the Hebrews*. New Testament Commentary. Grand Rapids: Baker, 1984.
———. *Exposition of the First Epistle to the Corinthians*. New Testament Commentary. Grand Rapids: Baker, 1993.

Bibliography

———. *Exposition of the Second Epistle to the Corinthians*. New Testament Commentary. Grand Rapids: Baker, 1997.

Klein, William W., Craig L. Blomberg, and Robert L. Hubbard. *Introduction to Biblical Interpretation*. Dallas: Word Publishing, 1993.

Klem, Arthur Wheeler. "The Biblical Doctrine of the Illumination of Scripture by the Holy Spirit." MA Thesis, Wheaton College, 1956.

Klooster, Fred H. "The Role of the Holy Spirit in the Hermeneutic Process: The Relationship of the Spirit's Illumination to Biblical Interpretation." Pages 451–72 in *Hermeneutics, Inerrancy, and the Bible: Papers from Chicago Summit Conference II*. Edited by Earl D. Radmacher and Robert D. Preus. Grand Rapids: Academie Books, 1984.

Koenig, John. "Vision, Self-offering, and Transformation for Ministry (Rom 12:1-8)." Pages 307–23 in *Sin, Salvation, and the Spirit*. Edited by Daniel Durken. Collegeville, Minn.: The Liturgical Press, 1979.

Koester, Craig R. *Hebrews*. The Anchor Bible 36. New York: Doubleday, 2001.

Koranteng-Pipim, Samuel. "The Role of the Holy Spirit in Biblical Interpretation: A Study in the Writings of James I. Packer." PhD diss., Andrews University, 1998.

Köstenberger, Andreas J. and Scott R. Swain. *Father, Son, and Spirit: The Trinity and John's Gospel*. Downers Grove: InterVarsity Press, 2008.

Kraus, Hans-Joachim. *Psalms 60–150: A Continental Commentary*. Translated by Hilton C. Oswald. Minneapolis: Fortress Press, 1993.

Kuyper, Abraham. *The Work of the Holy Spirit*. Grand Rapids: Eerdmans, 1956.

Kwok, Man Chee. "Benjamin B. Warfield's Doctrine of Illumination in Light of Conservative Calvinistic Tradition." PhD diss., Trinity International University, 1995.

Lane, William L. *Hebrews*. 2 vols. Word Biblical Commentary 47a-b. Dallas: Word Books, 1991.

Larkin, William J. Jr. *Culture and Biblical Hermeneutics: Interpreting and Applying the Authoritative Word in a Relativistic Age*. Grand Rapids: Baker, 1988.

Lemke, Steve W. "The Inspiration and Authority of Scripture." Pages 176–93 in *Biblical Hermeneutics: A Comprehensive Introduction to Interpreting Scripture*. Edited by Bruce Corley, Steve W. Lemke, and Grant I. Lovejoy. Nashville: Broadman & Holman, 2002.

Letham, Robert. *The Holy Trinity: In Scripture, History, Theology, and Worship*. Phillipsburg, N. J.: P & R Publishing, 2004.

Leupold, Herbert Carl. *Exposition of the Psalms*. Columbus, Ohio: Wartburg Press, 1959.

Lewis, John. *Revelation, Inspiration, Scripture*. Nashville: Broadman Press, 1985.

Lincoln, Andrew T. *Ephesians*. Word Biblical Commentary 42. Dallas: Word Books, 1990.

Lloyd-Jones, D. Martyn. *Authority*. London: Inter-Varsity Fellowship, 1958.

Lohse, Eduard. *Colossians and Philemon*. Translated by William R. Poehlmann and Robert J. Karris. Hermeneia. Philadelphia: Fortress Press, 1971.

Longenecker, Richard N. *Galatians*. Word Biblical Commentary 41. Dallas: Word, 1990.

Lopes, Augustus Nicodemus. "Calvin, Theologian of the Holy Spirit: The Holy Spirit and the Word of God." *Scottish Bulletin of Evangelical Theology* 15 (Spring 1997): 38–49.

Luther, Martin. *A Commentary on St. Paul's Epistle to the Galatians*. Philadelphia: Smith, English & Co., 1860.

———. *Martin Luther's Basic Theological Writings*. Edited by Timothy F. Lull. Minneapolis: Fortress Press, 2005.

———. *The Bondage of the Will*. Translated by James I. Packer and O. R. Johnston. London: James Clarke & Co., 1957.

MacDonald, Margaret Y. *Colossians and Ephesians*. Sacra Pagina 17. Collegeville, Minn.: The Liturgical Press, 2000.

Maier, Gerhard. *Biblical Hermeneutics*. Translated by Robert W. Yarbrough. Wheaton, Ill.: Crossway Books, 1994.

Marshall, I. Howard. *The Epistles of John*. The New International Commentary on the New Testament. Grand Rapids: Eerdmans, 1978.

———. "The Holy Spirit and the Interpretation of Scripture." Pages 66–74 in *Rightly Divided: Readings in Biblical Hermeneutics*. Edited by Roy B. Zuck. Grand Rapids: Kregel Publications, 1996.

Martin, Ralph P. *2 Corinthians*. Word Biblical Commentary 40. Waco: Word Books, 1986.

Matera, Frank J. *Galatians*. Sacra Pagina 9. Collegeville, Minn.: The Liturgical Press, 1992.

McGee, J. Vernon. *Luke*. Nashville: Thomas Nelson Publishers, 1991.

McKinley, David J. "John Owen's View of Illumination: An Alternative View to the Fuller-Erickson Dialogue." *Bibliotheca Sacra* 154, no. 613 (Jan.–Mar. 1997): 93–104.

McNicol, Allan J. "How Does God Give Guidance Beyond the Illumination of Scripture?" *Christian Studies* 16 (1996–97): 33–53.

Meador, Kevin. "A Study in the Role of the Holy Spirit in the Interpretation and Proclamation of the Word of God." DMin diss., Reformed Theological Seminary, 1998.

Meeks, Wayne A. "The Image of the Androgyne: Some Uses of a Symbol in Earliest Christianity." *History of Religions* 13, no. 3 (Feb. 1974): 165–208.

Melick, Richard R. Jr. *Philippians, Colossians, Philemon*. The New American Commentary 32. Nashville: Broadman Press, 1991.

Metzger, Paul Louis, ed. *Trinitarian Soundings in Systematic Theology*. New York: T & T Clark, 2005.

Migliore, Daniel L. *Faith Seeking Understanding: An Introduction to Christian Theology*. Grand Rapids: Eerdmans, 1991.

Moo, Douglas. *Romans 1–8*. The Wycliffe Exegetical Commentary. Chicago: Moody Press, 1991.

Morris, Leon. *New Testament Theology*. Grand Rapids: Zondervan, 1986.

———. *The Epistle to the Romans*. The Pillar New Testament Commentary. Grand Rapids: Eerdmans, 1988.

———. *The Gospel According to John*. Grand Rapids: Eerdmans, 1971.

Mueller, J. Theodore. *Christian Dogmatics*. St. Louis: Concordia, 1934.

———. "The Holy Spirit and the Scriptures." Pages 267–81 in *Revelation and the Bible*. Edited by Carl F. H. Henry. Grand Rapids: Baker, 1958.

Nebeker, Gary L. "The Holy Spirit, Hermeneutics, and Transformation: From Present to Future Glory." *Evangelical Review of Theology* 27, no. 1 (Jan. 2003): 47–54.

Bibliography

O'Brien, Peter T. *Colossians, Philemon.* Word Biblical Commentary 44. Waco: Word, 1982.

Oden, Thomas C. *Life in the Spirit.* San Francisco: HarperCollins, 1992.

Oehler, Gustav Friedrich. *Theology of the Old Testament.* New York: Funk & Wagnalls, 1883.

Oesterley, W. O. E. *The Psalms: Translated with Text-Critical and Exegetical Notes.* London: S. P. C. K., 1955.

Osborne, Grant. *The Hermeneutical Spiral: A Comprehensive Introduction to Biblical Interpretation.* Downers Grove: InterVarsity Press, 2006.

Owen, John. *A Defense of Sacred Scripture Against Modern Fanaticism* in *Biblical Theology.* Translated by Stephen P. Westcott. Morgan, Pa.: Soli Deo Gloria Publications, 1994.

———. *An Exposition of the Epistle to the Hebrews with Preliminary Exercitations.* Vol. III. London: J. Haddon, Castle Street, Finsbury, 1840.

———. *An Exposition of the Epistle to the Hebrews with Preliminary Exercitations.* Vol. IV. London: J. Haddon, Castle Street, Finsbury, 1840.

———. *Pneumatologia, Or, A Discourse Concerning the Holy Spirit.* Philadelphia: Towar & Hogan, 1827.

———. *The Holy Spirit: His Gifts and Power.* Grand Rapids: Kregel Publications, 1954.

———. *The Works of John Owen.* Vol. 3. Edited by William H. Goold. Johnstone & Hunter, 1856; Repr., Carlisle, PA: The Banner of Truth Trust, 1967.

———. *The Works of John Owen.* Vol. 4. Edited by William H. Goold. Johnstone & Hunter, 1856; Repr., Carlisle, PA: The Banner of Truth Trust, 1967.

Packer, J. I. *Keep In Step With The Spirit.* Old Tappan, N. J.: Fleming H. Revell, 1984.

———. "The Holy Spirit and His Work." Pages 51–95 in *Applying the Scriptures: Papers from ICBI Summit III.* Edited by Kenneth S. Kantzer. Grand Rapids: Zondervan, 1987.

Palmer, Edwin H. *The Person and Ministry of the Holy Spirit: The Traditional Calvinistic Perspective.* Grand Rapids: Baker, 1974.

Peifer, Claude. "The Experience of Sin, Salvation, and the Spirit as a Prerequisite for the Understanding of the Scriptures." Pages 3–20 in *Sin, Salvation, and the Spirit.* Edited by Daniel Durken. Collegeville, Minn.: The Liturgical Press, 1979.

Pinnock, Clark H. "The Role of the Spirit in Interpretation." *Journal of the Evangelical Theological Society* 36, no. 4 (Dec. 1993): 491–7.

———. *The Scripture Principle.* San Francisco: Harper & Row, 1984.

Plummer, Alfred. *The Gospel According to St. Luke.* The International Critical Commentary. New York: Charles Scribner's Sons, 1906.

———. *Second Epistle of St. Paul to the Corinthians.* The International Critical Commentary. New York: Charles Scribner's Sons, 1915.

Poehnell, Gray. "The Relationship of Illumination to the Interpretation of Scripture: An Exegetical Study of I Corinthians 2:14." MA thesis, Trinity Evangelical Divinity School, 1987.

Power, David N. "The Holy Spirit: Scripture, Tradition, and Interpretation." Pages 152–78 in *Keeping the Faith: Essays to Mark the Centenary of Lux Mundi.* Edited by Geoffrey Wainwright. Philadelphia: Fortress Press, 1988.

Poythress, Vern S. *God Centered Biblical Interpretation.* Phillipsburg, N. J.: P & R Publishing, 1999.

Bibliography

Preiss, Théo. "The Inner Witness of the Holy Spirit: The Doctrine of the Holy Spirit and Scripture." *Interpretation* 7, no. 3 (July 1953): 259–80.
Ramm, Bernard. *Protestant Biblical Interpretation: A Textbook of Hermeneutics for Conservative Protestants*. Grand Rapids: Baker, 1970.
———. *The God Who Makes a Difference: A Christian Appeal to Reason*. Waco, Tex.: Word Books, 1972.
———. *The Pattern of Authority*. Grand Rapids: Eerdmans, 1957.
———. *The Witness of the Spirit: An Essay on the Contemporary Relevance of the Internal Witness of the Holy Spirit*. Grand Rapids: Eerdmans, 1959.
Rehnman, Sebastian. *Divine Discourse: The Theological Methodology of John Owen: Texts and Studies in Reformation and Post-Reformation Thought*. Grand Rapids: Baker, 2002.
Roberts, Randal Raymond. "The Relationship Between the Perspicuity of Scripture and the Nature of Spiritual Illumination." ThM thesis, Western Conservative Baptist Seminary, 1984.
Ryle, J. C. *Expository Thoughts on the Gospels: St. Luke*. New York: Fleming H. Revell Company, 1858.
Ryrie, Charles Caldwell. "Illumination." Pages 590–591 in *Evangelical Dictionary of Theology*. 2nd ed. Edited by Walter E. Elwell. Grand Rapids: Baker, 2001.
———. *The Holy Spirit*. Chicago: Moody Press, 1965.
Sailhamer, John H. "Genesis." Pages 3–284 in *Genesis, Exodus, Leviticus, Numbers*. The Expositor's Bible Commentary 2. Edited by Frank E. Gaebelein. Grand Rapids: Zondervan, 1990.
———. *Introduction to Old Testament Theology: A Canonical Approach*. Grand Rapids: Zondervan, 1995.
Saucy, Robert L. *Scripture: Its Power, Authority, and Relevance*. Nashville: Thomas Nelson, 2001.
Sawyer, M. James. "The Witness of the Spirit in the Protestant Tradition." Pages 71–93 in *Who's Afraid of the Holy Spirit?*. Edited by Daniel B. Wallace and M. James Sawyer. Dallas: Biblical Studies Press, 2005.
Schaff, Philip and Henry Wace, eds. *St. Basil: Letters and Selected Works*. Vol. 8 of *Nicene and Post-Nicene Fathers*. Grand Rapids: Eerdmans, 1955.
Schlier, Heinrich. *Der Brief An Die Epheser: Ein Kommentar*. Düsseldorf: Patmos-Verlag, 1957.
Schnackenburg, Rudolf. *Die Johannesbrefe*. Freiburg: Herder, 1953.
———. *Ephesians: A Commentary*. Translated by Helen Heron. Edinburgh: T&T Clark, 1991.
Schreiner, Thomas R. *Romans*. Baker Exegetical Commentary on the New Testament. Grand Rapids: Baker, 1998.
Searle, John. *Speech Acts: An Essay in the Philosophy of Language*. Cambridge: Cambridge University Press, 1969.
Simpson, E. K. and F. F. Bruce. *The Epistles to the Ephesians and the Colossians*. The New International Commentary on the New Testament. Grand Rapids: Eerdmans, 1957.
Smail, Thomas A. *Reflected Glory: The Spirit in Christ and Christians*. London: Hodder and Stoughton, 1975.
Smith, Fred William. "The Pauline Doctrine of Illumination in the Light of Emil Brunner's Theology." MA thesis, Wheaton College, 1959.

Bibliography

Smith, Morton H. "The Doctrine of the Sufficiency of Scripture." Pages 1-30 in *Written for Our Instruction: The Sufficiency of Scripture for All of Life*. Edited by Joseph A. Pipa, Jr. and J. Andrew Wortman. Taylors, S. C.: Southern Presbyterian Press, 2001.

Sproul, R. C. *Scripture Alone: The Evangelical Doctrine*. Phillipsburg, N. J.: P & R Publishing, 2005.

———. "The Internal Testimony of the Holy Spirit." Pages 337-54 in *Inerrancy*. Edited by Norman L. Geisler. Grand Rapids: Zondervan, 1979.

Stein, Robert H. *A Basic Guide to Interpreting the Bible: Playing by the Rules*. Grand Rapids: Baker, 1994.

Stonehouse, N. B. and Paul Woolley, eds. *The Infallible Word: A Symposium by the Members of the Faculty of Westminster Theological Seminary*. 2nd ed. Phillipsburg, N. J.: P & R Publishing, 2002.

Stonehouse, Ned B. "Special Revelation as Scriptural." Pages 75-86 in *Revelation and the Bible*. Edited by Carl F. H. Henry. Grand Rapids: Baker, 1958.

Stott, John R. W. *The Letters of John*. Tyndale New Testament Commentaries. Leicester, England: InterVarsity Press, 1988.

Studebaker, John A. Jr. "'The Authority of the Holy Spirit' in Contemporary Theology with Special Reference to Authority in the Church." PhD diss., Trinity International University, 2003.

Stuhlmacher, Peter. "The Hermeneutical Significance of 1 Cor 2:6-16." Pages 328-47 in *Tradition and Interpretation in the New Testament*. Edited by Gerald F. Hawthorne and Otto Betz. Grand Rapids: Eerdmans, 1987.

Tate, W. Randolph. *Biblical Interpretation*. Peabody, Mass.: Hendrickson, 1991.

Terry, Milton S. *Biblical Hermeneutics*. New York: Phillips & Hunt, 1883.

Thiselton, Anthony C. *New Horizons in Hermeneutics: The Theory and Practice of Transforming Biblical Reading*. Grand Rapids: Zondervan, 1992.

———. *The First Epistle to the Corinthians: A Commentary on the Greek Text*. The New International Greek Testament Commentary. Grand Rapids: Eerdmans, 2000.

———. *The Two Horizons: New Testament Hermeneutics and Philosophical Description*. Grand Rapids: Eerdmans, 1980.

Thompson, John. *Modern Trinitarian Perspectives*. Oxford: Oxford University Press, 1994.

Thompson, Mark D. *A Clear and Present Word: The Clarity of Scripture*. Downers Grove: InterVarsity Press, 2006.

Toon, Peter. *Our Triune God: A Biblical Portrayal of the Trinity*. Vancouver: Regent College Publishing, 1996.

Torrance, Thomas F. *The Christian Doctrine of God: One Being Three Persons*. London: T & T Clark, 1996.

Vanhoozer, Kevin J. *Is There Meaning in This Text?* Grand Rapids: Zondervan, 1998.

———. *The Drama of Doctrine: A Canonical-Linguistic Approach to Christian Theology*. Louisville: Westminster John Knox Press, 2005.

Vanier, Jean and Frances Young. "Towards Transformational Reading of Scripture." Pages 236-54 in *Canon and Biblical Interpretation*. Edited by Craig G. Bartholomew and Anthony C. Thiselton. Grand Rapids: Zondervan, 2006.

Veenhof, Jan. "Holy Spirit and Holy Scripture." *Scottish Evangelical Theology Society* 4 (Fall 1986): 69-84.

———. "The Holy Spirit and Hermeneutics." *Scottish Bulletin of Evangelical Theology* 5 (Spring 1987): 105–22.
Virkler, Henry A. *Hermeneutics: Principles and Processes of Biblical Interpretation.* Grand Rapids: Baker, 1981.
Wainwright, Geoffrey, ed. *Keeping the Faith: Essays to Mark the Centenary of Lux Mundi.* Philadelphia: Fortress Press, 1988.
Wallace, Daniel B. "The Holy Spirit and Hermeneutics." No pages. Cited 22 October 2009. Online: http://www.bible.org/article/holy-spirit-and-hermeneutics.
———. "The Witness of the Spirit in Romans 8:16: Interpretation and Implications." Pages 37–51 in *Who's Afraid of the Holy Spirit?.* Edited by Daniel B. Wallace and M. James Sawyer. Dallas: Biblical Studies Press, 2005.
Wallace, Daniel B. and M. James Sawyer, eds. *Who's Afraid of the Holy Spirit?.* Dallas: Biblical Studies Press, 2005.
Wallace, Ronald S. *Calvin's Doctrine of the Word and Sacrament.* Edinburgh: Oliver and Boyd, 1953.
Waltke, Bruce K. *An Old Testament Theology: An Exegetical, Canonical, and Thematic Approach.* Grand Rapids: Zondervan, 2007.
Walvoord, John F., ed. *Inspiration and Interpretation.* Grand Rapids: Eerdmans, 1957.
———. *The Holy Spirit: A Comprehensive Study of the Person and Work of the Holy Spirit.* Grand Rapids: Zondervan, 1965.
Ward, Timothy. *Word and Supplement: Speech Acts, Biblical Texts, and the Sufficiency of Scripture.* Oxford: Oxford University Press, 2002.
———. *Words of Life: Scripture as the Living and Active Word of God.* Downers Grove: InterVarsity Press, 2009.
Ware, Bruce A. *Father, Son, & Holy Spirit: Relationship, Roles, & Relevance.* Wheaton: Crossway Books, 2005.
Warfield, Benjamin Breckinridge. *Calvin and Augustine.* Philadelphia: The Presbyterian and Reformed Publishing Company 1956.
———. *Revelation and Inspiration.* New York: Oxford University Press, 1927.
———. *The Inspiration and Authority of the Bible.* Grand Rapids: Baker, 1948.
Watson, John H. "The Holy Spirit and the Bible." *The Evangelical Quarterly* 23, no. 4 (Oct. 1951): 275–83.
Webster, John B. "Biblical Theology and the Clarity of Scripture." Pages 352–84 in *Out of Egypt: Biblical Theology and Biblical Interpretation.* Edited by Craig Bartholomew, Mary Healy, Karl Moller, and Robin Parry. Grand Rapids: Zondervan, 2004.
———. *Confessing God: Essays in Christian Dogmatics.* Vol. 2. London: T & T Clark, 2005.
Weeks, Noel. *The Sufficiency of Scripture.* Edinburgh: The Banner of Truth Trust, 1988.
Westcott, Brooke Foss. *Saint Paul's Epistle to the Ephesians.* Grand Rapids: Eerdmans, 1952.
———. *The Epistle to the Hebrews.* Grand Rapids: Eerdmans, 1892.
———. *The Epistles of St. John.* Grand Rapids: Eerdmans, 1955.
Williams, Donald T. *The Person and Work of the Holy Spirit: The Holy Spirit Effects In Us What Christ Has Done For Us.* Nashville: Broadman & Holman, 1994.
Williams, J. Rodman. *Renewal Theology: Salvation, the Holy Spirit, and Christian Living.* Grand Rapids: Zondervan, 1990.
Wolterstorff, Nicholas. *Divine Discourse: Philosophical Reflections on the Claim that God Speaks.* Cambridge: Cambridge University Press, 2005.

Bibliography

———. *Educating for Shalom: Essays on Christian Higher Education*. Edited by Clarence W. Joldersma and Gloria Goris Stronks. Grand Rapids: Eerdmans, 2004.

Wood, A. Skevington. *Ephesians*. The Expositor's Bible Commentary 11. Edited by Frank E. Gaebelein. Grand Rapids: Zondervan, 1978.

Yarbrough, Robert W. *1-3 John*. Baker Exegetical Commentary on the New Testament. Grand Rapids: Baker, 2008.

Yarkin, William. *History of Biblical Interpretation: A Reader*. Peabody, Mass.: Hendrickson, 2004.

Yarnell, Malcolm B. III. "The Person and Work of the Holy Spirit." Pages 604–84 in *A Theology for the Church*. Edited by Daniel L. Akin. Nashville: Broadman & Holman, 2007.

Young, William G. "The Holy Spirit and the Word of God." *Scottish Journal of Theology* 14 (1961): 34–59.

Zuber, Kevin D. "What Is Illumination? A Study in Evangelical Theology Seeking A Biblically Grounded Definition of the Illuminating Work of the Holy Spirit." PhD diss., Trinity Evangelical Divinity School, 1996.

Zuck, Roy B. "Application in Biblical Hermeneutics and Exposition." Pages 278–96 in *Rightly Divided: Readings in Biblical Hermeneutics*. Edited by Roy B. Zuck. Grand Rapids: Kregel Publications, 1996.

———. *Basic Bible Interpretation: A Practical Guide to Discovering Biblical Truth*. Colorado Springs: Victor, 1991.

———, ed. *Rightly Divided: Readings in Biblical Hermeneutics*. Grand Rapids: Kregel Publications, 1996.

———. *Spirit-Filled Teaching: The Power of the Holy Spirit in Your Ministry*. Nashville: Word Publishing, 1998.

———. "The Role of the Holy Spirit in Hermeneutics." *Bibliotheca Sacra* 141 (1984): 120–9.

Scripture Index

Genesis
2:15	88

Exodus
17:7	2n8
33:23	141n47
34:33–35	141n47

Numbers
12:8	141n47
22:31	85

Deuteronomy
29:29	25n44
30:6	90

1 Samuel
16:13	111

1 Kings
3:9	89n30

2 Chronicles
6:41	151n95

Nehemiah
8:8	89
8:12	89

Job
29:14	151n95
33:4	2n7

Psalms
1	85
19:7–8	25n44
51:11	89n32
119	89n30
119:17–24	84
119:17	85
119:18	6n17, 13n41, 84–85, 87, 94, 96, 168
119:33–34	6n17, 87, 96
119:33	87, 88
119:34	88, 89n30
119:73	89n30
119:105	25n44
119:125	89n30
119:130	89n30
119:144	89n30
119:169	89n30
132:9	151n95
139:7–10	2n6

Proverbs
4:23	57
30:5–6	51n141
31	ix

Isaiah
6:8–10	2n8
6:9	89n30

Scripture Index

Isaiah (cont.)

29:14	89n30
31:3	89n30
61:1	111
63:10–11	89n32

Jeremiah

31:31–34	2n8, 90–91

Ezekiel

11:19–20	6n17, 90
36:26–27	6n17, 90
36:26	91n40

Daniel

2:21	89n30

Joel

2:28–29	90–91
2:28–32	12

Matthew

5:1–7:29	98
5:17–19	30n65
12:28	109n114
13:13–15	121
15:16–17	98
16:17	120
22:37	93
23	39
28:17–20	40
28:19	3n10
28:19–29	2n8

Mark

1:8	109n114
7:18	98
7:34–35	93
8:18	121

Luke

1:15	109n114
1:35	2n6, 109n114
1:41	109n114
1:67	109n114
4:18	111
8:15	45
10:27	93
11:28	45
11:36	63
24:27	98
24:31	93
24:32	98
24:44	92
24:45	6n17, 13n41, 92–94, 98

John

1:9	63
3:5–8	2n6
3:9–15	39
5:39–47	39
5:39–40	30n65
6:63	2n7
10:35	30n65
14–16	95, 120
14:16–17	11
14:25–26	96
14:26	3n10, 6n17, 13n41, 28, 95, 99n75, 112
15:26	3n10, 6n17, 13n41, 97
16:5–7	12
16:8–11	11
16:13–15	1n2
16:13–14	3n10
16:13	2n6, 6n17, 13n41, 28, 98–99
17:3	114
17:17	98

Acts

2	12, 90, 94
5:3–4	2n8
10:38	111
16:6–11	3n10
16:14	93
17:11	169
17:18	105
17:32	105
26:24	105
28:25	2n8

Scripture Index

Romans

1:4	109n114
1:5	137
1:21	121, 140n41
1:28	140n41
3:10–12	35
3:23	35n83
5	133
5:5	150n94
5:12–21	133
5:12	35n83
5:16	133
5:18	133
6:6	151n95
7:6	132
7:23	140n41
7:25	140n41
8:1–30	1n1
8:1–11	6n17, 11, 132–36, 156, 167
8:5–6	134
8:11	2n7
8:15–16	66n56
8:16	82n124, 151n99
8:27	3n10
10:17	163
11:8–10	121
11:13–36	138n34
11:33–36	138
12:1–2	6n17, 137–40, 145–46, 156
12:2	151
13:12	150n95
13:14	150n95
15:19	2n6
15:30	2n8, 3n10

1 Corinthians

1–2	66n56
1:4–9	101
1:6ff	28
1:9	3n8
1:10–17	101
1:18–2:5	105
1:19	93
1:20	101
1:24	101
1:30	101
2:4–11	66n56
2:6–16	6n17, 13n41, 101
2:10–14	107, 115
2:10–11	2n6, 3n10, 101
2:10	101, 102n79
2:11	102
2:12–14	122
2:12	101, 104
2:13	103, 116, 154
2:14–16	134
2:14	101, 103, 105–6, 115–18, 120–21, 123–24, 154n110, 158n123
2:15	103, 154
2:16	101, 108
3:1–23	101
3:1	104n91, 154
3:3	104
3:16	2n8
4:5	63
9:11	154
10:3–4	154
12:1	154
12:11	3n10
13:12	109n115
14:1	154
14:37	154
15:44	154
15:46	154

2 Corinthians

3	143n60
3:1–11	66n56
3:3	55, 66n56, 141
3:6	55, 141
3:7–11	55
3:8	141
3:12–4:6	6n17, 13n41, 55–57
3:12–18	86n12
3:12–15	55
3:14	55–56
3:15	55
3:16–18	56
3:17	141
3:18	6n17, 140–44, 156
4:1–2	56
4:3–4	120
4:3	56–57
4:4	56, 121, 142
4:6	57, 66n56

187

Scripture Index

2 Corinthians *(cont.)*

4:15	v
4:16–18	143
13:14	2n8, 3n10

Galatians

3:27	150n95
4:6	66n56
5:1–15	144
5:6	150n94
5:16–25	1n1, 6n17, 144–47, 156, 167
6:1	154

Ephesians

1:3–14	57–58
1:3	154
1:13–14	109n114
1:13	150, 151n99
1:14	3n10
1:15–23	58
1:17–18	13n41, 58, 108–10, 151, 153
1:17	3n10, 6n17, 58–59, 102
1:18	6n17, 57–58, 59n27, 61, 63, 148
2:1–3	35n83
3:4	93
3:9	63
3:14–19	99
4:1	148
4:17–24	6n17, 147–52, 156
4:18	35n83, 59, 93, 148
4:22–24	150, 151n95, 152
4:30	3n10, 151n99
5:7–14	65
5:8	59
5:18	60, 167
5:19	154
6:12	154

Philippians

4:7	93

Colossians

1:5–6	150
1:9–14	153
1:9–10	153–55, 156
1:9	167
1:11–12	153n105
1:15–20	153
2:3	33n77
2:4	153
2:8	153
2:16–23	153
3:16	154

1 Thessalonians

1:5	99
5:8	150n95
5:19	167

2 Thessalonians

1:11–12	167

1 Timothy

2:3–7	150
3:14–16	150
6:3–5	150

2 Timothy

1:10	63
2:7	93
2:15–18	150
2:22–26	150
3:7–8	150
3:16–17	22, 28, 30n65
4:1–5	150

Titus

1:1–3	150

Hebrews

1:1–14	60
2:1–18	60
2:9	62
3:1–6	61
3:9	2n8
3:12–14	61
3:16–19	61
4:1–5:10	61
4:6	61
4:11	61

5:11–14	61
6:4	6n17, 60–63, 64
9:14	2n6
10:1–18	63
10:15–17	2n8
10:19–25	64
10:26–31	64
10:26	64
10:29	2n8
10:32–39	64
10:32	6n17, 63–65
11:1–6	163

James

1:22–25	45

1 Peter

1:2	109n114

2 Peter

1:3	28
1:19–21	22, 30n65
1:21	2n7
3:14–18	26n50

1 John

1:3	3n8
1:6	3n8
2:20	6n17, 13n41, 111–13
2:27	6n17, 13n41, 111–13
5:20	6n17, 13n41, 93, 113–14

Jude

19	106
20	167

Revelation

13:18	93
18:1	63
21:23	63
22:5	63

Subject Index

attributes, Holy Spirit, 2, 2n6
authority, 13, 29–35, 48, 52, 67, 70, 71n81, 73, 73n90, 74–77, 78–80, 98, 129

Calvin, John, xii, 13n40, 33n76, 36n84, 37n86, 59, 64, 69–72, 78, 88–89, 91, 94, 96, 105–6, 125, 137–8, 142, 149, 152, 154–55
cognitive meaning, 29, 38–41, 42, 43–44, 47, 157–59, 163–64
cognitive understanding, 39–41, 43–44, 46n119, 119, 126, 129, 134, 149, 154–55, 159–60, 163

deity, Holy Spirit, 1–4, 12n37

illocution, 39–40, 43, 46–47, 118, 159, 163, 169
inner testimony of the Holy Spirit, 23, 34, 54, 65–68, 70–72, 74–81, 128–29
inspiration, 21–24, 29, 32, 38, 48, 49–50
interpretive community, 14n43, 52, 168–69

locution, 39, 46, 118, 159
Luther, Martin, 26–27, 33n76, 65n53, 66–68

Owen, John, xii, 13n40, 36n84, 62–63, 65, 72–77, 83–87, 92n43, 93n49, 99, 105–7, 109–10, 112, 114, 136n30, 158, 167

perlocution, 39–41, 43, 46–49, 119, 159, 161, 163, 169
personhood, Holy Spirit, 1–4
perspicuity, 24–28, 38, 48, 50, 68, 74, 157

regenerate biblical interpretation, 5, 16n2, 42–47, 48–53, 83, 98, 108, 125–26, 129, 131, 133, 135–36, 140–42, 148–49, 156, 161–64, 165, 167
revelation, 16–21, 22, 23n39, 26, 33n77, 38, 42n104, 49, 51n141, 71–72, 77n106, 86, 92, 96, 107, 109n114, 110, 157, 160n129, 162–63

sufficiency, 28-29, 51–53, 73

transformative meaning, 29, 37, 42–45, 47, 119, 130, 160n127, 162–64
transformative understanding, 29, 37, 42–48, 119, 127, 129–30, 132, 134, 140, 149, 154–55, 160n127, 162–64
Trinity, triune, trinitarian 1–4, 6–8, 11–12, 30n67, 33, 46, 97–98, 100, 102
unregenerate biblical interpretation, 5, 16n2, 35–41, 106n101, 116–19, 119–22, 133, 135–36, 148–49, 157–61

www.ingramcontent.com/pod-product-compliance
Lightning Source LLC
Chambersburg PA
CBHW071514150426
43191CB00009B/1530